AF326789

WELCOME

THE DARK SHADOWS DAYBOOK UNBOUND

Patrick McCray

edited by Terri Boyles

For the Rons, of course:
McCray and Mikulak

Ah, but a man's reach should exceed his grasp, Or what's a heaven for?

"ANDREA DEL SARTO," ROBERT BROWNING

"I can do anything; I'm the chief of police."

MARTIN BRODY, AMITY ISLAND, JULY 1975

CONTENTS

Introduction   x
A Foreword Conclusion   xix
Who's Who   xxiii

PART ONE
1795   40

PART TWO
1967   72
1968   104
1969   163
1897   175
1970 Leviathans   239

PART THREE
1970 Parallel Time   265
1970 Ragnarök   275
1840   289
1841 Parallel Time   335

Epilogues   339

Afterword   369

INTRODUCTION

"A Morbid Child"
by MARK B. PERRY

"When I was in third grade, I was bitten by a vampire. Figuratively, of course, but bear with me. It was April 17, 1967, and I happened to be crossing through the den where my big sister was glued to our Philco. There, a monochromatic and maniacal young man was prying open a chained casket in a creepy mausoleum. Big Sis, her eyes never leaving the tube, explained that his name was Willie Loomis and he was looking to do a little graverobbing. She'd barely finished her sentence when both of us gasped in unison, gobsmacked. You all know that moment. That image. That dawn of a brand new vampire trope in all of its face-quaking, flesh-quivering terror. That eye-popping scene—a John Karlen tour de force—would become one of the most iconic in modern day gothic horror. It also happens to be my very own lightning bolt introduction to the seductive and spooky realm of Dark Shadows. And that, my fellow devotees, is how I was first bitten.

Now most vampirologists will tell you there are three possible outcomes of going throat to fangs with the undead. The bloodsucker may A. treat you like a cup of Maxwell House (for you kiddies that's "good to the last drop") whereupon you die and stay that way, or B. turn your carotid into a midnight buffet to be sipped on at leisure until you, too, become wholly unholy, or C. nibble just enough to keep you enslaved and hold you forever enraptured in their thrall.

No question about it: ol' Willie and I were most definitely hard Cs.

To further mangle this metaphor, Dr. Julia Hoffman would later discover that the supernatural affliction transmitted from predator to prey was not unlike a virus. In my case, I was soon to learn that pre-existing conditions could intensify the infection's potency. At eight years of age, I already had at least one comorbidity: a love of ghost stories and all things Halloween. That first exposure to Dark Shadows ticked all my Monster Kid boxes and sealed my fate. I spent that entire summer break of '67 in a delirious fever dream. With no school to run home from, my condition quickly became chronic. Come Autumn, I was incurable.

By the time I entered 4th grade at Brockett Elementary in Tucker, Georgia, I had already started a scrapbook dedicated to the show. I'd grab my mom's good scissors and cut out every article, review, advertisement, photo, and any other Dark Shadows what-have-yous I could get my tiny hands on. My sister's Tiger Beat magazines were reduced to Swiss cheese. I drew obsessive pictures of everything from the characters to the coffered drawing room doors of Collinwood. That winter, I wrote a six page, sixteen act play (neatly pecked on my dad's Royal typewriter) and convinced a very indulgent Miss Morris to allow me to produce, direct, and star.

We played one performance to a packed classroom, and in the opera house of my imagination, 9-year-old Mark B. Perry was Barnabas Collins.

DARK SHADOWS
(BASED ON THE DAY-TIME SERIAL)
ADAPTED FOR THE STAGE BY MARK PERRY
Act One
Narrator–"Dark were the shifting shadows that waxed and waned among the turrets and gables of the great house at Collinwood. Darker still were the shadows that deepened over the souls of those who dwelt within -- shadows of fear and evil and despair..."

Soon after, in art class, I used cardboard to make a nifty miniature coffin with a teeny-tiny plaque drawn on the lid bearing my name. Mrs. Johnson, a walking stereotype of the sourpuss southern schoolmarm, paused by my desk and drawled, "Mark Perry, you are a morbid child." What a compliment!

That six-sided coffin would turn out to be the inspiration for a full-size traditional four-sided casket constructed from scrap lumber in my dad's basement workshop. I painted its plywood exterior flat black and attached brass drawer pulls as pallbearer handles. I even fully lined the interior with an old, tufted pea green bedspread to make it extra comfy. To my delight, the finished product once spooked a hapless furnace repairman who, had he known I was "playing Barnabas Collins" inside, might have hightailed it back up the stairs three at a time, his hair turning shock white as he flew. I'd have liked that.

So devoted to the Dark was I that I'd hold the microphone of my parents' cassette recorder up to the TV speaker and record the episodes to play back again and again until the allowance-busting cost of cassettes forced me to dub over them. Years ago, I found one such tape and relived the sounds of Barnabas chatting with some lovely but ill-fated night worker on the Collinsport docks. Then, Bob Cobert's signature "Bomp bomp boooooooomp!" hammered home that thrilling moment when our hero reared his head back, exposed his maxillary cuspids, and got down to business. On the recording, the music was then lost in the sound of the microphone being dropped as my child self not only squeed but burst into applause.

And still, no one called Child Protective Services. I'm telling you, had a time traveler shown up from the future and given me a box containing every single episode—a box shaped like a coffin no less—I likely would never have been heard from again.

I was fortunate in that my folks just shrugged it all off. Sure, maybe they would have preferred that their cape- wearing kid emulate Superman and not a bloodsucking serial killer, but they never once said boo about it. Instead, my resourceful mom soon figured out the best way to punish me or get me to do virtually anything was to threaten to take away my Shadows. And that's why, to this very day, I'm still the best little boy in the world.

So in case you were wondering, those are my Dark Shadows bona fides. Which brings us to what I believe to be the reason Patrick McCray honored me with his invitation to be his warmup act. You see, Dan Curtis' brainchild was a major influence in setting me on my long voyage to Planet Grownup where I've settled in as a professional TV writer-producer with more hours of broadcast episodes than I care to (or probably even can) recall. I'm also the guy who's crazy enough to be trying to reincarnate Dark Shadows as a sequel series. Because, as I say in my pitch, I'm determined to see the show restored to its rightful place in the pantheon of great gothic horror television. As it turns out, that's at least one mission I share with the inestimable author of the pages to come.

McCray's quest to understand the show's magic was sparked not by mere fandom, but by something truly spiritual he can best explain himself. And just as I am driven to repair the disrespect and damage done to the show by a certain $150 million dollar insult discourtesy of Messrs. Burton and Depp, so, too, is McCray. I with Dark Shadows: Reincarnation and he with his vast catalog of works devoted to pop culture's quirkiest and most uniquely addictive phenomena. Of course, he expresses this far more eloquently when he writes of that ill-advised film, "...the 2012 creative team didn't have the soul to show Dark Shadows fealty or the wit to mine the genuine humor for its predicaments." Yeah. What he said. Though I think "creative team" is just his way of being a gentleman.

The show is not now and never was a campy "vampire out of coffin" romp. Instead, as McCray puts it with such elegance: "It's Shakespeare writing a Greek tragedy commissioned by Rod Serling." And that is the respectful perspective from which he waxes about all things Dark Shadows. The good, the bad, and the Leviathans. As I read McCray's scholarly take on these episodes one by one, I realize that my Dark Shadows mania has always been childlike and blissful in its ignorance of the show's overarching themes and metaphors and dramaturgical nuances. I mean, I've always known the show was the coolest thing since The Twilight Zone, I just never knew how cool. Maybe because I never really stopped to think about it, as opposed to McCray who apparently can't stop thinking about it. And that's something for which we can all be quite thankful indeed, but you already know that or we wouldn't be all snuggled together here in these pages.

But back to me for a moment. As established, I'm a lifelong fan of the show, but I'd never really embraced its fandom until these past few years developing the sequel. Shortly before I "came out of the coffin" and started to connect with other monomaniacs in the DS community, I took great pride in watching all 1225 episodes. It took me a couple of years, with a rather lengthy hiatus somewhere in the loooooong Adam/ Frankenstein arc, but my mission was at last accomplished. Brief digression #1: I wish I'd read McCray's book before my rewatch. His thoughtfully word-smithed tribute to that storyline and Robert Rodan's portrayal of the creature not only opened my eyes but pulled tears from them, dammit.

While still in my pre-McCray era/ignorance, on my own initiative, I (thought I) came up with the idea to start a new rewatch but this time beginning with the 1795 origins storyline through to Victoria Winters being hanged as a witch, then jump back to 210 for the introduction of Barnabas Collins. I was intrigued that the character released into 1967 Collinsport bore little resemblance to the man he had once been and was destined to become again. I started to ponder what 172 years of sentient inhumation might do to an undead person's disposition. How it might have turned the hopeless romantic 18th Century Barnabas into the 1960s sartorial villain who ended every scene handwringing to some variation of "(insert character name) must die...and soon!" How clever I (thought I) was!

Ahem.

Enter Patrick McCray. I don't recall exactly what combination of words I fed into Google that summoned him into my awareness, but once he arrived on the scene, I realized I'd been holding his beer without even knowing it. Of course he'd already done the 1795-rewatch-jump-back-to-1967 thing, and the only face-saving consolation for me was that our theories explaining B'bas' cantankerous mood swing more or less jibed. At least I felt somewhat validated. And then there's the ultimate beer-hold: a full decade earlier, he had famously watched all 1225 episodes. Only He did it in 45 days. Just calculating the daily hours involved in that undertaking is beyond my mathematics. The very thought of such an endeavor conjures images of Malcolm McDowell's eyes-pinned- wide-aversion-therapy-treatments in Kubrick's A Clockwork Orange. So I think it's pretty safe to say McCray pioneered—if not outright invented—the binge watch before it had a name. And he did so with the ultimate bender. Is there any other single series with more produced episodes available on DVD or streaming? I think not. And he emerged from that sensory overload chamber with some pretty darn profound insights into the show we all love.

Let me put it this way: if Dark Shadows were a language, I could speak and understand it well enough to get a taxi or order a burger at the Collinsport Inn without humiliating myself. Whereas McCray, who achieved his fluency through the total immersion method, would be holding court at the Blue Whale, surrounded by every Sam, Carolyn, and Harry in town, cracking wise and making them all laugh until they were hyperventilating.

Which brings me to a point I've been anxious to get to while having so much tangential fun. Those of us in the DS universe often hear that Dan Curtis and his team would sometimes ignore plot inconsistencies and production bloopers because they were pretty sure nobody would ever see the episodes again, let alone re-watch the entirety of their work in order. Moreso, to their way of thinking, who in their right mind would want to? (Digression #2: If that were true, one has to wonder why Curtis saved all the tapes—but that's a discussion for another time.)

Now, I've been in many a writers' room and I've also been a showrunner on more than one TV series. In those thirty-plus years, my experience producing just 22 or more 45-minute little movies in ten months is a hair-on-fire exercise. Remember the I Love Lucy episode where Lucy and Ethel get jobs in a chocolate factory? Where they're working the assembly line and it rapidly goes from easy-peasy to chaotic hilarity? Well that, my friends, is exactly what it's like to produce a TV series—only you have to replace hilarity with blind panic. It's a relentless conveyor belt of breaking story, writing, studio notes, rewriting, network notes, more rewriting, director meetings, casting sessions, still more rewriting, more meetings, pre-production, production, and then trying to fix it all in post. And the conveyor belt never slows or stops until the season order is completed. Now try to imagine an overlapping conveyor belt where you're doing all of the above while simultaneously in pre, pro, and post on several other little boxes of chocolates. Only this time, *the season order has no end in sight*. It's not just multi-tasking; it's *omni*-tasking. And like Lucy's chocolate factory, some of your darlings will come out perfect, a few will be a little beat up, a handful you'll eat, and the rest you'll stuff down your pants.

With that in mind, this TV veteran has to confess I cannot wrap my remaining brain cells around how the writers of *Dark Shadows* produced five episodes a week, 52 weeks a year, without a single rerun and only five preemptions from 1966 to 1971. I mean, their conveyor belt must have been a Clive Barkeresque steampunk version of Lucy's. And despite that, they somehow managed to produce—as McCray is fond of saying—one complete, epic, and satisfying story. Honestly, it's hard for me to imagine anyone having the time to put a tenth of the thought into creating their work as McCray puts into his analysis of it. The original writers even admitted they sometimes got so lost in their own tangled web that they'd have to ask the schoolkids congregated outside the studio for clarification.

So the big question for me is: Were they aware of all the resonating subtleties and elegant callbacks and character nuances or the blend of comedy and pathos that McCray so artfully unearths? In their story conferences at each other's Manhattan homes, where they'd create their "flimsy" scene-by-scene episode beat sheets working from Sam Hall and/or Gordon Russell's master plan, were they spinning all that gold on the fly? One of these talents, Violet Welles, recalled in an interview that they also spent a *lot* of time on the phone, laughing hysterically as they tried to recall if Quentin was alive or dead that week or who had done what to whom in 1840. In the center of their daily maelstrom-like grind, were they hiding all those Fabergé Easter eggs that McCray has found in his archeological dig, or were they just sprinting to make sure ABC didn't go dark at four o'clock every weekday afternoon? All the while chanting their mantra *"it's okay because no one will ever see our work again!"*

After reading what lies just a page flip away—McCray's brilliant, insightful, and often laugh out loud blend of reverence and its more mischievous alter ego—I think we can safely conclude the *Dark Shadows* writers may not have always known exactly what they were doing, but they were all so whip smart literate that they did it anyway. By second nature. Part damn good crafts-*person*-ship, part happenstance. But one takeaway from McCray's analysis is that you can't have those happy accidents if you're not already on the right path. He makes a masterful case that he's not retrofitting excellence, it's already baked into the show's DNA, whether intentional or as the result of a collective savant-like genius among Dan Curtis and his scribes. And we're all very fortunate indeed to have Patrick McCray—Mr. *Dark Shadows* himself—to sort it all out for the rest of us.

Now get out of here and go binge this book. If you're like me, you'll be bitten all over again.

Mark B. Perry was born and raised in Atlanta, Georgia, and earned his BA in broadcast journalism from the University of Georgia. An aspiring writer and filmmaker, he moved to Los Angeles in 1986 and worked as an office temp until he wrote a script on spec for the top-ten show The Wonder Years. Not only did this writing sample lead to a freelance assignment and a staff position on the series, it was also purchased and produced as the opening episode of the 1989-1990 season, entitled "Summer Song." Its premiere was the number three show for that week in the Nielsen Ratings, outranked only by the venerable Roseanne and The Cosby Show. Mark went on to write and produce such diverse television series as Northern Exposure, Picket Fences, Moon Over Miami, Law & Order, Party of Five, Push, Time of Your Life, Pasadena, First Years, That Was Then, One Tree Hill, Windfall, and What About Brian. After helping successfully launch the second season of ABC's Brothers & Sisters in 2007, Mark was then a co-executive producer on CBS's Ghost Whisperer. Finally, in 2011, Mark began two gloriously venomous seasons on the ABC hit Revenge before resigning to complete his debut novel, City of Whores. As a producer on the first season on David E. Kelley's Picket Fences, Mark and the other producers received an Emmy Award for Outstanding Dramatic Series (1993). For his episode of Party of Five entitled "Falsies," he was nominated for a Writers Guild of America Award for Best Achievement in Dramatic Writing (1997). And for his writing and producing services on that same series, he shared a Golden Globe Award for Best Drama (1996). He is best known to fans of Dark Shadows as the creator/executive producer of Dark Shadows: Reincarnation.

In this author's opinion, Dark Shadows has found in him what Battlestar Galactica found in Ronald D. Moore.

A FOREWORD CONCLUSION

Take 1225 steps back. Look at the whole series. What's the story?

When Barnabas appears in 1967, we think he only wants one person: Josette. But that's not who he wants. She loved him for what he represented. Rather, he wants his sister, Sarah, who loved him for who he was. Who he still is. Maybe. When she finally appears to Barnabas, she castigates him for his newfound reliance on force, brutality, and terror. He must be good, she tells him. Only when he is, will she appear again.

The currency of human interaction is trust, and trust is a myth that only exists until we screw up. Some people pride themselves on never screwing up. That must be nice. For the rest of us, transgressions identify us far more than our triumphs. And then it becomes the job of stories to clean up the emotional mess that results.

Separating sins from sinners is anathema to us. Look at our news. We thrive on real-life exposés of supposedly-good people who are revealed to be the worst of us all. Mistrust is a fundamental human survival skill, so those moments of revelation justify our fears.

While mistrust, especially of the self and of our own character, might help us survive, it does not help us evolve. It's a road that leads to safety, but not happiness. Not joy. And ultimately, not love.

It's a choice that keeps us, literally, in the dark shadows.

The movie Magnolia is another look at what pulp historian Gordon Dymowski calls "intergenerational trauma." In it, we are asked, "What can we forgive?" Well, what is the basis for forgiveness?

Forgiveness is an act of faith. It's a statement that just because someone has done something fundamentally bad, it does not follow that they *are* fundamentally bad.

Similarly, doing good deeds does not make you a good person. How many dispensers of good deeds are tirecome creeps? Exactly.

The ultimate defining act of a good person is recognizing the worth in another human when they don't expect it.

Barnabas makes a mistake. He uses someone without valuing their humanity or his own. He treats Angelique as a commodity. He treats Josette that way too… she's a means to a business end. And why should he not treat either woman that way? That's how he treats himself. That's how his family treats him.

It's literally no way to live. As a vampire, he stands outside of the social world where they treated him like a prop and encouraged him to treat others like props. Until he doesn't. After a fashion, he finds purpose in doing good deeds. First as a human reborn, but even more as a vampire… but a vampire by choice.

And we think he's mastered that at the end of 1897. The reward? He becomes a human again for the second, arguably third, time. He's learned his lesson, and all's right with the world.

So what's up with him becoming evil again with the Leviathans? I'm not talking about the literal truth of the storytelling mechanics. He wasn't privy to the story sessions. I'm talking about the metaphorical truth of someone who is ignorant of those show-building realities.

His second fall is as much a metaphor as anything.

It's a signal that the story isn't over. It's because he still has not forgiven Angelique. He's congratulated his cleverness, but he cannot surmount the challenges of his wounded heart, his deafening pride, and the damage it has done. Because Angelique remains.

And yes, yes, we know that he should forgive her, but why? How can either truly atone? What's on the other side of that action? Just… "for its own sake"? Man, the eleemosynary patina of professionally Saving Collinwood must really bring out the natural luster of that Broyhill, huh?

And here we come to the point.

When Sarah finally speaks to him, hundreds of episodes before, she tells him that he must "be good."

Barnabas interpreted this as "doing good." And like a good superhero, that's what he does. But if you asked him, regarding Angelique, how a fundamentally good person would relate to her, he would probably say, "Forgive her. But I can't do that. Ergo, it makes me a bad person."

In 1840, Barnabas has lost everything again, but on a scale so grand it consumes not just the house, but the future. Seeking refuge in yet another page of the past, he is again faced with Doing Good versus Being Good. The difference lies in the most impossible choice imaginable for Barnabas: forgiving Angelique.

But how? His sister's death. His mother's death. His uncle's death. Her acts are unforgivable. But so are his. And the two of them just keep living, anyway. Often in Hell, either literal or metaphorical. But they've lived. That cannot be said for many others.

Forty-five years and nearly two centuries later, they are the last to bear the scars. And the guilt. Who else can understand the centuries of umbrage? Who else feels the uniquely dire need for forgiveness? Of course, they are united in anger. And pain.

And guilt. And, yeah, sure, love. But it's easy to lie when you say, "I love you," especially to yourself. Love means so many things because it describes a feeling rather than a definable result. If that were not the case, unemployed divorce lawyers would roam the land. Because only in matters of love is "for now" pronounced "forever."

But forgiveness? That's an end point. Future actions can stamp "I love you" as null and void. But you don't fall out of forgiveness, and if someone tries to take it back? That pretty much invalidates the authority they had to grant it.

Sarah wants Barnabas to *be* good. Doing good is to love Angelique. Being good is to forgive her. At last, Barnabas is good.

We know that he always was. But will he remain good, even after Trask kills Angelique and robs Barnabas of his inspiration? In our last moments with the Great Man, he is between fury and despair. To what will it drive him?

To what would it drive us?

For hundreds of episodes, we've been able to second-guess his judgment. Because we knew better, and we knew that he'd be in years of episodes to come. That's more security than any of us enjoy in "real life." But when he returns from 1840, there are no more episodes for B. Collins, esq. For the first time, Dark Shadows presents a cliffhanger that can never be resolved.

Rather, it can only be resolved by the choices made by those of us living on the other side of the screen.

- PATRICK McCRAY

WHO'S WHO

I've been told that the first book was easily enjoyed by those who had no familiarity with Dark Shadows. At the same time, a friend suggested that a character index wouldn't hurt. Wise man. The year listed usually refers to the year we first met them. It's a selective field guide, at best, alphabetized by first name except when it isn't. By the way, for those who came in after the credits, "PT" is a term used throughout the book, and it means "Parallel Time," a mirror universe.

Abigail Collins (Clarice Blackburn):

Barnabas's aunt and humorless, religious zealot. We can thank her for the witch trial and Trask. 1795

Adam Collins Lang (Robert Rodan):

A Frankenstein's Monster, created by Eric Lang and sparked to awareness with the "life force" of Barnabas Collins. Thus, Barnabas is cured of vampirism as long as Adam lives. They also seem to share a sense of physical pain. 1968

Aristide Plantagenet (Michael Stroka):

Sleazy fop and enforcer for Count Petofi. Had a thing for puppets. 1897

Angelique Bouchard Collins Rumson (Lara Parker):

Assumed name of Miranda Duval, a woman who gained occult powers in the 1600's. Disguised as a maid to the Dupres family in 1795, she has an affair with Barnabas, marries him, and then curses him with vampirism in response to a musket ball wound. 1692, 1795, 1840, 1897, 1968, 1970

Barnabas Collins (Timothy Gordon, Jonathan Frid):

Son of Collins family patriarch, Joshua Collins, and heir to Collinwood. Cursed by Angelique in 1795, Barnabas is a vampire, off-and-on, several times. Released from a chained coffin in 1967 by Willie Loomis, he is initially smitten with Maggie Evans, who resembles his late fiancée, Josette. 1795

Bruno Hess (Michael Stroka):

Sleazy fop and enforcer for the Leviathans. 1970

Bruno Hess PT (Michael Stroka):

Sleazy fop and composer for PT Angelique. 1970PT

Brutus Collins (Louis Edmonds):

Collinsport's 1580's business tycoon and bearded occultist who so dislikes infidelity that he curses all future Collinses to sacrifice one of their own to a haunted room because his wife, who was not a Collins, cheated on him. People, you know? 1841PT

Ben Stokes (Thayer David):

Brutish-but-gentle criminal who winds up in indentured servitude to the Collins family, particularly Barnabas. 1795

Beth Chavez (Terry Crawford):

Collinwood chambermaid and sometimes lover to Quentin Collins. She is a beloved fixture in the life of Edwardian heir, Jamison Collins, whose oldest child bears her name. 1897

Ezra Braithwaite (Edward Marshall, Abe Vigoda):

Silversmith who, as a very young man, makes a vaguely protective pentagram for the Collins family before transforming into the hunky Abe Vigoda. 1897, 1969

Bramwell Collins (Jonathan Frid):

Barnabas's son in PT. A loner. A rebel. 1841PT

Clarence "Burke" Devlin (Mitch Ryan):

Rakish business tycoon, framed for manslaughter by Roger Collins. And get this, he's bent on revenge. 1966

Carolyn Stoddard Hawkes (Nancy Barrett, Diana Walker):

Daughter of Elizabeth Collins Stoddard. Has a thing for guys who are bad news. 1966

Catherine Harridge Collins (Lara Parker):

Bride to Morgan Collins. Lover to Bramwell Collins. 1841PT

Cassandra Blair Collins (Lara Parker):

The pseudonym used by Miranda Duval (who also used the alias, "Angelique") when she comes to 1968 to bed Joe, marry Roger, and kill Barnabas. 1968

Charles Delaware Tate (Roger Davis):

Smock-frocked artist who inherits the power to turn his paintings into reality. 1897

Chris Jennings (Don Briscoe):

If my calculations are correct, he's the great-grandson of Quentin Collins. As the eldest male of his generation, he inherited the werewolf curse. He has no idea that he is actually a Collins. Neither does his young sister, Amy, nor his twin brother, Tom. The same can be said for his cousin, Joe Haskell. 1968

Cyrus Longworth (Christopher Pennock):

Friend to the Collins family in 1970 PT and creator of a Jekyll/Hyde formula that transforms him into John Yaeger. 1970PT

Daphne Harridge Collins (Kate Jackson):

Catherine's sister, Morgan's sister-in-law, and Bramwell's wife. He doesn't love her, ergo, she is intensely loyal. 1841PT

David Collins (David Henesy):

Allegedly the son of Roger Collins, although he and Burke have a lot more in common. Hmmmmm. 1966

Dr. Dave Woodward (Robert Woods, Robert Gerringer, Peter Turgeon):

A local physician who becomes confident that Barnabas is a vampire. Just to teach him a lesson he won't forget, Barnabas has Julia kill him. At least, I think he does. Yeah, I'm pretty sure. Anyway, he asks too many questions and winds up dead. Word to the wise. 1967

Dr. Eric Lang (Addison Powell):

A scientist of rather extreme passions and even more extreme results. He cures Barnabas of vampirism and creates new life out of the kibbles and bits of various cadavers. I love this guy. 1968

Diabolos J. Bonacker (Duane Morris):

It's how they spell Satan in the south. 1968

Dirk Wilkins (Roger Davis):

Mustache-toting handyman and be-gloved groundskeeper for Collinwood. This guy can't get a break. He's made the hypnotized love slave of an Egyptian fire goddess before becoming the most profoundly diabolical vampire in the history of the show. 1897

Edward Collins (Louis Edmonds):

Quentin's upright and repressed brother, Edward is the very picture of Victorian propriety. Over the course of his storyline, we see him mellow, gain dimension, and become the greatest monster hunter of his age. Or perhaps any other. Possibly my favorite character on the show. 1897

Edith Collins (Joan Bennett):

Miserable wife of Gabriel Collins, eventually the grandmother to Quentin, Edward, Judith, and Carl. Keeper of the "family secret." She does all of this while simultaneously being dead. Well, kind of. 1840, 1897

Elizabeth Collins Stoddard (Joan Bennett):

"Present Day" matriarch of the family, she is alternately warm and austere, having spent nearly two decades guarding the nonexistent corpse of husband she unknowingly failed to kill. 1966

Gabriel Collins (Christopher Pennock):

Ostensibly disabled son of Daniel Collins, Gabriel is bitter, scheming, pathetic, and often intentionally hilarious. He left Fox News in February 2021. 1840

Gerard "Hair" Stiles (James Storm):

Pseudonym for Ivan Miller, fashioning himself as the best friend of Quentin Collins I. He also occasionally claims to be psychic. Eventually, he will be possessed by Judah Zachery, who will continue to appear as Ivan's ghost well into the 20th century. 1840

Buzz Hackett, CPA (Michael Hadge):

Messiah. 1966

Hallie Stokes (Kathy Cody):

The niece of Professor Stokes, dropped off to live at Collinwood so the Professor can continue his lifestyle of occult investigation and sybaritic delights. 1970

Istvan, Chad (Henry Baker):

Mute bodyguard for King Johnny Romano. 1897

Jamison Collins (David Henesy):

Son to Edward, he is the beloved nephew of Quentin Collins II. He's also the father of Roger and Elizabeth. 1897

Jason McGuire (Dennis Patrick):

Charismatic and manipulative con-man, he leverages Liz's guilt over her husband's non-murder into a near-wedding. 1967

Jeff Clark (Roger Davis):

Identity kind-of assumed by Peter Bradford when he is drawn to the present day by love and the promise of endless hot breakfast buffets. 1968

Jenny Rakosi Collins (Marie Wallace):

Abandoned wife of Quentin Collins and sister to Magda. Her death at Quentin's hands will lead Magda to curse Quentin and his heirs to lycanthropy. 1897

Jeremiah Collins (Anthony George, Timothy Gordon):

Barnabas' stalwart uncle, near age-peer, and best friend. Naturally, he marries Barnabas' intended. But it's all Angelique's fault. 1795

Joe Haskell (Joel Crothers):

Hardworking fisherman and boyfriend to Carolyn. Little do they know that they are related. Nutty. Later, boyfriend to Maggie. 1966

John Yaeger (Christopher Pennock):

The evil side of Cyrus Longworth. Looks like Bob Goulet. 1970PT

Josette Duprés Collins (Kathryn Leigh Scott):

Sugar heiress whose engagement to Barnabas earns her the wrath of Angelique, who's slumming it as her maid. 1795

Joshua Collins (Louis Edmonds):

Father to Barnabas. Proud and unyielding in his defense of virtue and principle, he will oversee the efficient and prompt destruction of all he holds dear. 1795

Judah Zachery (Michael McGuire, James Storm):

Occult supervillain tried and executed for witchcraft by Amadeus Collins. His curse on the family reverberates for hundreds of years. Judah trained Angelique in the black arts and later returned to America in a glass box. Well, just the head. But as a gift. (Of course.) 1692, 1840, and arguably 1970

Judith Collins (Joan Bennett):

Quentin II's humorless sister and spinster for hire. Of course, she inherits the family fortune. Of course, she marries a Trask. 1897

Julia Hoffman, MD (Grayson Hall):

Badass psychohematologist. In love with Barnabas. Comes to Collinwood to find the man who kidnapped Maggie. Stayed for the vampire. 1967

Kitty Hampshire, Lady (Kathryn Leigh Scott):

Con artist and nefarious sweetie, she is the ultimate and true repository for the ghost of Josette. Finally. 1897

Laura "The Phoenix" Stockbridge Collins (Diana Millay):

A being who appears every hundred years to give birth to a Collins heir and then burn him alive. 1897, 1966

Leticia Faye (Nancy Barrett):

Cockney psychic at large. She's the boho chic version of 1897's Pansy Faye. 1840

Magda Rakosi (Grayson Hall):

Charismatic gypsy and sister to Jenny Collins, she avenges her sister's murder by cursing Quentin with lycanthropy. 1897

Maggie Evans (Kathryn Leigh Scott):

Diner waitress and later, the tutor to David Collins. She looks exactly like Josette. 1966

Morgan Collins (Keith Prentice):

Stiffnecked husband to Catherine, driven mad by Brutus Collins. Very loud. 1841 PT

Bathia Mapes (Anita Bolster):

An occult warrior unable to defeat the demons of Collinwood. 1795.

Naomi Collins (Joan Bennett):

Despondent and boozy mother to Barnabas, she's the best of us. And we see where *that* gets her. 1795

Nicholas Blair (Humbert Allen Astredo):

Warlock or Demon? Yes. He's often assigned by Diabolos to craft a terrestrial army. Unsuccessful, but darned natty. 1968

Nora Collins (Denise Nickerson):

Daughter of Edward and niece to Quentin, she serves as the latter's conscience and moral voice. 1897

Pansy Faye (Nancy Barrett):

Psychic music hall performer and card-carrying member of the cockney strumpet's union who follows up her engagement to Carl and murder by possessing a fundamentalist. She's like Leticia Faye by way of Spencer's Gifts. 1897

Peter Bradford (Roger Davis):

A stalwart jailer who recognizes Vicki's innocence and defends her in the witch trial. His love for her draws him to 1968, where he assumes the identity of Jeff Clark. What a guy! 1795

Petofi, Count Andreas (Thayer David, David Selby, David Henesy):

Jovial and amoral mage whose desire to escape the wrath of gypsies leads him to hijack Quentin's future-bound body. 1897

Professor Eliot Stokes (Thayer David):

A strutting stag of a man, he is the true Master of the Mystic Arts. Men want him. Women want to be him. 1968

Quentin Collins I (David Selby):

Rakish supernatural scientist and irresponsible dad. 1840.

Quentin Collins II (David Selby):

Rakish supernatural adventurer and irresponsible dad. Future werewolf, ghost, and swinger. 1897, 1969

Quentin Collins I (PT) (David Selby):

Rakish voice of reason and irresponsible dad. To someone, at some point. 1841PT

Quentin Collins (1970PT) (David Selby):

Rakish business tycoon and irresponsible dad. 1970PT

Rachel Drummond (Kathryn Leigh Scott):

Governess to Jamison, she's the first Josette duplicate in 1897.

Roger Collins (Louis Edmonds):

Elizabeth's brother and David's father. He goes from being a real sourpuss to an occult hero when he kills a cult thug with big hair. He accidentally marries both a fire demon and a witch. Oh, he also killed a guy while driving drunk and then sent Burke to jail. But he got better. Roger, not the accident victim. 1966

Sarah Collins (Sharon Smyth):

Barnabas' inexplicably young sister, killed by Angelique. Sarah returns as a ghost and perhaps catalyzes much of the story. 1795

Sky Rumson (Geoffrey Scott):

Tall, dark, and vacant, Sky is a wealthy publisher and cult member. Married to Angelique in 1970. He may be inflatable. 1970

Tad Collins (David Henesy):

Son to Quentin I. David Henesy's last part. Not… much… else. 1840

Tim Shaw (Don Briscoe):

Former graduate of Worthington Hall and now one of its teachers. Set on revenge against Trask, he is turned into the perfect assassin with hypnotic mischief. He later gets the Hand of Petofi and blows a wad of cash on a fine wardrobe. 1897

Tom Jennings (Don Briscoe):

Homespun handyman, turned into a vampire by Angelique. 1968

Trask, Gregory (Jerry Lacy):

Religious nut job who runs a repressive boarding school and marries into the Collins family. 1897

Trask, Lamar (Jerry Lacy):

Religious nut job who leads the witch trial against Quentin I. 1840

Trask, Orville (Jerry Lacy):

Religious nut job who leads the witch trial against Vicki Winters. 1795

Vicki "Victoria" Winters (Alexandra Moltke, Betsy Durkin, Carolyn Groves):

An orphan who may secretly be Liz's daughter. She is David's tutor and the original protagonist of the show. 1966, 1795

Wilbur Glenworthy, Reverend (Jonathan Winters):

The Blessed Reverend of Whispering Glades Memorial Park in Beverly Hills, California. 1965

William Hollinshead Loomis (John Karlen):

Troubled author and husband to Carolyn Stoddard. 1970PT

Willie Loomis (James Hall, John Karlen):

Troubled sea tramp and buddy to Jason McGuire. He unleashes Barnabas, who thanks him by beating him into having a conscience. He may be the heart of the show. 1967

IN THE 18th CENTURY...

PART ONE

Call to Adventure

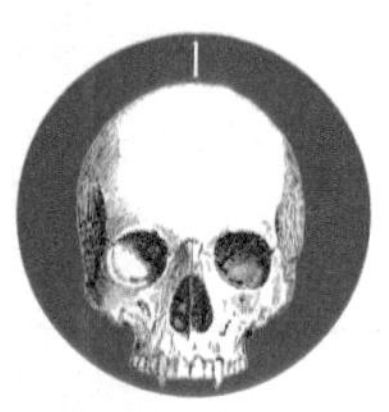

1795
Reluctant Heroes

And a beginning is a very delicate time, Ms. Irulan.
Especially three hundred and sixty-five episodes in.

Barnabas was never intended to be a hero, and we can learn volumes about the evolution of a tv show by studying his journey to heroism. Ratings hit. Can't kill him. Kids love him, anyway. What to do? And there are those who see the later Barnabas as a betrayal of his initial persona.

But that's just one perspective. When Dark Shadows is contemplated as a finished work with its own, goofy, lovable internal consistency, Barnabas was always the hero, even while we awaited his liberation. He just had a bad wake up call after an involuntary entombment of many, many decades. Who among us is truly human before the first shisha that heralds the morning? Exactly.

After 1795 reveals his origin, It's hard to view him quite so ominously. In fact, the most helpful thing for me is to go back and watch those first episodes with this storyline in mind. But who has time for that? I got two shows in Vegas tonight, so let's *get this straightened out. The faster and more fascinating approach to Dark Shadows is to begin in 1795, see who Barnabas is or was or will be and then unchain him. It adds poignancy to his fall from humanity and gives us a point of aspiration.*

EPISODE 367

Vicki's impromptu trip to 1795 might end with religious fundamentalists setting her clothes on fire, but her troubles are just beginning. Abigail Collins: Clarice Blackburn. (Repeat; 30 min.)

Abigail awakens Victoria with the news that the young time traveler is probably just an agent of Satan. The time traveler then visits an unfinished Collinwood and meets the dashing Jeremiah. Despite Abigail's misgivings, the family hires her on as young Sarah's tutor. Victoria has a bright future 175 years in the past.

367 is an episode that holds a strange magic. Victoria is in 1795, and, instead of just fainting and being carted off to her room, actually takes action exploring the world and carving a little place in it. She even challenges Abigail on the insanity of her religious fanaticism. In the space of 22 minutes, Victoria shows more gumption, drive, and nerve than she's probably displayed in the entire series and finally earns legitimate recognition as the heroine of the show. Since Barnabas will spend months as tantamount to a hapless victim, if not officially a hapless victim, Victoria becomes the lead we've been hoping to see for the past sixteen months.

The prior episode, which introduces Victoria to 1795, is even more magical, but it is so surreal and intoxicating that it feels like the dream for which Vicki mistakes it. In 367, we awaken from the dream, as does Victoria, and we find that it's still real. Bracingly so. From the start of 367, the show is off to the races. 366 finds Jonathan Frid trying a bit too hard to be the Blue Boy come to life, playing a wide-eyed innocence that is incompatible with his mordant, Canadian wit. An episode or two in, and Frid will be in his element.

The only one in 367 who seems as ill-at-ease is Anthony George, and it never seems to take for him. Contrast this with Clarice Blackburn, who finally has a part worthy of her pointy and acerbic talent. She's like the bitter, hypocritical wives in the domestic W.C. Fields movies, and she will find a way to keep that shtick fresh until Barnabas does her in, months from now. Of course, Joan Bennett is finally playing to her strengths and reads as if she walked right off the set of Man in the Iron Mask. All of this lends a touch of MGM grandeur to the proceedings. Most of all, Louis Edmonds is completely transformed as Joshua. It's the toughest role in the storyline to play. It requires him to be a stiff, unyielding representative of the double standard while still having a compassionate heart buried deep somewhere. His take on the job interview with Victoria lacks a script as funny as the one that will be perfected for the 1990 series, but the strange mixture of fairness and frugality in it makes for great TV.

Likewise, Lela Swift is composing shots and using lighting with a creativity and sense of art far beyond what we usually expect from hurriedly assembled daytime soap operas. There's a unique thrill for Dark Shadows fans in seeing Collinwood still under construction, and the early morning sun with which it is lit gives an old set a brand-spanking-new aura. Back at the not-yet-Old House, in the scene where the family is considering whether or not to take on Victoria, Swift paints one meaningful screen picture after another. She lines up the characters from most skeptical to least, often balancing the screen picture with them. These are small touches, completely unnecessary for the practical job, but they have a sense of art that is clearly inspired by the unique nature of the episode. An incredibly complicated set of given circumstances is communicated with economy and panache.

1795, as a storyline, is as much about the mixed-blessing necessity of compromises as it is about anything. Barnabas compromises with Angelique. Hell, the entire family compromises with Abigail until it's too late. But we also see Victoria compromise with Joshua and her own sense of honor as she lies her way into survival. A new skill for the unusually honorable governess. She's spent a year and a half as the measure of purity against which we judge the dirty hands of her fellow characters. Now, seeing life in a true survival mode, she'll finally gain the skills and make the choices to ultimately understand. And figure out how to play the clavichord.

This episode hit the airwaves November 21, 1967.

EPISODE 368/369

When Barnabas is reintroduced to Angelique, can he resist her temptation to stray from Josette or will the charming chambermaid distract him with an unforgettably new direction? Angelique: Lara Parker. (Repeat; 30 min.)

Barnabas is elated to find that Josette has arrived. However, when the news comes from Angelique, his old flame, he is reminded that his fidelity is precarious. Angelique does what she can to persuade him to stray, and his refusal to do so is a clear invitation to the dance for the sorceress.

One of my favorite clichés in the Daybook is about "this being the official first episode of the series." Another one is, "this is the perfect place to introduce someone to the series." Far be it from me to let you down; this episode does both!

In the previous few episodes, we are just dealing with temporal jetlag and the thrill and shock of seeing the show take on the wild ambition of 1795. The installments are certainly necessary for flavor, but when it comes to advancing the plot, this episode is all meat. As always, to find the beginning of a story, study the ending and work backward. In fact, that is the core of David Ball's Backwards and Forwards play reading technique. When you read a play backward, the context of the entire script is brought into crystal clarity. You "begin" by seeing the final, deciding choice made by the characters, the choice that sums up the entire story. By then, it's the only choice possible. The rest of the plot is about exploring how all other alternatives fell away until you reach the beginning of the play when everything is and should be possible.

Just as Dark Shadows has one or more beginnings, it has at least two endings. One, at the end of 1840, and one at the end of 1841 PT. And both of those endings have a single thing in common: Jonathan Frid and Lara Parker are in each other's arms. Seen this way, this show is about getting them there.

After seven months of hearing about Angelique, today she enters. So, no pressure, Lara. You only have to live up to a half year of build-up. No portrait. No ghost. No voice at a séance to tease the audience with your laughter. Nothing but Jonathan Frid and language.

Oh, and she is entering as the first new female character to greet the ensemble in a year or so since Diana Millay. Yes, I realized that I left out Grayson Hall. I read that as a testament to the strange gender neutrality of the part, and this is what I mean; Julia is not a creature bound by the tropes and clichés typically used as shorthand to represent the standard TV women of the era. Yet Millay is swathed in those tropes, and she entered into a tight ensemble of women, each of whom had a distinct identity and place in the storytelling. And I know, it's just me, but she never really fit. I mean, she was fine as flame flinging fire spirit women go. But Millay kind of feels like an intruder into the pre-established chemistry of the show, and it's an alienness that benefits the storytelling.

With that as the only basis of comparison, Lara Parker gets to work. Given the results, I imagine that the last words a stagehand heard from her before she made her first entrance were, "Think that's a tall order? Hold my daiquiri," as an invisible timpani began its roll.

Is she nervous? Is she confident? It doesn't matter. The moment the camera records her, she transforms the program with a beauty, sense of truth, intelligence, eroticism, and dark integrity that feel absolutely real and wholly unique in television. The casting of Lara Parker was the single most important decision Dan Curtis ever made. Not to slight Jonathan Frid, but his job was made easier than you might think by the costume and the lyrical writing, the props, the Old House set, and the fact that he is playing a vampire. But who made the badass a badass? This challenge is far more sophisticated. And Lara Parker had no fangs (at this point). Her costume had to represent eighteenth-century refinement with a dishwater lack of glamor. Did she get an Inverness cape? Did she get a cool ring and a nifty cane? No. She got a handkerchief and Jeffersonian G.I. Joe. All of the power that she mustered had to come from within. And although she manifests no such abilities in this episode, the potential energy is clearly there. I think that's true for viewers even if they somehow missed the context laid out in the conversation over 1967.

Now we know why Barnabas became what he… will be. And with that, we know that the story can be told. It's clear why Barnabas fell in love with this woman and her unique mix of capable strength, diplomacy, and emotional honesty. With that established, there is, at last, a pilot at the stick of this plane. That build-up actually means something. The program has an actor who can make us believe that we are witnessing history rather than a reenactment.

The episode works in every regard, showing us a world of hypocrisy destined to fall. This is the "before" prior to countless little afterimages of disaster and triumph. We see all of the assumptions that will create the controlled demolition of Collinwood before it even enjoys its grand opening raffle. This begins with Joshua's dismissal of love as fit only for women, not men. This should, according to him, be a world of sensible, arranged marriages designed only to enhance commerce. Take that conflicted thinking, wrap it in the alluring regality of Kathryn Leigh Scott, and it's easy to see the rationalizations that led to Barnabas's downfall. His continued pursuit of Josette nearly two centuries later isn't love; it is his desire to earn his father's approval by projecting a very specific type of masculinity. He just happens to be a great romantic, anyway, so he will do his best to merge his natural instincts with a strategy to keep Joshua off his back. Thanks to Jonathan Frid's natural disinclination toward the erotic, his immediate and conflicted attraction to Angelique reads as far more personal than simpleminded priapism. When Barnabas loves, it's clear that he's responding to a woman's deepest essence. It's no wonder that Angelique responds as she does. Rejecting her is an act of brave determination, one commensurate with the brave determination shown by her. The pursuit of Barnabas forces her to hide her powers even longer. Not easily done after she risked everything to return to America via a sea voyage in the most inclement weather of the year. What makes it worth it? Angelique could have anyone. But Barnabas is hardly just anyone. And she has the right number. Say what you will, Angelique is not a stalker, deluded into thinking that Barnabas is something he is not. Angelique doesn't just get the memo, she binds them for the Library of Congress, forgetting nothing. If Victoria exists to find ever-new things to not understand, Angelique resides at the opposite end of that spectrum.

Her willingness to fight for that love is made all the more admirable when we contrast her with the shallow and arrogant Countess Natalie, easily pleased with her title and the cruel privileges that it makes possible. When we meet Naomi here, day-drinking to distract herself from Joshua's world, we glimpse an even darker surrender. It is a surrender of greatness that makes Angelique's determination even more astonishing. She understands exactly what she will be fighting for.

Eventually, in 1840, she will take a bullet for that belief. And she will finally die. But it will be on her own terms, having proved Barnabas's love and the worthiness of her own character. It begins now.

The episode hit the airwaves November 22, 1967.

We have no choice. It's all about "cool."

Long before Marlon Brando and others like him made "cool" cool, WASPs perfected the science of it. After all, what is "cool"? Total invulnerability. It's a Keanuvian "whoa" to the decimated Statue of Liberty... rather than George Taylor damning us all to Hell.

In the latter half of the past century, acting went from conjuring emotion to showing as little as possible. Maybe that's an appropriate response to ever-widening film screens. Maybe old- school emoting would have been overwhelming in Cinemascope. There's probably a reason that Stanley Kubrick didn't put Charlton Heston on the Discovery. Have you seen his teeth?

The central joke of the past seven decades has been watching comical characters aspire to cool when they are anything but. This is especially true on Dark Shadows. Its funniest moments come when they insist that we move along because there's really nothing to see. White Anglo-Saxon Protestants have a noble tradition of meeting calamity with stalwart denial. Despite the Irish name, no family on television WASPs like the Collinses.

397 sticks a glittery baton in the hand of that idea and puts it at the front of the parade. Barnabas is desperate to disavow anything peculiar about his blood-drenched wedding, an attempt that becomes impossible as the script plays out. If you wonder why I think Dark Shadows is an intentional comedy, watch 397, and we'll chat it up over brunch.

EPISODE 397

It's wedding bells for Barnabas and Angelique, but will Barnabas's dead uncle catch the garter? Reverend Bland: Paul Giles. (Repeat; 30 min.)

Barnabas is understandably mordant to accept that his bride is missing on the wedding day. He explains this to the reverend while rationalizing away the various haunted events from Jeremiah that interfere with the pre-nuptial wait. Meanwhile, Angelique is nearly buried alive by the ghost of Jeremiah before the presence of Ben Stokes grants a reprieve. At the wedding, more cursed events take place, and despite the wine turning to blood, they marry. The wedding night is disrupted by Josette's music box and the sight of a mocking Jeremiah.

Predictably, the social event of the year is also one of the most hilarious as the Dark Shadows writers have their wedding cake and smear it over the faces of proper expectations at the same time. They've always excelled at mixing horror with the ridiculous and the sublime, depicting situations that are monstrous for the characters, frightening for most audiences, and blackly satirical for the cast and savvier viewers. Best of all, the characters in 397 are vastly aware of this — especially Barnabas and Ben. And with Paul Giles's doddering Reverend Bland, it's infinitely clear that Sam Hall does, as well. Grayson Hall is clearly a woman of deep wit, and a script like this could only have come from the guy she chose to keep up with her. Considering that, I'm not surprised that the show allowed itself these sardonic side-quests; no... I'm amazed that it reserved them *only* for, you know, weddings.

In the midst of it all is Angelique, getting a taste of her own gris-gris with the twisted genie of Jeremiah refusing to go back into the bottle. (With this monkey's paw, I thee wed....) Of course, it leads her to pledge to do only good, which is what one often does after nearly being buried alive. And, of course, all it takes is Barnabas clutching Josette's music box like Darren

McGavin with the Leg Lamp to lead her away from the ledge and back into fiery jealousy.

This is all after Jonathan Frid's bone-dry Canadian wit gets a thorough workout alongside Reverend Bland, who struggles to find anything good to say, struggling to make wildly inaccurate statements about the admirable loyalty shown among the Collinses. Barnabas keeps his straightest face ever, explaining away breezes coming from closed windows, etc., like a Benny Hill character on a date with a flatulently deflating love doll hidden in the closet. Jeremiah does his best to ruin the wedding, and its proper vengeance for a ghost who's been through what he has. If anyone shares the hero spot of the episode, it's the villain, which is par for the Collinsport course.

This is a wedding I used to forget about when I would see the entire show over the course of years. However, it's perhaps one of the three or four most pivotal moments in the mythos. Setting up a payoff that no one knew would come in the 1840 storyline, it's a wedding of two people who love each other despite every reason not to, and Lara Parker and Jonathan Frid pull off the ambiguity with a humanity that transcends common sense. In other words, a wedding. And it's not so horrible that it nukes their relationship in the long run. If anything, it strengthens it. It's one of the shared disasters that bonds people rather than atomizes them. And it's exactly the disaster that (and you knew this was coming) would be my focus if I were King of Big Finish. They've taken the stories in another direction, and I can't complain. Imagine this as an episode of after-dinner tales. Because these are the stories the grandkids finally hear when they come back from college and can have that cognac after the meal, pulling it off as if they've always done so. Maggie and Quentin get misty-eyed talking about their nude wedding at Club Med, laughing at the fact that the only attendees were Roger Collins (who insisted) and Willie Loomis (who was inexplicably there at the time). Then, of course, the kids ask about Barnabas and Angelique's wedding. And they laugh. Protest. Roll their eyes. And tell the story. And it ends sentimentally. Which it should. Because it was all worth it.

And there are moments of warmth in the episode that ring with inevitability. Naomi, never the snob, accessorizing Angelique's wedding dress. Ben Stokes, the first and last man standing, now the best man, as well. Because, as Barnabas says, he is. In every sense in 1795, he truly is.

I'm 48 and unmarried. Episode 397 is a checklist of the good and bad that will need to happen before I am.

Well, maybe not all of it. But you get the idea.

This episode hit the airwaves January 2, 1968.

I have no idea about the cast's drinking habits. However, I have rarely met an actor whose elbow wasn't either permanently bent or at least spring-loaded like a 1970s action figure. How do they respond to shooting something like this after New Year's Eve... in 1967... New York?

EPISODE 400

Barnabas might have Trask in his crosshairs, but will Angelique's fireworks throw off his aim? Barnabas: Jonathan Frid. (Repeat; 30 min.)

Barnabas allows Trask to perform a witch-hunting ritual, confident that nothing will result but the proof of Trask's idiocy. Unfortunately, a fire spell by Angelique sends Vicki running, seemingly proving the reverend's case. Afterward, Barnabas concludes that, like the Darrens to follow, he may be married to a witch.

Can you believe these people had to work on New Year's Day? Thanks, Dan. Let's just get that out of the way right now. And we're not just talking about a regular New Year's Eve the night before. We're talking about a New York New Year's Eve. So, you can just imagine. Not only that, but they were on the hottest show on daytime television, relatively speaking. One that had gone from a storyline one year prior that was not necessarily their best, involving the Phoenix, to an entire flashback time travel sequence built around the character no one had imagined a year prior, introduced to be a villain, and now the defender of reason, commonsense, and the character — Vicki — who, until recently, was the protagonist! So, there's that. The immediate game that I played while watching this episode was trying to determine who, among the cast, was the most hungover. There are some cast members, no names please, who always look somewhat hungover, and this creates a natural confusion. However, such a sport is a fruitless effort. Because in trying to determine it, you are left with two realities. The first is that these are actors, and that is a breed that exceeds the most stalwart of the Royal Navy when it comes to the capacity to operate with absolutely toxic levels of alcohol in their systems. But the second point is that these are actors, and not just actors, but good actors. These are pros. So, if I found out that none of them were hungover, I would not be a bit surprised. Also, there was a lot of shouting and screaming in the episode. Especially by Jerry Lacy and Alexandra Moltke. And they simply would not be able to do that schnockered. So that leaves as candidates Lara Parker and Jonathan Frid. They generally are performing rituals or are involved in some kind of deep introspection in the episode, which can be done fairly quietly. But I don't believe either one of them was reeking of the sauce because their performances are just too smart and too disciplined on this day. Which means, they might've had a fairly dull evening the night before. And I think perhaps we should all have a moment of silence in recognition of their sacrifice.

I've long maintained that most of Clan Collins are secular, probably owing to the memory of the Bedford witch trials. They rarely invoke any kind of religion, leaving that to Quentin (who'll worship anything), Julia (and I lay money on her being a lapsed Catholic), and Willie (who gets religion to the degree of the threat he faces or the woman on whom he's macking). Barnabas seems to have no need for it, voicing sentiments that Joshua probably mutters only out of earshot of Aunt Abigail. If you want evidence, look at Barnabas's disdain for Trask. Not only that but look at his confidence that Trask's bizarre ceremonies will assuredly humiliate the Reverend and be the end of it. Unfortunately, give a Trask enough rope, and he'll use it to hang the governess. But this doesn't occur to Barnabas, who has no lack of credulous imagination. It says something that he'll believe Vicki's story about time travel before 2,000 years of Scripture. I can only imagine that if Jesus showed up in 1795 as the governess from the 1960's, they'd all be in a real quandary. Let's see Trask deal with that.

Barnabas has a lovable overconfidence in common sense and the essential decency of human beings… it all smacks of the Enlightenment. As the series goes on, this naiveté will lead to his frequent downfalls while also being his inspiration to rise just as often. On Dark Shadows, the bad guys are destined to win, except when they don't, and the good guys are destined to somehow survive, except when Matthew Morgan pushes them off a cliff. If the show has any emotional message, it is to revere perseverance. The victory of evil is statistically assured. The only bulwark against good's eradication is its refusal to acknowledge it, despite all evidence to the contrary.

Did I mention this is an election year?

William Faulkner asserted that every great story written after Don Quixote is a retelling of it. The Many Quests of Barnabas Collins is all the evidence we need. Most poignant in the brotherhood Barnabas shows with the great knight are their similar trips on windmills. Cyclical, often downward, but only until blessed ignorance lifts their spirits to fight another day. In 400, Barnabas experiences an entire cycle, unaware that Trask and Angelique are in a strange alliance. By the end, as he spins earthward, he contemplates the truth that his wife may very well be the seed of evil in Collinsport making Trask a fellow fool, if on the other side of the windmill. But wait. The stars will soon replace the rocks below as Fortuna spins the wheel of inevitability.

For the sake of auld lang syne, if only for one day.

This episode hit the airwaves January 5, 1968.

Roger Davis may be the most controversial personality associated with the show. He had a reputation for cutting up on the set. Some people liked that. Dan Curtis was a fan.

Some did not like that. This is America, though.

He was very different from the other men on the program. He had a different look. He had a different energy. He's the tonic to their gin.

And he's from my hometown, which immediately puts me in his corner. I grew up in the shadow of his building projects. In fact, that's how I first knew of him. He rebuilt the hotel where Tom and Daisy got married, so says The Great Gatsby. He was the second Dark Shadows cast member I ever met. I was sixteen and he was just a fireball of friendly. I mean, he stood there and talked to me like I was his long-lost nephew. It felt effortless.

The next time I saw Roger Davis, it was at the very end of the 50th-anniversary convention. He alluded to the fact that he was not feeling particularly warmed by love from the event. Maybe he had earned it. Maybe he was the victim of misperception. Maybe it was about stuff that took place 50 years ago.

There was a lot he didn't say. But he didn't have to. There was an emotion there that I understood. There was weariness. There was a sense of loss. There was some muted anger. None of it would be resolved.

These dark moments are familiar to most funny people, and he's a funny guy. I know that my own jocular nature can get on peoples' nerves. It's a defensive move that covers profound insecurity. (Hint... if someone is cracking jokes around you, take a look in a mirror because you're probably scaring them.)

Despite the bad day, he was kind. This continued over the years. As I mentioned in the last book, he read one of my essays and liked it enough that "Colonel Tom" Hotz arranged a phone call. Roger was very positive about the piece, and he was very specific.

Hearing that exactitude of response is a prized rarity.

And then he called me out of the blue, two years later, and held court with edgy affection. Profoundly funny. Emotionally generous. Totally honest. He's working on a book right now that is somewhere between a novel and a memoir. He read a section that was witty, poignant, and marvelously balanced.

Like all artists, he's a complex man. Writer, actor, architect.

Like all of his cast-mates, there's a lot to admire.

EPISODE 404

Does Vicki have the power of witchcraft after all? All bets are off when a smitten jail guard quits his day job to become Collinsport's newest lawyer for her defense. Peter Bradford: Roger Davis. (Repeat; 30 min.)

Judge Madigan goes from defending Vicki against Trask to distancing himself when she reveals her anachronistic origins.

From the wings, a handsome young gaoler named Peter Bradford volunteers to defend her innocence. Meanwhile, Barnabas is interrupted by a spying bat when he attempts to tell Josette the true identity of the witch.

If the Monolith from 2001 had taken a break from filming his upcoming Valentine's Day special across the hall, he would have dropped in on this episode of Dark Shadows. Apes at his feet. Golf club over his shoulder. "Thanks for the Memories" wafting around him thanks to Bob Cobert. Why? Change must be heralded. And to be certain, change is arriving. Dark Shadows, a cauldron of moral ambiguity, is about to get its first, pure hero. Ladies and gentlemen, join me, Richard Strauss, and the Also Sprach Zarathustra Dancers as we welcome Mr. Roger Davis.

Specifically, Peter Bradford. A character unlike any that the show has introduced in 400 episodes. He's a capital-R Romantic hero in the midst of a Greek tragedy. Both the actor and character bring everything right to Dark Shadows, filling needs we never knew the show had until now. It's appropriate that this segment of the show should feel even more like a Greek tragedy than Dark Shadows normally does. And that's saying a lot. If this program were any more Greek, it would be smashing plates and awaiting the Pierce Brosnan musical number. The show may have been low in budget, but the stakes in the drama are inventive and gripping.

The forces opposing Victoria Winters are like those tormenting Gods themselves. They are relentless. Vast to the point of institutional. And inevitable. Vicki's journey is a maddening cycle of hopes dashed, raised, and dashed again. The arrival of Peter Bradford is part of that cycle, but it also feels like the storyline is finally bucking with unexpected defiance toward fate. Vicki deserves it. It's awfully cheeky of the universe to pick on Victoria in the first place. Did it not have a worthier target? This is the person famous for saying that she doesn't understand. I love her to death, but I think few could argue that Vicki could get stuck on a broken escalator. As always, I ask why is she back there? Why was she chosen?

Especially with her growing fascination with Josette and her era, Vicki makes an ideal witness. She departs for the past as something of a Collins fangirl, herself. Her reverence for the Collins family puts her in a perfect position to be let down by the clay-footed reality. The mighty must fall. It's what makes high drama so satisfying. Besides, we can't get the deposit back on the periaktoi, so we might as well use them. Pure as they come, Victoria is untouched by the tragic flaws creating the forced implosion of the Collins family. She's an outsider. (Then again, so are Angelique and Josette.) It makes sense that an outsider would be her undoing.

Everyone admits that Trask is full of monkey feathers, but they seem incapable of honoring the wisdom of Susan Powter and stopping the insanity. She is surrounded by ineffectual voices of wealthy, enlightened reason consistently subordinated by a superstitious redneck. In this episode, it looks like she'll be getting the best lawyer in town. Complete with judiciary superpowers, Addison Powell might as well enter nude and greased up on a wrecking ball to save her, just like Miley Cyrus did, and Kate Smith, before her. The day is saved until she makes the mistake of telling the truth, and then the needle scratches off the record with cosmic inevitability.

Enter Peter Bradford. This guy's different. He doesn't even look like he belongs in a Dan Curtis production. Tenor, not baritone. Sandy-haired, not dark. Physically proportionate rather than elongated and looming. The Dan Curtis taste in casting men who look suspiciously like, well, Dan Curtis, has trained us to expect a pattern, and Roger Davis breaks it. In doing so, he feels like an ambassador from the real world, and we instantly trust him. As he offers a tearful Vicki his help, seasoned viewers wait for the music or lingering shot that would normally signal a hidden agenda. Wait all you want; we finally have a genuine mensch. If Dark Shadows is a universe where the average person harbors secret hazards, then the very presence of an average person implies statistical outliers. One would be a Trask, who is nothing but a public menace. And now, we meet his opposite. Just as rare. Seemingly, just as inevitable.

In his debut, Davis does what few actors can: he makes doing the right thing actually interesting. We see a compassionate strategist in Davis, with a purity of purpose that suggests a man who will not back down. That very sense of dedication hints at a man of both love and principle, who will, by turns, be equally feral and contemplative. His benevolence has a necessary edge, and Davis's native senses of intelligence, passion, and mischief are precisely the elements that define the program's unpredictable bravado.

Vicki may finally have a fighting chance. As Dark Shadows explores its power to push beyond limits, it also finds new limits to push.

This episode hit the airwaves January 11, 1968.

EPISODE 406

Can Angelique cure Barnabas of the curse before he escapes to Josette and rises again? Angelique: Lara Parker. (Repeat; 30 min.)

After cursing Barnabas, Angelique immediately regrets her choice and tries to cure him, despite his desire to flee to Josette. Meanwhile, Josette's neck bleeds in exactly the spots where Barnabas was bat-bitten. Angelique tries to restrain Barnabas, explaining to Ben that if he rises, he'll become one of the living dead.

The threat of indentured servitude didn't do much to dissuade Ben Stokes from murder, but at the time, he didn't know he'd also have to referee for Barnabas and Angelique. Through serving as marriage counselor-by-default, he comes across as the real hero of the episode, and weirdly, so does the witch, herself. There is a nuance in the Dark Shadows story that gets lost, and it's in 406. Angelique truly wants to undo her curse. Is it selfish? Well, in the words of Mother Teresa, isn't everything? Your Honor, in defense of Angelique Collins, I submit that she had been shot at the time said curse was laid. Who among us does not have fairly strong feelings about a musket ball burning a hole through his chest and ruining his best negligee? She didn't know she'd wake up and still be married to him. If she had known, she would have cursed him with the scent of bay rum and to always like her friends, no matter how late they stay over watching reruns of The Real Housewives of Logansport while drinking his Drambuie without replacing it. But she didn't know, and that's why he's becoming a vampire.

Nothing on the show is as simple as it would seem, nor is it easy. Angelique continues to haunt Barnabas with the kind of searing hatred that can only be attributed to true love. I continue to wonder about her inability to remove the curse in 1796, but then kind of be able to in 1897, and totally be able to in 1840. My guess is that her powers increase and diminish depending on her standing with Diabolos and how much energy it takes her to travel. The Angelique who cures Barnabas without so much as a Samantha Stephens nose-twitch has the benefit of being on Diabolos' good side, thanks to 45 years of wandering the countryside generally doing evil and staying out of church. Those batteries are full, as is the case for any magic-user who hangs around Michael Stroka for long.

But when we later meet her in 1968, the temporal journey has taken a lot out of her, and she has no interest in mercy. In that timeline, she skipped 1840 without Barnabas's return. Warren Oddson speculated on Angelique's timeline in a fantastic essay in the 1840 Concordance. In it (to my memory), he posits that Angelique's timeline goes 1795-1840, 1968, 1897, and finally 1970. This means that the 1840 Angelique is possibly the most powerful version — not as experienced, but not as ravaged by time travel, stints in Hell, and diabolic deals for parole.

As their history continues, Barnabas only tries to kill her occasionally, kind of like an incredibly patient parent who nevertheless has a breaking point. For the most part, he puts up with her rather successfully when we know full well, she's only one tiki torch away from being a stain on the road. Her insistence on curing him in this episode, to the extent of trying to keep him from packing and leaving, must have influenced his indulgence, despite his statements to the contrary. I feel for Angelique. We've all had moments of overreaction followed by the inability to retract them. What follows (for the series) is not only continued anger at Barnabas but anger at herself, as well. His survival is a constant reminder of her wrath, and the memory of her wrath is the memory of its inspiration. He won't love her. But he also won't have the decency to die and stop reminding her of the curse. Of course, she is the curse's ultimate victim, and perhaps that is as much a motivation for the cure as anything. Say what you will, but she loves him.

This episode hit the airwaves January 15, 1969.

EPISODE 427

As Victoria's trial begins, will Peter turn the tables on Trask by placing him on the witness stand? Trask: Jerry Lacy. (Repeat; 30 min.)

As the trial begins, Victoria learns that her allies in the Collins family will be of no help. When it seems as if Vicki was in two places at once, Trask's victory seems assured. Upon investigation, Peter suspects that Ben knows more than he is saying.

Jerry Lacy further establishes himself as an instant star on the show, giving us a far more strategic Trask than we've seen of the ranting loon thus far. But there is an even more dramatic element to 427. Lighting. The star of 427 is lighting. The show had used gobos off and on from the beginning to project, yes., dark shadows on the actors. In the courtroom, they cast a rounded window's mullions over the witness stand, casting Victoria in a perfect spider's web. Unsubtle? Absolutely. But if you're looking for subtlety, this isn't the show for you. TV's first (fictional) witch trial began on this day, and Sam Hall & crew are to be championed for rationalizing how that could possibly happen in 1795. The sluggish pace of the soap opera is often a whipping boy here at the Daybook, but this is an object lesson in the medium's greatest strength. Thanks to the gift of time, storylines can be lacquered up, and the ridiculous becomes the norm. Not only does this allow them to credibly insinuate the incredible plot elements into a comparably normal world, it makes the show resemble real life, where exactly the same thing happens. Except not with witches and vampires.

Okay, not with vampires.

The second payoff is for longtime viewers. As the show progresses, so does the pace — Parallel Time notwithstanding. By the time late 1968 rolls around, we accept the rules of Collinwood, and the storytelling picks up to match our familiarity with the bizarre... which has become the norm. 1840 may seem rambunctious for some, but for others who prize the chance to watch every day, it is laudably rich with daily turnabouts and surprises. In some ways, that storyline takes even more time, although what has preceded it is so baroque that it works even more. In 1795, it took them only three months to get to the climactic witch trial; in 1840, they wouldn't reach it until the fourth.

On this day in 1968, Arthur Miller's Tony-nominated play, The Price, opened on Broadway. Like all plays by Miller, it was a searing indictment of, you know, prices. Miller loved a good, searing indictment.

This episode hit the airwaves February 13, 1968. This is one of those essays where I had to skirt around condemning organized religion because the show skirts around condemning organized religion. Successfully. They could've gone further by showcasing a "good" member of the clergy, but that would have been pandering, and they were too tasteful for that. It was a rare case of a risky program having it both ways.

EPISODE 437

Victoria takes the stand for a final showdown with Trask, but will she be any match for the reverend's secret weapon? Nathan Forbes: Joel Crothers. (Repeat; 30 min.)

Trask extorts Forbes into testifying that Vicki bewitched him, a choice both would later regret. Afterward, Victoria gives her final testimony where she reveals her origin, the origin of the book, and the fact that she traveled back via séance. Hearing this, the court sentences her to hang.

The "trial of the century" — or at least, the ratings stunt of 1968 — comes to an end, and Trask plays suspiciously dirty for someone who has God on his side. Blackmailing Forbes? Is that necessary? Of course, he doesn't know that Vicki is going to do something crazy, you know, like tell the truth under oath. Victoria and Trask transcend realism (and maybe humanity) to become walking, talking metaphors, and in this sense, Dark Shadows absolves religion of evil. Religion's not the problem. If Trask and Vicki evolve into polar opposites, what is the thing that separates them? On one level, Trask lies, and Victoria tells the truth. Of course, she does; she's a teacher. Why does Trask do what he does? This is the most fascinating incarnation of the reverend. All are impulsive bigots, but the Reverend T. is the most ideologically motivated. He is there to impose the truth he knows; Victoria is there to report the truth she discovers. Close up, if 1795 is "about" something, it's a study in jealousy. Take a few steps back and look at it in the context of the series' end: it's about truth. Barnabas refuses to acknowledge his true feelings.

His mind is made up. Trask refuses to concede that the Enlightenment has transformed humanity's interpretation of God. Vicki, the hapless and professional victim that she is, stands as both an ambassador of the modern world and a counterpoint to the 1795 fad of willful ignorance. She is honest to a fault, even if it means confessing a story so lurid and fantastic that it will guarantee the noose. Vicki is compelled to tell the truth — although she could win without it — as much as Trask is compelled to twist the facts — although he could win without it.

It's a compulsion that is driven by the need To Make a Point more than human realism, but this was the era defined by Chayefsky and Serling. These writers didn't have time for realism; reality just got in the way of the truth.

Blood and thunder rule the actors today, with Davis, Moltke, and Lacy in a cutthroat race for Daytime Emmys. But what choice have they? The stakes are enormous for all, and the consequences, shattering. In between the Loud Noises is Joel Crothers. As an actor, Crothers is somewhere between Gregory Peck and Major "Q" Boothroyd from the Bond movies. No matter what he has done before, he always invents new ways to command the stage with quietly focused, intense humanity. In moments of almost no dialogue, we see Forbes grow and say more than other actors do with hundreds of lines. Any rewatch of the series reveals new heroes, but few champion the integrity of the storytelling as does Joel Crothers.

This episode hit the airwaves February 27, 1968.

EPISODE 450

In 1795, there is one force that can stop Angelique, and it just arrived at Collinwood. Bathia Mapes: Anita Bolster. (Repeat; 30 min.)

Bathia Mapes arrives to determine the nature of the curse and its solution. Meanwhile, Joshua deals with a mad Millicent, and Barnabas is drawn back to the tower room. There, Mapes begins a battle with the force cursing Barnabas.

When we first learn about the supernatural as kids, it is the quintessence of the mysterious. We've spent a year of awareness learning the rules, and here is a system of action that breaks them. To what is it connected? What possibly explains it? When I first saw Dark Shadows, I was in quiet awe of the vast mythology that explained how the house "got this way." I was in equal awe of the cosmology that empowered those forces. Could it ever be explained? Of course not. And when you're a kid, everything is inexplicable. Like magnets or the electoral college, this makes about as much sense as anything else.

Then, the paranormal all loses its sense of wonder because we pretend to understand it to death. It becomes like religion, systems of reincarnation, or D&D. We either discover or make up all manner of elaborate, insert-tab-a-into-slot-b instruction manuals for how a paranormal universe works. This crystal cures this. This orc can be killed only by that. This star cluster absolutely means you're gluten intolerant. And so on. It's just as true for monster media. Vampires have about as much written about them as do dogs and cats. But in the name of celebrating our sources of wonder, we accidentally kill them with comprehension.

Dark Shadows, perhaps due to hurried writing for a medium that "no one's going to see again," defies that. Yes, there's a lot to understand and bicker about and make charts and graphs over. I do it a lot, myself. But at its best, the show is about the opposite. It makes all of us Victoria Winters out of confident Joshuas. We make fun of Vicki for not understanding, but that's the point. She's never meant to genuinely understand what's going on. We are never meant to understand what's going on. Our job is not to understand what's going on; it's to connect through the experience of not being able to do so.

Bathia Mapes reminds us of that. Just when the show is at the outer end of strange, and Barnabas is summoning the voices of ghosts, and Joshua has lost all control of the Newtonian harness of causality, she shows up. The lighting is suddenly a dark and textured expression of the new dimension of Joshua's world, plunging us into a Rembrandt painting. The dialogue has a sudden and Marlovian urgency and poetry. On a show accustomed to talking around problems, implicating it with extreme prejudice, this episode speaks to the very heart of them. And yet, only one person knows what's going on, a strange and confident sorcerer/ precursor to Elise in Insidious.

In a show where the supernatural frequently bullies the Collinses around, it takes a formidable person to give it what for. Even Stokes would concede that there are none like Bathia, looking and acting for all the world like the EC Crypt Keeper prior to death. She gives DS mythology new depth and familiar resonance by again treating a curse as a curse. On most of the show, the curse is considered the causal agent for the real problem, vampirism, and the only cure is a stake to the heart. Mapes treats the curse as the ongoing crisis itself. She warns the Countess against being loved by him, and suddenly we get why Julia survives for as long as she does. Masks drop with thunderous noise. In no other timeline do we go from sacred denial to profane truth as we do in 1795, where the Enlightenment smolders down to a muted hell over four and a half months? As the characters go mad from the truth, and Barnabas roars with the voice of Angelique, we finally get one character who knows what's going on. It is the greatest testament to Angelique's awesome ability that she doesn't last long.

But it's Jewel Box Epic of a battle. These episodes won't be matched for sheer pain until we learn of Quentin's son's death or the eventual death of Angelique. And even then, I'm not sure that this is a sustainable quality that the show can ever rival again.

This episode hit the airwaves March 15, 1968.

EPISODE 458

Naomi faces the ultimate choice when she discovers her son is one of the living dead. Naomi: Joan Bennett. (Repeat; 30 min.)

After seeing Millicent with Barnabas, an increasingly agitated Naomi discovers that Joshua may have found a relief to the curse in Boston. She nonetheless responds with pessimism. After writing a note, she visits Vicki, who remains concerned about Peter's freedom. Vicki feels as if her visit with Naomi is the last she shall have, at which point Nathan arrives to take her at gunpoint, unmoved by her admission that she, not Peter, killed Noah. Naomi drinks a draught of poison and then visits Barnabas, who confesses all. Despite his pleas to the contrary, she persists in her love for him. Joshua enters and cradles her as her body grows cold.

And then, it got really dark.

Naomi is one of Dark Shadows' stronger, more willful characters. Every bit the equal to Joshua, which is saying somethings — she is admirably strong, honest, and loyal. These are all qualities that make her suicide either a show of defiant self-determination or a betrayal of her essence. Forgive the politics, and apologies to those whose loved ones have made that terminal selection (I rank among you), but I see it as the former. Romantic literature might not... or might. These are Barnabas's last moments before being sealed into semi-suspended animation, so, this event and example, this disposition toward death, heavily influences the man we see rise in 1967. Death is both an option *and* simply one more choice. When he murders, perhaps he is consigning others to what he sees as an inevitability that exists without shame. These are very existential questions, and when you look at them in little bits, without considering the big picture, they are easy to ignore. Just as heroes in real life don't go about spouting their ontologies like characters out of Chayefsky or Rand, nor do those on this show. Still, we can and, as responsible fans, should discern what we can about the philosophies of the characters from their actions. With Barnabas, that's a sticky wicket. Not only does he evolve, appearing in more episodes than anyone, but his perspective changes depending on whether or not he's under the influence of what I refer to as the Beast. Critics of Barnabas are quite right. He can be the master of the double standard, easily rationalizing like a machine. In the balance, his life, abilities, options, threats, and nature of existence change violently and frequently. The choices he has to make, and the range of shifting tools and consequences tied to those choices, are rarely the same. The consequences demand categorical thinking. Seeing that his own mother held death as a choice galvanized Barnabas's thinking, I believe. If it were not a shameful destination for her, it is not a shameful destination for anyone. Of course, she chose it and Barnabas's victims do not, but if it becomes a questionable destination, then his actions to consign others there become equally questionable. Thus, Barnabas must maintain a casual attitude toward the undiscovered country. Kids don't try this at home.

This episode hit the airwaves March 27, 1968.

This is one of the first pieces where the series came into acutely sharp focus for me while writing the column. In the immortal words of Floyd Gondoli, "I am a simple man of simple pleasures." I am far too easily distracted by the bright colors and exotic noises of 1897 to properly remember and appreciate 1795. The upside of this is that the sequence always strikes me as remarkably fresh and profound when I cycle back to it again.

EPISODE 459

In the wake of his mother's suicide, Barnabas Collins vows to take revenge… if his father doesn't shoot him with a silver bullet, first. Joshua: Louis Edmonds. (Repeat; 30 min.)

Hearing that his mother is dead because of revelations by Nathan Forbes, Barnabas goes about the business of revenge. Meanwhile, Forbes retorts with a crossbow.

In 1795, the cherished friends and beloved relatives around Barnabas Collins have been dead for years. Barnabas was, too. Until, and you see this coming, he died. This would all be "electrocuting a dead horse" except that this arc mentions the concepts of death and life constantly.

When Jonathan Frid delivers the line telling Forbes that bullets will have no effect because he's already dead, he's savoring the words with unusually deliberate relish. In fact, he is at his most Shakespearean in this episode. Not because of an accent. Not because he stands around posing in tights, using archaic language. No, for legitimate reasons. Listen to his treatment of the sincerely grand statements. Words are stretched into multisyllabic wrappings over decisions and discoveries of cosmic import. He's not only getting the most out of their intentional weight. He has found the dreadful music of death and revenge and the language that describes them.

We take death for granted on Dark Shadows. In 1795, it's not just a consequence. It is the subject of philosophical heft without weighing the audience down with ascetic and academic self-consciousness about it. Death is both a metaphor and a very real state of being. For once, it has, by explored implication, been given proper attention… and by implication so has a meaningful life. We stand on the battlefield of fallen characters who have no voice. Well, except for one.

By finally standing outside of life, there are no more appearances to keep up. Indeed, all the rules of the living are what cost Barnabas his life. Was he in love with Josette? Perhaps social class taboos and a marriage prospect with a business prospect chaser kept him from confessing his true feelings, even to himself. I don't call that living.

The fact that Barnabas walks and speaks, and feels is all of the proof we need that, on this program, death simply releases a cursed figure to explore living. Joshua, on the other hand, is a prisoner of his expectations. His need to appear in control is so pervasive and toxic that it takes being in the throes of death for his wife to say she still loves him.

Of course, the real journey of the storyline belongs to Joshua, reluctantly exploring and admitting the moments of humanity forbidden to him otherwise. It's unclear how Joshua became so incredibly stoic, but I will guess that life at sea, having to coexist among pirates and slavers, changes a man. His charting of an underdeveloped sense of humanity exists less on the page, and so Louis Edmonds must be lavishly praised for his efforts to do so. In theory, it's a broad part. Shouting. Taking umbrage. Being at a loss for words on a nearly hourly basis. You know, those things are easy. They are a puckish southerner's spoof of New England finery. Underneath that is a keenly focused, gently urged character evolution. Frankly, if the actions of Angelique could not bring that about, the character would lack humanity, completely.

More than anywhere else, we see the effects of the curse.

Exactly what she said: those he loved would die. But why make him a vampire at the same time? Of course, so that he could be the cause. The triple somersault of irony is that, outside of the domain of the living, subsisting by the ethics and standards of the dead, Barnabas would eventually live to a point where he realized he loved Angelique. And that's the one part of the curse that, in 1840, she forgot to lift. This isn't a soap opera. It's Shakespeare writing a Greek tragedy commissioned by Rod Serling.

On a technical level, it's not a soap opera either. An episode like this is the payoff that we somehow knew was possible while making our way through often hundreds of episodes of semi-repeated exposition with a sidecar of looming implication. Every time Dark Shadows has an episode like that, it carries with it an implicit promise for something more. This episode is as tight and propulsive as anything written for prime time. Frid, Edmonds, Joel Crothers, and Thayer David glide through the action with equal parts of passion and confidence. There has never been better chemistry on the program than with Jonathan Frid and Louis Edmonds as Barnabas and Joshua. Opening with the immediate fallout from Naomi's suicide, and with the ticking clocks of Victoria's fate and the oncoming sunrise, it manages to go about solving its problems (and inventing new ones) with purposeful urgency that never devolves into sloppiness or panic. It's too busy addressing the problems of the living with the insight of the dead.

This episode hit the airwaves March 28, 1968

PART TWO

DEPARTURE

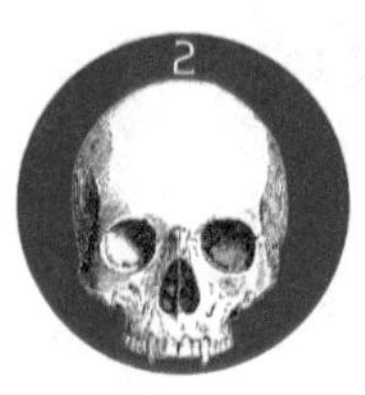

1967
CROSSING THE THRESHOLD

"Night has fallen over the Great House of Collinwood..."

Welcome to the actual first episode of the show and the traditional "first episode" of the show. The former gets the series running, as Vicki arrives in Collinsport for the first time. The latter introduces Barnabas to the 20th century, turning the pilot on its head. In Episode 1, an orphan comes to the family, hoping to find her future in the Collins' past. Willie has similar goals... if more materially oriented. Both find venerable black sheep. Liz, is one because of what she did. Barnabas, for what he was. If we begin with Vicki and Liz, everyone is sympathetic. The only mystery to solve is when the matriarch will spill the tea about her wrought-iron divorce. However, if we begin with Willie and Barnabas, the mysteries are vast and metaphysical and redolent with cosmic justice. Let's with sympathetic.

EPISODE 1

A sophisticated New Yorker gives up big city life for the charm of rural America. Will she find colorful locals and a talking pig... or terror? Mr. Wells: Conrad Bain. (Repeat; 30 min.)

Victoria Winters ventures from Manhattan to Collinsport to assume the position of governess in a forbidding mansion whose owners are ambiguous about her arrival. Along the way, she meets a brooding business tycoon, quietly obsessed with her future employer's isolation. A charismatic diner waitress, Maggie Evans, joins in the chorus of those who warn her away from Collinwood.

Okay, so technically it's the 56th anniversary of the first episode of Dark Shadows.

Except that it really isn't. It's the 56th anniversary of the first episode of Shadows on the Wall. After all, if Art Wallace had any idea that the show would've wound up as it did, there's no way that this would have been the pilot. That doesn't make the pre-Barnabas episodes inferior, but I do see them as a separate series; I think it's helpful to look through that lens.

How to introduce Dark Shadows? I mean, really. This sets a certain atmosphere, but I'm not certain it's an atmosphere that works with the ultimate point of the show. And yet it's still a marvelous piece of television storytelling.

This is both a small and large episode. It exists at night, with small ghostly characters surrounded by vast swaths of darkness. Yet, it's an expansive episode, almost an epic compared to the rest of the series. It has 11 characters which is over twice the norm of the program. It takes place on trains and at the Blue Whale and at Collinwood and in New York and in the Collinsport Inn lobby and at the attached diner and even on a lonely street corner. It takes two cities to tell this story and uses abundant flashbacks, thus told over multiple days even though it's also just a tiny slice of one endless night.

As the next episodes go on, they will all be taking place over this "day." And yet this day begins after dark, and if that's supposed to be in early to mid-June, during some of the longest days of the year, how long is that evening? That strange timelessness creates a wonderfully surreal slice of pure atmosphere. And pure atmosphere is what powers the entire story as we learn about Victoria Winters and her quest for home and meaning and identity, so yes, it's the 56th anniversary of the first episode of Shadows on the Wall. And without that, we would have had no Dark Shadows. Let's celebrate it as its own animal. And yes, I know it's all one big text and it's one big story. And yes, I am violating my own rules by looking at this as more of a slice of real-world production than the first piece of a 1,225-piece puzzle. But what's analysis without a little internal contradiction, right?

It's fun to watch how Art Wallace deploys the characters, sets, and information that viewers will need. It gives a clear view of his priorities… and what did or did not hook audiences.

As the episode begins, Vicki is introduced as someone in search of meaning, having to find out as much as she possibly can about… everything. That singular need makes her oft-repeated mantra of, "I just don't understand" feel more grating for her to say than for us to hear. Meanwhile, Roger is preoccupied with the danger of bringing a stranger into the house, while Liz seems determined to do so. When we consider that Liz is the one who has been isolating herself for 18 years, this situation becomes intentionally absurd. That is a quieter mystery than Vicki's quest. It's one to be revealed under the skin of the story, but it's more profound than any of the others.

Painting Roger as an angry xenophobe may be the only sour note here. After all, the trial and Burke's imprisonment were over years ago. Unless Roger is obsessed with Burke's return, he's in a pretty comfortable place. The later Roger — of Dark Shadows — would be thrilled at someone new coming into town. And from a dramatic perspective, having him in a place of smug comfort might have been a good height from which he could fall with Burke's return. But it wouldn't give the character anywhere to go, and it sets up one more mystery — why is Roger such an intense sourpuss?

As a character, Collinsport is depicted in a suitably dreamlike fashion; the conductor says that there are normally no regular stops there, making the town seem beyond isolated for a place with a major business within. We wonder how it can possibly hope to exist. Not only has Liz isolated herself, and not only is Collinwood a fortress from the outside, but the entire town seems insulated from any kind of external influence. We understand why Burke calls it "the beginning and the end of the world." In her flashbacks, Vicki keeps hearing the question, "What are you going to do?" And her answer is the answer of the 20th century; to take action is to step into a void of nothingness, hoping for the best.

Even though the episode is in black and white, and it uses it magnificently, its investment in the symbolism of color is still essential… such as when we hear about what Burke and Vicki have physically brought to Collinsport. Burke is saddled with two black bags, literally representing his copious personal baggage and their ominous contents and weight. Vicki has only one piece of luggage: red. Her desirability or her heart or her intensity or sense of life? Or maybe Art Wallace just liked typing the word "red." But it's a passionate color, making her a tad less virginally naive when she meets her Collinsport counterpart, Maggie.

At this point, Burke and Vicki split up. Vicki stays at the inn… a place of nourishment and comfort, where people know Burke with a fond warmth incongruous with his cold demeanor. And Burke? He goes off to a bar, which says it all. He leaves the girl with the red tote and journeys to the Blue Whale. A color both sad and obscene, attached to the largest animal on the planet. Is he Jonah or Ahab or both?

Each learns valuable information from possible allies. Or not. Vicky meets Maggie, who so little resembles the later character of Maggie Evans that the part might as well be played by Danny Trejo. Maggie is a wonderful foil for Vicki, worldly and edgy and keeping nothing to herself. They are both seemingly working class and yet nothing alike.

At the bar, Burke learns that Elizabeth has been isolated for 18 years. That's big news for the audience, but upon reflection, it seems odd that Burke would not know some of this. He hasn't been away that long. But the mystery of Collinwood pervades. It feels as if Vicki's impending danger is printed in bold on every page as the pilot moves her closer and closer to Collinwood.

Just like Barnabas would, 211 episodes later, give or take, Vicki knocks on the door under the portmanteau to gain entry. It's a very specific shot repeated for significant characters entering Collinwood… ones who seem to have more of a place there than many of the actual residents. Liz ushers her in, and the episode's abrupt end brings our attention to what we still long to know.

As the camera pulls away from the conversation to follow, we feel like voyeurs yanked back into the anonymous night. It's a directorial move telling us that we have only gotten a brief glimpse. It's a world meant to be guarded and cloaked. If we're lucky, maybe we will be allowed back in, just as Vicki was allowed in. Will our stay be as brief?

It's a terse, suspenseful inauguration. What would that series have been like if it had been a success as envisioned? Within two years, Vicki would be not only lost in space but in time as well. Her mysteries would mount rather than diminish. Perhaps Maggie never loses her brass as she gains texture and nuance. It takes grit *and* glamour to win the attention of television's brainiest, most diabolical beaus. I don't see Nicholas and Barnabas on the menu at this point, but I'm happy to hang around for them. Shadows are made to reveal surprises. Nothing could have surprised viewers more than what awaited them in the ones cast here.

This episode hit the airwaves June 27, 1966.

EPISODE 210

Willie's scheme to rob the Collins family of its wealth may cost him far more than riches when the dead rise to take vengeance. Barnabas Collins: Timothy Gordon. (Repeat; 30 min.)

As Liz pays off Jason to leave Collinwood, Willie escapes the house to plunder the Collins' mausoleum. As he cracks open a sarcophagus behind a hidden door, a hand from within the tomb grasps him by his throat.

This is the first episode that most of us in the pre-streaming generation ever saw. It may not have been the first Dark Shadows episode, but in every way that matters, it's the first episode of Dark Shadows.

We generally avoid thinking of it as the pilot of the series, because, let's face it, it isn't. To the delight of literalists and pedants everywhere, the first episode is cleverly entitled, "Episode 1." (And my favorite part is where Burke Devlin has to talk David into the pod race so that he can get a sample of his blood.) But 210 is the first that matters. Yeah, I said it. And I'm not just being a Weisenheimer. If you start with today's episode, are you really missing much? Clearly not. We didn't see those early episodes for decades, and it didn't slow us down at all.

More than most other shows, Dark Shadows is true theater. It deals with consequences rather than causes. That means that there is always some kind of past we didn't see. There are always, even for completists, "unaired episodes" being referred to. Victoria's Sanka is barely in the cup before she finds herself over a decade behind (if dealing with Burke and Roger) (or twice that time if dealing with Liz, Carolyn, and the case of the slightly bent fireplace poker). We've always missed something on the show. Isn't that the very core of the haunted house mythos? Protagonists in stories like that only exist because of what they don't know. Because of the threats, they're trying to solve threats that came from someplace else. Usually wrapping them up in problems they weren't even alive to help create.

The Dark Shadows that begins with this episode was a success to the extent that, 55 years later, you're reading about it and I'm writing about it. So, it stands to reason that this episode contributed to that success in a unique way by, you know, starting it. Most people might look at episode 210 and conclude that it works because of its last five seconds. While you would think it's appropriate to give the hand a hand, it works as a pilot in other regards. In more important regards. Barnabas is hardly the first vampire we see in the episode. In fact, all of the men in the episode are vampires to one extent or another. Jason is exploiting Liz. Willie is exploiting Jason and attempting to exploit the Collins Legacy. And while the women are largely victimized by this, I'm not sure that you can call them victims. They certainly don't act like it. Liz legitimately thinks that she is ending the situation, and she comes off as a matriarch who seems very good at ending situations; she wants to see buried in a sea chest in the cellar. This is probably why Roger had gas logs installed in the fireplace. Still, Liz clearly has secrets, and Jason knows them to the extent that he's calling way too many shots for a man with a hat like that.

Villains and heroes are immediately evident. Liz is dancing for Jason like his name's Bob Fosse, and that immediately roots us in a world where aristocracy is a ramshackle lie. But Jason also seems under the thumb of his own underling's unpredictability. He's the one pleading to Willie to come clean about his secret plans, and Willie taunts Jason with his ignorance of them. Jason's sole power, we quickly see, is in Knowing Things, so this stymies our would-be heavy to a point where he seems downright human. Perhaps more so than the austere Liz. Certainly, more so than the vaguely sanctimonious Victoria. These may be the forces of good, but evil seems more compelling and strangely identifiable. Because evil is just as powerless as we are in the face of a raw stupidity that is too dim to see the limits of its own great ideas. Hence, we see Willie's ability to keep everyone subordinate... even more than the show's blackmailing mastermind or the bedrock of Old Money American Power.

Even before the long pantomime of Solving the Puzzle of the Mausoleum, we are treated to a compelling story about the collapse of American power and the strange charm of moral corruption via Jason's Irish lilt. But it's more than that. All of these people in the power chain have fooled themselves into thinking they are the top dogs while being knowingly undermined by the guys right underneath. That's the paranoia that defines the American identity. Live by the redneck, die by the redneck. The only one who didn't get the memo is Willie, whose clues to the family jewels are the ultimate wardrobe of Emperor's New Clothes. They will only lead him to death, that is all that's below him on the ladder down from the Olympus of Collinwood.

Sure, Willie. You go exploit the rich. Spend it fast, baby. What you don't know is that death has a lot of plans for you. And we love the ending because we all know what it's like to be taken advantage of. Maybe this episode of Dark Shadows is strongest as a standalone, ending in a profoundly Rod Serling-esque place. Seeing it end like this is to see that at least one person isn't playing the game. Barnabas has no moral inversion because a dead man has no need for moral order at all. It's a relief that the cold and misanthropic universe — the one that gives cancer to infants — will also turn its relentless, cruel inevitability toward even the worst. The Willies of the world may think they have it by the ass, but death truly does come for us all.

It's just that in 210, we can finally shake death's hand. You know, after it chokes the life out of He Who Thought He Could Get Away With It. The painting of Barnabas serves as a warning of this, but no one is paying attention.

People in the house see the regalia on Barnabas and talk about how he liked to wear jewelry. But that's not jewelry. He's bedecked in the honors of war. These are the medals of a soldier. A decorated one. Barnabas Collins represents the strength that built Collinwood. A strength whose apparent absence allows a grubby second-hander like Jason to victimize Liz, and for Willie to keep Jason equally off-balance.

Only, it's a strength that is not absent. Just patient. It is a strength so undeniably resilient that even death is powerless to stop it.

Through it, in a fashion, Liz has her revenge. Willie is trapped by the literally unthinkable, and we know that it's only a matter of time until Jason is, as well.

Perhaps we didn't tune in to episode 211 to see if Willie survived. Perhaps we tuned in to make sure that he didn't.

And then everything changed.

This episode hit the airwaves April 17, 1967.

My interest in men's issues is strictly based on insecure retaliation over nothing. That, and a sense that I have been drafted into a team-versus-team competition without even getting a helmet. If a competition is going to exist, Dark Shadows dribbles the puck past the jockey and into a solid home run. Rather than take sides, it seems to have a perverse interest in nuance and contradiction.

Although it takes them a while to get there, fathers come off as important and beloved figures on Dark Shadows. Roger certainly evolves into one. Joshua, as well. And Edward. And Daniel. Basically, anyone played by Louis Edmonds. Of the many turning points experienced by Quentin Collins, the discovery of his fatherhood is arguably paramount. In fact, excluding Justin, who is more of an adopted father (at his best), almost all of the fathers transform from right bastards and into occasional paragons. In a show that focuses so intensely on family, seen now in an age where so many television fathers are fifty shades of grating, this is a refreshing representation. Even Paul Stoddard transforms. But if there is a #1 dad in Collinsport, it's single father extraordinaire and world-class alcoholic perjurer, Sam Evans.

EPISODE 235

With Maggie's life in balance, Sam Evans will stop at nothing to save her. But how can you fight the impossible? Sam Evans: David Ford. (Repeat; 30 min.)

Finding bite marks on Maggie's neck, Sam wrestles with the origins and implications of Maggie's assault. While a nurse is distracted, Maggie vanishes from the hospital by way of an open window.

It's easy to get used to good acting on Dark Shadows. So much so that it often goes unmentioned. But then there's David Ford. Like so many alumni of the show, he was also a vet of Broadway; his transposed appearance in the film of 1776 further evidences his acumen. (Theatre insiders who saw his impressive Dickinson report that it was even more outstanding than his Hancock.) The measured intensity of Sam Evans in 235 sells the terror of Barnabas as much as Jonathan Frid, himself.

Although Dark Shadows very quickly becomes a paean to outsiders, it starts out very differently, as it should. The early months establish the twisted norms of Collinsport's inner societies, high and low. The show then convincingly throws that world into uncertainty and peril with the arrival of vampires and phoenixes. Eventually, it moves entirely to the other side of the coffin lid. But before we get used to Barnabas and Quentin, we see how disturbing it is to be a mortal among gods, and few are more mortal than Sam Evans.

This episode could easily have turned into a tired-yet subtle lecture on masculine arrogance. Not with Sam. He both represents ostensible male authority and displays perseverance in the face of its reevaluation. The show's perspective on masculinity is not sexist, it's Shakespearean. Does anyone know how to properly protect Maggie? Of course not.

In a poorly written episode of the modern era, Sam would have been advised of the possibility of supernatural threats from the get-go. Of course, he would have rejected them. And of course, the implication would have been that he was blinded by rigid, masculine inflexibility, thus leading to his failure as parent and protector, etc., etc. Ron Sproat doesn't play that game. The show skirts near implicating the fallibility of men, but instead does the more universal job of depicting fallibility, period. Because anyone would have made Sam's choices. Or Joe's. Or Woodard's.

The attacks on Maggie become a rape metaphor with very little imagination. In a ham-fisted episode, someone would have warned Sam about a potential attacker as he waved it away in a whiff of omniscient privilege. But there is no warning. To Sam, in his innocence, an attack like that is more than unthinkable; it doesn't even exist. He's a true naïf, but so are they and so are we. None in Collinsport can conceive of this attack as even possible. Maggie is the ultimate victim here, and right behind her is Sam.

No one is implicitly or explicitly to blame for anything except being in the wrong place at the wrong time, regardless of role or gender. By making no move in that regard, the show makes a fascinating and bold one. Bold in the 1960s. Arguably beyond progressively egalitarian, now, because of how tempting it would be as fodder for painfully "relevant" commentary.

Bearded and robust, Sam Evans looks like the love child of Brian Blessed and God, making him a seeming straw man for a Statue of Liberty-sized misandry. The perfect target, he's just as perfect at side-stepping the accusation. Opinionated at times, but never without a heart the size of China (and twice as fragile), his masculinity is a nourishing one, not toxic. Sam Evans is both parents, and he represents the best of them on the show, despite the alcoholism.

And he increases the intensity of the program's terror, as well. With no agenda except to love his daughter, his reactions inform us about the magnitude of the horror in Collinsport... of the terror of Barnabas and all of the ensuing transgressions. Sam sees the bite marks. He knows what they are. We know what they are. Fiction is now fact. You don't just witness the generic parent of a dry-toast-plain attack victim. You meet a man whose boundaries of safety and definitions of reality are stripped away. If vampires are real, what the hell else is out there? It's the job of a parent to stretch the truth when they say that everything is going to be okay. But few have been on the business end of the boogeyman as Sam Evans. There is no limit to the possible danger now. Realizing that, Sam shuffles into battle with hapless terror as his only weapon.

The show never could have sustained this level of existential dread, but by rooting us in it, it bolsters our fidelity in the story's sense of humanity. This establishes an emotional and ethical baseline, and as wild as the action becomes, we never stray from the terror experienced by everyone, including the monsters. We all share a fundamental need for safety, and safety is grounded in the footing of knowing what's possible. That knowledge is tenuous in Dark Shadows, even demons graduate from the show with more questions than answers.

The ambiguity-fueled panic first strikes a parent, and that is a crucial choice. Sam's job as an artist makes him even more vital as our lens. It's not only his job to represent reality, it's a metaphysical statement of who he is. He informs us early into the series that he's not an abstract painter. He is Collinsport's quintessential everyman and quite the counter to the ruling family. Liz has such power and guilt that it's hard to sympathize with her. Sam's guilty, too, of lying on the witness stand, but the pressures and weaknesses experienced there are a tad more understandable. He's a parent, not a paragon. Artist and father, he's joined in the dawning horror by Joe, who must be a realist to survive on the high seas. With them, and most tragic of all, perhaps, is Dave Woodard. He fights to understand the problem from every angle but the mythic. As a physician, with the most power and responsibility, his late attendance at the party of the possible carries with it the most culpability for Maggie's fate. Burke's in that mix, as well. Materialists all, but not insensitive ones, their best estimates of reality leave them without a body, just an empty hospital bed. Robbed of all ability to protect, they are even void of the evidence of their failure.

Ron Sproat's script is an admirably balanced mix of propulsive and meditative. In the wrong hands, it would have devolved into a tired lecture. Is it a warning against arrogance? No. Episode 235 spins the strange comfort that true horror will come when and where we know it shouldn't be possible. We are all together in that predicament, and while that connection may be scant, scarcity equals value. More than any genre, horror can unite as much as divide or critique. In 235, it has the chance to do the worst of the latter. Thanks to Ron Sproat and David Ford, it does the opposite.

This episode hit the airwaves on May 19, 1967.

EPISODE 245

When Woodard needs a condemning sample, will Barnabas put the squeeze on reluctant Willie? Dave Woodard: Robert Gerringer. (Repeat; 30 min.)

Barnabas guilts Willie into giving a sample of his blood to Dave Woodard, having stolen and swapped a clean sample sometime earlier. He eventually reveals this to Willie and warns

*him that he will not always be so protective. Woodard speaks
with Burke and Vicki about the unholy goings-on in Maggie's
blood.*

Joe Caldwell had to be stopped. Dave Woodard had to be killed off. Daytime TV could have survived neither. With all due respect to St. Sam and St. Gordon, this is the best-written episode of the series, and any more of it and the show would have collapsed under its own eloquence. Sam Hall and Gordon Russell had a series to write. Caldwell crafted a masterpiece, and that's an accomplishment so situationally dependent, it would be rare to see one again.

Based on the plot alone, it is a tight and intense story of anti-heroics and suspense, where you respect Barnabas's realpolitik skullduggery while simultaneously admiring the incredible curiosity of Woodard. I don't know what he saw in that microscope except for pure anti-life and the beginning and the end of the world.

Beyond that, the episode works because of its relentless and dark poetry. Most outstanding is the mind game that Barnabas plays and plays and plays with Willie. Ultimately, after an understandable background in the betrayal department, Barnabas is going to test and punish and punish and test Willie until he's satisfied with the results, and then he's going to do it some more. Back in the good old days, you'd just send Riggs out back to horsewhip Ben Stokes like banging a jar lid on the counter to loosen it. But, you know, you can't do that now because "progress." And because the cops are after you, so you don't need extra attention. Why? Because you got your house back. And because you may get your fiancée back. And because, along with it, some people are going to make their exits a little prematurely. Um, sorry. Yes, it's a shame. It's not like he doesn't jump at the chance for a cure. Between here and there, it would be nice if Willie just, you know, put the seat down occasionally, and stopped with the betrayal business. He is letting off some much-needed steam here, and if he lets Willie dangle in uncertainty, it's probably a fraction of the paranoia Barnabas suffers as he lies trapped in a wooden shell from the lethal rays of the sun while humans do Diabolos- knows-what in full view of the kids. I'm amazed that Roger is the alkie.

The real star of the episode is Robert Gerringer as Dave Woodard. It's a human performance, both urban and urbane. The type of grownup we don't see anymore. This was a generation of writers and actors who cut their teeth on Eugene O'Neill and have no compunction about mixing their poetry with their realism. It's almost as if he and Barnabas get into a flowery Introspection Duel, like a Profundity Slam as they talk about blood and the entity responsible for all of it. They share a bizarre duality of loathing and admiration. Woodard marvels at the unnatural progress of the biochemical rite. Barnabas all but confesses to the crimes. Woodard speaks with bizarre admiration, "It's the peculiar magnificence of the human spirit that's required to provide the potential for such corruption."

Barnabas adds that such a man must be, "at the same time, more than a man and less than a man."

Woodard asks if he feels sorry for that person, and Barnabas answers that he instead loathes him "very, very deeply."

At the Blue Whale, Vicki's take on life is at its most apocalyptically realistic. Woodard visits and rounds out the episode with a strangely aroused disgust at the unholy union going on in Maggie's veins, and how her blood hastily accepts the corruption offered.

The metaphors run rampant, but at the core of it, there is a distinct feeling that Woodard is describing naughty sexy time, and he can't bring himself to say it's bad.

Mind games. Sexual metaphors. Probably homosexual metaphors. There is a bounty to unpack, all with a sense of inevitable doom for the entire town and maybe all of existence. Barnabas at this time is like a lingering rot, eating away at the pretenses of decency, and he is doing so openly compared to what the series has offered thus far. He is somewhere between a Ken Russell movie and a Prince album in his relative frankness, and although he would endear himself with a demand for mothering later on, at this point, Jonathan Frid is playing Barnabas Collins as pure sex in a world where only a Hefner would be such a thing. That openness is one world ending and another world beginning. Woodard admires it a little too much but can't take part. Barnabas can. And right now, he knows it.

This episode hit the airwaves June 2, 1967.

EPISODE 251

When Barnabas wakes up to a homicidal, stake-wielding Maggie, will he finally swipe left for dear life? Maggie: Kathryn Leigh Scott. (Repeat; 30 min.)

Barnabas rises to find Maggie hovering over his coffin, ready to stab him. Understandably, he excuses himself to speak with Vicki, who has a clear love for, and perhaps a connection to, the past. When he later shows her a lace handkerchief belonging to Josette, she is smitten with its history. This sparks Barnabas's interest. Returning to the Old House, he warns Maggie that she will die if she does not embrace her identity as Josette.

Then there's that time when the gentle guardian of Sarah… and David and Amy… threatened to kill his kidnap victim, Maggie Evans, because she wasn't more easily hypnotized into willingly becoming the reincarnation of someone she never met. The only French she speaks has the word 'fries' after it. But there she is, anyway.

For defenders of Barnabas, it's a tough sequence to come back from. It's easy to see why so many have a taste for the ruthless and manipulative Barnabas and feel detached from the vaguely prissy and avuncular hero he later becomes. But as someone who is vaguely prissy and avuncular myself, I would tell them that they have to just deal with it. As long as, you know, I was sure they'd still like me. Then I'd apologize somehow. Barnabas, perhaps, spends the rest of the series doing just that.

Bad Barnabas is one of Jonathan Frid's three characters in the series, along with Good Barnabas and Bramwell. I'd wager it's the easiest. The objectives are a clear and wicked joy to play, and there is an ambiguity here that gives the part a challenging texture. It's clear that if he really wanted to kill Maggie, she'd be dead. Is it her beauty that stops him from doing so, or is it the fact that, while he knows he may have it in him to off her, it would still be wrong? Both Maggie and Barnabas find themselves cast by fate to role-plays for which they are profoundly unqualified. Maggie has no interest in Josette. Barnabas is not by nature a violent man. But she looks like Josette. And he's an emotionally ruined and unwilling vampire and a completely unintentional, one-way time traveler. He's gone from a world of fishing and finery to curses, betrayal, threats, and suicide.

In theory, nothing matters now, and life would be easier if he became as bad as the Angeliques, Trasks, and Forbeses who stuck him here. They always win, anyway, and he clearly can't rely on anyone to stake him… unless it's at one of those worst possible times. He makes a good show of being a "big meanie," but he can't seal the deal. We know this because his attempts to do so are as self-sabotaged as Roy Hinkley's attempts to escape from the Island.

Because he can't mind-control Maggie, setting her free isn't an option, so he may simply have to kill her for his own good. A lifetime sentence for him is no laughing matter.

His encounter with Vicki in the episode only complicates things. In Vertigo, the story from which this is clearly based (far more than Dracula), the Barnabas character, played by Jimmy Stewart, never recognizes that his ideal woman is right in front of him — Midge, played by Barbara Bel Geddes. Dark Shadows complicates this because Barnabas indeed recognizes that Vicki may not be a ringer for Josette, but she gets him. With no coercion. Unfortunately, Barnabas, through the embarrassing use of force, has committed to the idea of reviving Josette in Maggie. His ego won't let him easily withdraw from that. And yes, shame on him, and how sad. This chiding ignores the fact that his ego, which is simply the comfort he takes in his own judgment, is all he has left. Sacrificing that means sacrificing everything. Until he has the certainty of hope, that is a lot to ask of anyone. Just because Barnabas is an undead monster doesn't mean he's inhuman.

This episode hit the airwaves June 12, 1967.

EPISODE 271

If it's wedding bells for Liz and Jason, why is she ringing them with a bloody fireplace poker? Paul Stoddard: Dennis Patrick. (Repeat; 30 min.)

Liz explains why she cannot marry Jason in a flashback depicting her attempted assassination of Paul Stoddard. 18 years prior, after using the fireplace set for a rather extreme couples therapy role-play to respond to his attempts to leave, she seemingly murdered Paul, whose body was ostensibly buried in a trunk in the basement.

At this point, I really don't know how most people watch Dark Shadows, or if there even is such a thing as "most people." With DVDs largely dead as a medium and streaming packages insisting on separating the pre-Barnabas episodes as a weird (but potentially telling) afterthought, I really can't responsibly begin this essay the way I would have a few years ago. Therefore, I shall.

When most people watch Dark Shadows, they begin with the unleashing of Barnabas, and immediately, it's clear to anyone that he is not the villain of the series. It may be television's greatest morality trick. I mean, yes he's a kidnapper who kills people, but he's no JR Ewing. He's doing the former simply because he has to eat. He's doing the latter because he thinks, in some way, he can release the true, inner spirit from some sort of weird, working-class prison of internally mistaken identity. Well, OK, he also beats the shisha out of Willie Loomis on a regular basis, but everyone has to have a hobby. And considering where he came from, that's simply how you maintain a home appliance, like knocking a television on the side (back when they had sides) or whacking something with batteries in it to do... Whatever that's supposed to do. Teach them manners or something.

Realistically, the villain is obviously Jason Maguire. Jason does what he does not just out of greed, but because he legitimately enjoys torturing Liz. Maybe it's class envy. Maybe it's deep-seated, Irish Catholic rage aimed at someone who is more than likely an atheist. Or a Protestant. And to Jason, they're probably the same thing. We don't know much about the alleged death of Paul Stoddard, but we know that Liz has basically made herself serve 18 years with Matthew Morgan's cooking with no time off for good digestion. It's clear that she feels bad and that she has done more than her share of time served. So, we naturally feel sorry for her, and that makes him all the more hateful.

What's worse is that Dennis Patrick is quite probably the most charming actor to ever darken the towels of Collinwood, and while it won't be the first thing out of my mouth if I ever see a cast member again, I suspect most of them would agree with me. So, we wind up with that weird animal of "the villain you love to hate."

And pardon me if I digress from my digression, but doesn't that phrase seem a little turned around? Shouldn't you take a certain modicum of satisfaction in having the ethics to, if not love the act of hating a villain, at least have no compunction about hating them? Now that I think about it, the expression that is probably more accurate is, "the villain you hate to love." Because you know that you should just like him, but he's such an ingratiating person that, honestly, I often find myself thinking, "well, if I'm going to be married to a hateful parasite, at least he's fun to be around."

Liz has been alone for 18 years. She has more money than she knows what to do with. I'm not saying that she should fall head over heels for every extortionist who helps to bury a murdered spouse, but now that I'm thinking about it, I sort of wonder how bad life with Jason would really be. I mean, I'm sure marriage would be terrible. Especially because all of my married friends tell me that. But... I've seen close-ups of Bill Malloy's beard. And no, I'm not talking about Mrs. Johnson. I'm just saying that she could do worse. I see people get married for money all the time, and I have to give props to Jason for at least being honest about it.

And you can't say that Liz doesn't mind slumming it when it comes to husbands. I always detected a class difference between Liz and Paul. There are never any references to the mighty Stoddard belt loop empire or whatever it is that people make their fortunes with. (I hear rumors that it has something to do with hard work, but I haven't the nerve to try it.) And besides, give Jason a mustache and cut off his supply of Grecian Formula, and you have yourself one Paul Stoddard with a more familiar accent.

So even with all of that, Jason's moments of sadism are striking enough that they overcome even Dennis Patrick's effervescence. (Which, ironically, makes him all the more adept as an actor.)

As a Dark Shadows viewer, this episode, and the ones that immediately follow it, are some of the first most reassuring moments for most viewers that the show will deliver. Because at this point, Barnabas has given up on Maggie, probably because he thinks she's dead (but not in the right way). So that entire storyline vaguely feels like it went nowhere. But this one had to go somewhere. It's a bit of terrestrial nastiness that can only end in a wedding.

The show does such a masterful job at reiterating the source of Liz's anxiety that, even if we have not followed it from episode one, we still feel a profound satisfaction at seeing the flashback to Paul's murder. As a kid, I didn't think they would ever show something like that. And you only got it once, unlike everything else on the show, where the same pivotal moments are often repeated at least five times so that everyone, no matter what day of the week they see it on, gets the thrill. This felt like a genuine reward for paying attention and tuning in every day. It was somehow both the Easter Egg and the entire basket.

Coming about one year and a week after the show went on the air, it had to be even more luxuriously satisfying for viewers who'd been with it from the start. It takes four more episodes for the complete dénouement. It seems like a typically excessive length until you combine it with the typically excessive build-up. At which point, the five-episode payoff feels almost generous.

Watching the hand of Barnabas rise up to crush Jason's life was a quick and brutally satisfying moment, as well. It's a gesture that becomes a force of nature. For Willie, it was a moment that created his new life. For Jason, it means something else. But it makes the force within Barnabas seem like something out of Greek mythology, a cruel and honest crucible responding to an intruder's essence. In some ways, it almost feels as if that force within Barnabas has a judgmental autonomy completely divorced from the great man. (A bit like Count Petofi's capricious hand would be several years later.) Because both times, the gesture is basically just Barnabas's instinctive response to having someone throw open his bedroom door without even knocking.

And although the coffin was not necessarily rocking, Willie and Jason really should have at least greeted him from his sleep with a newspaper and some toast.

This episode hit the airwaves July 10, 1967.

EPISODE 305

When Sarah takes David on a tour of her home, will there be room for one more in the mausoleum? Sarah: Sharon Smyth. (Repeat; 30 min.)

A weakening Barnabas kvetches about the side-effects of Julia's injections, although she seems delighted. Meanwhile, Sarah shows David a hidden coffin.

Curses are blessings on Dark Shadows, and that's not always limited to the story; it's also true for the production. Truth time: the soap format slides easily into something that, without love and context, is unwatchably slow and dull. There. I said it. But it is not without its advantages, also. Usually, the directive to stretch out the storytelling is a mandate for repetition. But in certain cases, the writers found fascinating eddies of implication to explore, and 305 is an example of why people kept watching — it asks the questions we have, too. In this case, about the afterlife and the practicalities of the paranormal.

The episode is vaguely split between Barnabas & Julia and David & Sarah. Both involve a human dealing with the vagaries of supernatural lifeforms, unwittingly or not.

Barnabas is developing impatience with Julia's conversion process. He's tired of the perpetual hangover intrinsic to being human, and I think he's beginning to suspect that Julia either has no idea what she's doing or is purposefully dragging things out. Barnabas has had remarkably good health for nearly two centuries, so we can understand his disappointment. He's reacting as if she's spiking his sherry with saltpeter, and for all we know, she might be. Julia's savoring his lack of vitality, crossing weird lines between doctor, mother, and lover, promising that "she'll take care of Burke Devlin" her own way. Cue images of Rosa Klebb's clumsy attempt at a lesbian seduction in From Russia with Love. Well, it takes a very special lesbian to win the heart of Burke Devlin.

Meanwhile, outside, David and Sarah discuss her knack for divulging Collins family secrets, and she tantalizes him with the promise of a whopper. This leads to a marvelously acted dialogue where Smyth mixes simple honesty with beautifully strategic ambiguity, struggling to explain where she lives in the afterlife. Sarah never claimed to be alive; she just uses the metaphors of living. Here, it's clear that Sarah knows what she is, in the clearest terms she can muster, how she perceives existence. She's not being coy. David is simply not hearing her. I have no idea if the young actress considered the strange weight of the netherworld in her implication, but whether she did or didn't, Sharon Smyth quite simply kicks ass. For a child actress understandably BFF's with the teleprompter, Smyth shows remarkable sophistication in this episode. The result may be one of Sarah's best, most empowered performances in the series. Dark Shadows, in this era, excels at hinting. Everything is offstage. There are huge casts of characters we've yet to meet. To hear about the afterlife only heightens our curiosity.

Dark Shadows takes a unique approach to horror, showing us the inner workings and practicalities of the horrific from internal perspectives. The denizens of the damned have inner lives, too. So do children. Thus, the David/Sarah relationship is one of the most poignant on the program. Each is as lonely and lost as the adults on the show. (In that regard, Carolyn, Joe, and Maggie only seem like the least lonely… until they aren't.) Sarah's overall game may be to curb Barnabas's opportunities for evil. Or, drawn from death's domain by her brother's resurrection, she may simply want to have a friend the way that Barnabas wants a lover. Vicki will recognize physical resemblances when she goes to the past. Does Sarah see the same thing in the present, equating, say, Liz to her own mother?

By making Sarah the most realistic ghost in horror, the show raises all of the right questions, and ones we never knew we had.

This episode hit the airwaves on August 25, 1967.

EPISODE 328

After sending Julia to turn Willie into a stiff, Barnabas gets a rise out of the sheriff and then maintains it with the help of a carefully placed ring. Julia: Grayson Hall. (Repeat; 30 min.)

Can Willie bounce back from five gunshots to the back? The question gives Barnabas all new sources of agita. Because if anyone would have that kinda luck.... Meanwhile, Julia insists that she's in no position to help kill the potential snitch. Barnabas nonetheless prevails, and he lays a trap for the visiting sheriff to "accidentally find" Maggie's ring under a candle in Willie's room. The moon-drenched skies seem clear until Barnabas learns that Willie is emerging from his coma — despite or because of Julia's oversight.

Barnabas plunges to new heights as the aristocratic everyman and to-the-manor-born Joe Lunchbox in 328, one of the show's funniest episodes up to this point. If Barnabas ever wrote a biography, it would share a name with mine, "A Life Under Siege," and if you can't identify with that, well… I don't trust you. If you have any doubt that Dark Shadows is often an intentional comedy, just imagine this one with a laugh track. But even without it, Jonathan Frid and Grayson Hall are definitely playing "set-up/punchline/reverse" with relish.

No one has less authority than the one in charge, as Barnabas learns. It should be so simple. He's working with a doctor whose hands are getting dirtier by the episode. She has plenty to gain by killing Willie, and for Barnabas, it's the only thing to do. He's an eighteenth-century dandy, and the home appliance called Loomis is beyond the repair stage. You can't even donate him to Goodwill. No, the Loomis must go, and it should be obvious. But every time he sends Julia out to do the wrong thing, she comes back with the news that the lad's health is actually improving. It's a cacophony of counter-intuition. She claims he's under too much supervision. Barnabas responds that she's a doctor, and they kill people all the time "by accident," despite layers of oversight. She nags him into planting even more evidence against Willie. The Great Man vaguely goes along with it but surprises Julia by eventually insisting that Willie still needs to die, no matter the evidence.

His insistence doesn't really come from a fear of exposure. It's based on simple, inhuman indecency. Why is he being questioned on something this simple? When will he be trusted instead of second-guessed? If he's going to take the rap, he might as well have the authority to prevent it. Otherwise, like a community theater director, he has all of the responsibility and none of the power in the repeated, comic lesson the show teaches with a stinging regularity. Come on, Julia. It will take the appearance of Angelique, a dream curse, and a Noel Harrison hairdo to turn her around. In that sense, Julia's hair is a good indicator of her stance on Barnabas. It's like the Sisko-Beard Rule. If Sisko has a beard, it's a good episode of DS9. If Julia looks like she's modeling John Hurt's coif from I, Claudius, then Barnabas probably has a friend. But right now, she can endanger no one's life but his, and he's the boss!

We and he wish. The episode is a study in contrarian, cosmic inevitability. Barnabas Collins is decidedly not the boss. In fact, he's not even Tony Danza. But the old boy gives it his all, anyway.

Of course, the art is in concealing the art, and Barnabas's terrible line readings when he's "guiding" the sheriff and Sam through Willie's things make him a priceless popinjay. I said Barnabas's terrible line readings, not Frid's.

The more gullible that his quarry becomes, the more Barnabas channels the cosmic Eddie Haskell, "Gee, a candlestick toppled. Look. There is a ring inside. However, did Maggie's ring get there?"

"Oh, no. I'm falling over.
Oh, I'm falling over again."
— *A. Danger Powers, OBE*

Barnabas is like a Kid Diabolos on Anton LaVey's birthday, drunk on how easily he led the Sheriff and Sam straight to the evidence, warmed by how little cleverness he had to exercise in doing so. Can we blame the regal rascal? If he can't get Loomis whacked, Barnabas can at least feel like a smarty-pants about something. And it looks like the episode is going to end on a note of quiet triumph for our hero, but the universe still has a surprise or two under the tree. An inevitable deputy comes running back to ruin Barnabas's rebounding mood with the news that Willie is coming out of his coma.

And why shouldn't Young Loomis? He's with Julia. As always, the good doctor's Hippocratic Oath extends to everyone but the guy who needs it most: Barnabas!

If ever an episode of Dark Shadows needed to end with the theme from Curb Your Enthusiasm ...

This episode hit the airwaves September 27, 1967.

EPISODE 365

When Sarah begins appearing in David's bedroom, Vicki travels back to 1795 to straighten out the ghostly girl's haunted hash once and for all. Vicki: Alexandra Moltke. (Repeat; 30 min.)

To address Sarah's ubiquity, Barnabas reluctantly agrees to participate in a séance. Of course, a blackout results in Vicki changing places with the original governess, Phyllis Wick... from 1795. This is precisely where Vicki finds herself.

We are one episode away from 1795, which is when the future began.

Dark Shadows is taking a television show on vacation for the first time since Lucy went to Hollywood. If only Ricky had jumped off the balcony of the Tropicana Club, Ethel had tried Harpo Marx for witchcraft, and Fred Mertz had posed around the set in Nathan Forbes' first trousers (don't claim you don't know what I'm talking about), I Love Lucy and the 1795 storyline would be synonymous. Agreed? My work is done.

The flashback is also a move more daring than the introduction of Barnabas, himself. We are now sampling the core of Dark Shadows as Dan Curtis forges new alloys with the metal found in this mine. If this is the show's first ultimate trip, 365 is like watching the main characters pack. Of course, only one of them is traveling, and yet they are all going, in a certain sense. Here, Curtis and his company are not just giving us a last glimpse before the trip, they are also getting things ready for next spring and Vicki's return. Let's get ready for 1795 by leaping over it.

Looking ahead, that return to the present will be nothing short of a reboot for the show. Yes, it will be Dark Shadows, but it will finally know it's Dark Shadows. It's aware that their real bread and butter is Barnabas, and he's evolved into a hero. Of course. (Villains make the best heroes because their amorality opens up more options, and thus, there have a greater capacity for action.) They are tempering Barnabas with this in mind, and giving him dialogue that demands a flashback to explain it. In 365, he soft-pedals the evil in favor of confiding that this undead life is not one that he chose.

Gee, Barnabas, what do you mean? And…. cue time travel.

It almost makes me wonder if Sarah's recent appearance was a cosmic preparation for the journey back. Not to prepare the characters so much as the audience. And why not a séance as the time machine? Dark Shadows never exactly ran on practicality. Here, more than anywhere, it runs on metaphor.

In 365, we see a mix of who the characters have been and who they'll become upon Vicki's return. Roger is fussy and particular, and yet he has a winning enthusiasm for the whimsy of a séance. Carolyn is merging debutante sophistication with a more sober kind of confidence that comes from being the preferred weapon for Barnabas. She will need that increasing sense of backbone to deal with Adam. Barnabas and Julia are still at each other's throats, but the impression of stalemate has never been stronger. Fate has them both by the shorthairs, and they will eventually need each other there to survive. They are not yet friends. It will take threats like Angelique to forge that relationship, but the potential is finally there.

Sarah is again the catalyst for this major action. It's appropriate that they exorcize her with this. Indeed, after 1795, I don't recall her even being mentioned. It's as if the pipe to the afterlife is clogged up, and all it takes is a séance-driven time trip to unplug it and let the kid through to a better place. Sarah is the quintessential Little Girl Lost, and that figure is the driving metaphor of the show until Willie opens the coffin. So many are similarly lost. Liz, lost to guilt. Maggie, lost to an alcoholic father on the wrong side of the lobster boat dock. Carolyn, lost to being on the *right* side of the lobster boat dock. And Vicki, completing the Lilith Fair of the Lost lineup that inaugurated the show, is so lost she just doesn't understand. It's a central premise to the show and the ultimate thematic ambassador to their prime demographic, lonely women at home. Do they see themselves? Goodness, no. Ultimately, this demographic wanted a view (of Jonathan Frid) rather than a mirror. It can only further the exploration of the lost by completely by taking Vicki away in time as well as space.

The Collins family rarely met a problem that couldn't be addressed via séance, and 365 runs with the notion so far and fast that it drops Vicki off in 1795... maybe just because. Perhaps

Sarah just wants a friend, and this is an easier commute than constantly showing up as a ghost. But it's a visit, not a curse.

We never see Sarah again, perhaps because she only has one more charge left in the battery, just enough to get Vicki back to 1968. How does she know to do this?

Ghost Time is relative. It could be that her *first* act as a ghost was to send Vicki back home after the 1795 trip. Sarah's engineered time travel before, just kind of backward. Few, if any, shows discover themselves as this radically different than they were in their inception. But is it? For Dark Shadows, variety is the point. Where does Vicki go? Dark Shadows? From where has she come?

Exactly.

This episode hit the airwaves November 17, 1967.

An open letter to the *Collinsport Star*…

Dear Editor:

And that's all well and good, but the finer points are about as clear to understand as that Huckleberry Finn audiobook read by Rosie Perez.

I come to praise Dark Shadows, not to bury it. However, it might get a little bit of dirt on its shoes. But I promise, it'll come right off by the end of the essay.

I'm going to ask you a very straight question: how does the whole time travel seance thing really work? And why? Because, while it's easy to say, "because Dan Curtis wanted it to happen," I think we can probably do better than that.

The science behind the 1795 chronoportation is so nonexistent that it makes the Parallel Time room look like something even Richard Dawkins could love. And this always bothered me. Fast and loose, thy name is the Dark Shadows writing staff when it comes to certain aspects of temporal mechanics. At least 1897 and 1995 have external tools and locations that can explain the temporal Terpsichore, but 1795 is unhampered by the Curse of Causality.

While putting the finishing touches on this book, I rewatched episode 364, where Sarah visits Barnabas, and I saw things in it that were completely fresh and new. There is enough in that episode to fill an entire Daybook collection, he exaggerated. OK, that might be going a bit far, but I had a profound reaction to what I saw. Bottom line, I continue to see Sarah as one of the most intriguing characters on the series. We only underestimate her because she appears to be a child. And while she seems to behave like one in many ways, she has an agenda and can be impressively stern when executing it.

Whenever I encounter one of the thornier questions posed by the series, episode 364 usually alludes to an answer. And given that it takes place just prior to the time travel séance, I don't find that to be a coincidence.

I always had the suspicion that Sarah was responsible for the temporal displacement experience by Vicki, but that was largely, you know, because I said so. It seemed neat and tidy, but I couldn't really explain why it also made sense. Now, I think I can.

When Sarah appears to David, she says that the dead are angry and hints that the result may not be a Whitman's Sampler of Love. My immediate thought was that she's talking about Quentin and Judah Zachery. And that very well could be. But what ghosts? We have not seen the ghost of Josette for quite a while, and we won't see the ghost of Quentin for about two years, so what is she talking about? The widows? They seem to have moved to Miami. Finally. Well, don't tell her I said this, but the only angry ghost I see around here is Sarah, herself.

So what if that's the case? Why is she angry? Well, you know, she died in powerless agony, which doesn't sound like fun. Once dead, her spirit then watched her beloved brother turn into the worst version of himself. Oh, and she also got to see her mother commit suicide. So, I suspect she's got an advanced case of the Permanent Mondays as a result. That, and when Barnabas gets a second chance at life, somehow he's even nastier than he was when Joshua chained him up. So much for the healing power of alone time. I guess that online test was wrong, and he's not an introvert, after all.

(Newsflash: you probably are not an introvert, either. But it takes less time to say "introvert" rather than say, "literally doing nothing is preferable to hanging out, but having a doctor's note makes doing so feel that much nobler.")

As it turns out, I guess being buried unalive under the mocking, paralytic image of the God who abandoned you does not mellow a guy out the way everyone hoped. Well, there went those 172 years! So, the ghost of Sarah, sustained for nearly two centuries by the comforting hope that her undead brother might rise and again be her friend and companion, is in an understandable snit.

But that's not all, Sarah. If you call in the next ten minutes, you'll also get a complementary realization that the evil sorceress responsible for your death, his curse, your mother's suicide, and, I suspect, the harrowing hand of Hamburger Helper, is about to show up as Roger's new wife. Yeah, Angelique is on her way, and will most likely bring her Thomas Kincaid collection with her. It's a nightmare. This has to be stopped.

What better way than to take the girl Barnabas is crushing on, drag her back in time, give her an e-ticket tour through Barnabas becoming a vampire, and top it off with the woman she'll eventually have to call "boss" framing her for occult crimes against good taste?

Sarah Collins needs a flaming sword of justice. And now that Vicki finally understands not just something, but everything, is justice coming?

Determining this will be the ultimate test of the wisdom of Jack Austin, astronaut, "Knowledge is power... for real!"

Sincerely,

McCray: Stool #3.
The Blue Whale

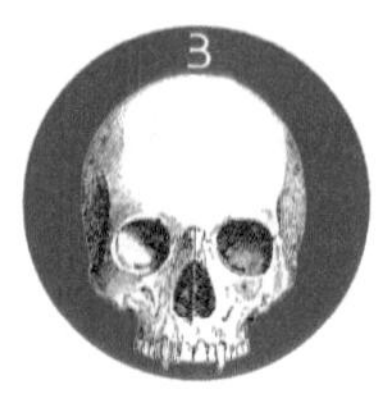

1968
THE ROAD OF TRIALS

"Night has fallen over the Great House of Collinwood..."

So, you already read about 1795, and that's plenty. Between the prior episode and the one coming up, Vicki came and went from 1795.

We now re-join our twentieth century, already in progress.

EPISODE 469

Julia and Lang square off when she learns that he has both the cure for Barnabas... and his loyalty, as well. Julia: Grayson Hall. (Repeat; 30 min.)

Jeff, Julia, and Vicki open the coffin in the secret room after Jeff reveals that he somehow knew the latch was there. The coffin is empty. In the hospital, Barnabas has excruciating blood pangs, and Lang explains that he may have a permanent cure. Later, Julia visits Lang, who brags that he can care for Barnabas far better than she. As she leaves, Julia passes Jeff Clark. Lang is furious that he is being associated with Clark. Jeff explains that he saw Julia at Eagle Hill. Lang says the bodies there are far too old for his purposes. It's clear Jeff is being blackmailed.

With more than a week of revolutionary plot advancement under the show's belt, the staff now settles back into a standard pace. In an interview with Violet Welles, I read that she, Sam Hall, and Gordon Russell would plot out the show months in advance, finally getting it down to a map spanning week-by-week, episode-by-episode, and scene-by-scene. The process was surprisingly meticulous. I think the formula breaks down a bit like this:

10% Last scene of the prior episode.

30% Covering prior plot points.

10% Review and advance secondary plot.

30% Revelation of one new plot point in prime storyline.

10% Foreshadowing future plot point.

5% Debate about prior decision or confession.

5% Major new decision or confession.

In this case, we spend a lot of time in the mausoleum as Vicki and Jeff sort of remember segments of 1795. The major new ground we cover is that Jeff is going to graveyards for Dr. Lang… and that the bodies in Eagle Hill are too old for the job. Hint hint. The discovery, of course, is that the coffin is empty inside the secret room… and that Lang may be able to permanently prevent Barnabas from having any relapses.

But is that a revelation? No. Lang never said that Barnabas is permanently cured. This is the trick that Dark Shadows does. It doesn't reliably deliver new information. Instead, it reiterates old information with slightly more context. The characters sometimes act like it's the first time they've heard things, but in the case of Barnabas and his blood pangs, he has no reason to be surprised. Barnabas may have "seen" the recent episodes, but not all viewers have. And for more seasoned viewers, the show still entertains by covering old ground in new enough circumstances that it feels like the first time. Usually.

The hot scene in this one is the conversation that Julia has with Lang. This may be Julia's real turning point. Up to this moment, Barnabas has been a thorn in her side that she's niggled about to their mutual masochism. She's poisoned him. Blackmailed him. Lang senses this. He revels in pointing out the legitimate truth that he can care for Barnabas better than Julia. After all, he cured him in less than a day. It feels like two pimps arguing over an, um, employee. They both pretend to have his best interests at heart. They both pretend not to be engaged in vicious combat. One pretends not to be weaker. One pretends not to be gloating over it.

(Technically, this was a cue for Big Papa Dan to stride onto the set, slam down his chalice, and settle things by reminding everyone that Jonathan Frid, that Shakespearean drizzle of Sweet Canadian Maple, was, and forever would be, HIS foxiest earner.)

Julia loved Barnabas; has she lost him? He was close enough for her to bully, torture, and be tortured by. He was a problem, yes, but he was all hers. She contemplates losing him to someone who can actually pull off the stunt she only speculates is in her wheelhouse. Not only that, but it's someone who offers none of the minuses of romantic jealousy. She's suddenly behind an eight-ball the size of Collinwood. If she gets out from behind it, her relationship with Barnabas will never be the same. She'll have to tap into her humanity, not her guile. They might even wind up equals.

On this day in 2063, Dr. Zephram Cochrane and the town of Bozeman, Montana will welcome the Vulcan surveyor T'Plana-Hath on what will be appreciated as First Contact Day.

This episode hit the airwaves April 10, 1968.

To "get into" the Angelique/Barnabas relationship requires two things. You have to imagine them getting along. And it's not difficult. If you can imagine them getting along, we are home free. The other thing you need to contend with is the fact that these are murderers, many times over. It helps that neither of them is entirely human when they make most of their lethal decisions. As Christopher Lloyd says in Buckaroo Banzai, "It's not my goddamn planet, monkey boy." Indeed. And humans are no longer their people. They exist beyond time. They exist beyond the need for normal nourishment. As one of the living dead, Barnabas has a set of priorities that may overlap with his former instincts, but his moral compass about his new food source is completely different. I think it's the same cognitive dissonance that humans have when they continue to eat meat even when they realize that steak had a mother. Also, we have no idea what Angelique really is. I know that Barnabas asserts that she's not even human in 1840. I'm not saying we shouldn't mourn the lives they took or hold them accountable, but they see humans entirely differently than we see ourselves. We are built to die. They are not. They are built to have an influence that will last for centuries, if not more. We are not. So, to them, it's no big deal if they shave off a few decades from our lives. We probably weren't going to do much with them, anyway.

EPISODE 473

When Roger takes a wife and Angelique takes her place at Collinwood, will Barnabas take extreme measures or a one-way ticket to Windcliff? Cassandra Collins: Lara Parker. (Repeat; 30 min.)

Roger enters with his new wife in tow, a dead ringer for Angelique named Cassandra. Brittle conversations ensue as Roger and Liz fume at one another, and Cassandra pretends to have no idea who Barnabas is. The episode ends with Cassandra alone, tintinnabulating a familiar laugh.

I think everyone has at least one Angelique.

As she returns (for the first time) in 473, we get the feeling why. That's a tribute to the script by Sam Hall and the everything else by Lara Parker.

Barnabas has been dreading it, but even with the bizarre stuff he's seen in Martinique, 1795, and the sixties, I don't think he believes she will reappear. As he opines that witches never die, etc., I think he's doing it so that he can turn around and say, "Well, guess I was wrong. Ding-dong and all that."

It's hard not to impose inner monologues while watching the show, perhaps because Angelique is a living Rorschach blot of a character, drawing out the true intentions of everyone she meets. Wonder Woman needs a lasso. Angelique just needs to stifle a judgy little laugh. Whether it's lust, violence, respect, or jealousy, the veils come off others in her presence. And that's such a refreshing thing on the show. Everyone else is dedicated to keeping and/or inducing secrets. Yes, she's awfully evil, but she's evil in the name of love, and we all have impulses to go there once or twice in our lives. And each audience member secretly suspects that, as long as they weren't in her way and kept up some lively chat, they'd be spared, right?

It's her ultimately romantic intent that redeems her. Do any of us really dread that she's back? No. Finally, a woman at Collinwood who knows the score. Heck, just someone at Collinwood who knows the score. She's what we've been waiting for since Jason McGuire — an agent of action, change, humor, awareness, and love. I just imagine, alone with Angelique for the first time in 473, Barnabas sitting down with her and catching up on "how crazy it's all been" before remembering she's a monster he's obligated to hate.

Lara Parker really must be given ample credit for this effect. The good stuff, not the monster part. Holding multiple college degrees, beauty rarely seen this side of the Louvre, and a balance of genteel, southern refinement and canny, metropolitan wisdom, Parker enlivens the wickedest dialogue with equal parts pathos and play with unerring instincts.

Her arrival signals the last major tonal shift we've been awaiting in the show, and you saw it here, first. Up to now, it's a story about 1960s mortals interacting with gods. With Angelique joining Barnabas to form the dysfunctional, time-trekking, immortal First Couple of Collinwood, the situation is now reversed. The story of Dark Shadows is finally one of gods weaving through fields of mortals. That's an important factor to consider when passing moral judgment on Barnabas and Angelique. They may have impossible crimes, but they also have impossible spans of time to pay impossible prices. Us? Short timers.

This episode hit the airwaves on April 17, 1968.

I hope you can tell that I have a real ax to grind with people who complain about the acting on the show. These are the sorts of critics who confuse Dark

Shadows' limited production values with the performances. Don't make that mistake. How are you supposed to act this stuff? There is no sense memory exercise for anything the show has to offer, even if Thayer David is a memorable feast for all five.

EPISODE 481

After being caught snooping in the garden, Angelique has no choice but to steal Dr. Lang's Secret Anti-Witch Medallion. But first, she'll need a good lawyer — to hypnotize! Tony Peterson: Jerry Lacy. (Repeat; 30 min.

As Julia nearly calls the cops on Barnabas and Lang, she is reminded of Dave Woodard's murder. Later, she and Barnabas fence over Lang's plan, keeping the threat of Angelique in focus, which is easy because he catches her snooping on them. Later, she notices that Tony Peterson looks like Reverend Trask and relishes the irony of making him her slave to fetch Lang's Secret Anti-Witch Medallion. Lang is duped into leaving his home, and when he realizes the deception, rushes back.

Reliable histrionics rule the day as Grayson Hall explores a completely understandable meltdown for Julia as she tries to decide whether to drop a dime on Barnabas for perhaps the last time. Not to be outdone, Addison Powell is again topping everyone, combined, as he reels with the news of missing medallions and dummy requests to render medical aid. Addison Powell was a serious actor, and yet… I have to wonder if anyone on the show asked him to tone it down because his singularly athletic acting approach makes Keith Prentice sound like Ricky Jay at his most Atlantic School wooden. I think Powell would have just said, "The part said mad scientist, so I'm playing a mad scientist. What else am I supposed to play? 'Bemused resignation'? By the way, once we go off the air in the afternoon, our prime demographic's biggest concerns are cooties, geometry tests, and meatloaf."

Amazingly, Addison Powell plays a character who seems to know he's trapped on a soap opera named Dark Shadows and has adopted a defensively broad acting style to dupe producers into thinking he's not in on it. He just needs to pull out the aces when the time is right.

In short, Roger Davis is about to get his face ripped off, and Julia decides to call the cops, even though Barnabas needs the face.

And then life wasn't so easy. Dark Shadows is a frustrating show by design because it's reliably realistic in the way that matters. Like life, we know how it's supposed to go. And unlike life, we know where it's going. Julia and Barnabas are friends, and once the show comes back from 1795, it's a different program and they're pals very fast, right, because that's the good part and we like the good part, right?

The tone above gives the answer. Of course, it's not that easy. From the most macroscopic perspective, this is true because we need it to be. It tells us that we are not alone in our frustration with progress toward the inevitable. Life should not be two steps forward, three steps back, but it is. It's what makes Dark Shadows frustratingly slow, infinitely watchable, and the most identifiable production on TV.

Actors like Jonathan Frid and Grayson Hall excel at navigating this peculiarly existential angst. As the episode begins, Julia contemplates what would have once been no dilemma at all. Face stealing is a crime, after all. Now? She's so far down the rabbit hole, it's an option to be debated with her soon-to-be best friend, Barnabas. Together, they are the Oliver and Lisa to Collinsport's Hooterville. But, as Lang might do in an "experiment," it reverses the genders. Grayson is Oliver, trying to impose the last wisps of order on a maelstrom of weirdness. The more they try, the more they fail. Barnabas learned long, long ago to just go with it. Yes, Barnabas is our Eva Gabor. But I don't need to tell you that.

At the same time, Barnabas Collins is the man that Angelique made him. Is he a paragon? In some senses. He's also a hero who kills in cold blood and then sucks it dry as a warning to anyone who might dream of crossing him. He's a benevolent gentleman — and he's also the most brutal, sadistic, and vindictive dweller of the night to stalk the small screen. That Angelique should warm to Jerry Lacy's vaguely bewildered Tony Peterson is obvious. It's not that she has the opportunity to romance the great witch hunter. No. She finally unites with the man who joined in to inaugurate the undead living nightmare that binds him nearly two centuries later. When Barnabas grabs Angelique and scolds her in front of Julia like the sitcom snoop she's become, the destined bond of Trask and Bouchard is upgraded to inevitable.

Why Barnabas? I mean, I know literally "why," but Dark Shadows is a celebration of punishments that exceed their crimes by infinite degrees. So, why Barnabas? Why ANY of us? One of the reasons that Dark Shadows speaks to us is that it features characters trapped in a dishonorable world that nonetheless trumpets honorable standards, regardless of those trapped in the chasm of the disparity. Depending on the storyline, Liz, Victoria, Maggie, and even Neo-Roger sit with heads high and noses higher as everyone else fights backstairs battles quietly enough to not disturb the sherry break, taking it into the hall or Parallel Time if necessary. Barnabas is the ultimate victim of circumstance, as are we all.

But poor Tony Peterson may take the urinal cake of cosmic suffering in this one as we kick off what would go on to become the most artistically successful spin-off of the Dark Shadows Universe, and that's the perverse chemistry of Lara Parker's evolvingly impish Angelique with the long-suffering everyman, Jerry Lacy's Tony Peterson —the Man with Trask's Face — as they team up in the finest of the Big Finish productions, from the pen of the masterful Mark Passmore. It's the least likely pair on the show, but with the two most unpredictable and autonomous characters in the ensemble, taking things beyond Bewitched and perhaps even beyond Westworld. Peterson handily inherits the throne of "callin' shenanigans" from Harry Johnson's fugitive father, Bill Malloy. But unlike Malloy, he hasn't the luck of being thrown off a cliff by Matthew Morgan. Stuck with someone — Angelique — whose kindness comes only when it's convenient, we have the one sap in Collinsport incapable of doing (much) wrong. He and Barnabas are strange brothers orbiting around Angelique, vaguely trying to do something right and receiving the proportionate punishment for it. But don't we all? And by seeing it on Dark Shadows, that strange spook house progeny of James Whale and W.C. Fields, we can just barely survive it.

This episode hit the airwaves April 29, 1968.

EPISODE 482

When Lang is in search of a new assistant with nerves of steel, Barnabas can think of only one man: Loomis. Willie Loomis. Barnabas: Jonathan Frid. (Repeat; 30 min.)

Barnabas suggests Willie to Lang as his new assistant after Jeff Clark quits. Jeff is compelled to appear at Maggie's and hear the dream. That night, he has it.

Barnabas Collins reveals himself to be master of the game as he delivers the greatest blow possible to Eric Lang. When the greatest scientific mind in the Western world, abandoned by Roger Davis, needs an assistant for the most important experiment in human history, Barnabas knows just the man. The assistant needs only "good hands and a lot of nerve." Who's up? Joe Haskell? Buzz Hackett? Ross "The" Skipper?

No. No, my friends. For such a mission, there is only one man.

Who better than the cravenly, hysterical, alcoholic, multiple bullet wound survivor and PTSD poster boy, William H. Loomis, Esq. late of Windcliff Sanitarium? This, to me, is proof positive that Barnabas has no real interest in a cure. Yes, Roger Davis — who now has friends in Collinsport, and good for him — is an impossible act to follow, but is Willie the preferred weapon here? The best part is that Lang hears that the lad is in a mental institution and has absolutely no qualms about using him. It just goes to show what you can accomplish when you have the lowest (or most conveniently expedient) standards possible. With this one decision, and perhaps it's a test by Barnabas, they both fail. In doing so, Lang reveals himself to be the Hal Needham of mad science. Completely daring and utterly artless. And THAT'S why he gets things done. If only Mike Henry had played Adam.

Then Maggie answers the door in an oven mitt.

It may be the single most ghastly costume piece ever forced on a performer on Dark Shadows. When a skirt made from the Collinsport Afghan is too muted and tasteful, look to Ohrbach's, my friend. And when people want to know what women wore in the era, they can look to certain scenes on Dark Shadows. This is a garment so eye-popping that no one would have kept it. No one would revive it. No costume designer would try putting a star in it for some period piece. It is a skirt lost to history. But no agendas existed then except to sell stuff from Ohrbach's, and thus, the show again serves a new purpose, that of time capsule. Like David's Major Matt Mason toys, Dark Shadows is an accidental portrait of so much that would otherwise be lost to Newer and Better. And what else are you supposed to wear for Roger Davis to appear at your door, asking you about your dreams?

The dream curse is truly up and running now as we have our first viral transmission of it… and glimpse the shtick that will rule the show for the next few weeks. It both builds and consistently backfires as the reach of the show's special effects falls short of its practical and budgetary grasp. This is a problematic era for the show, at once a pure example of it and the first major storyline that gets vague derision from certain fans. Still, it serves an interesting set of purposes, psychologically. First, of course, it's a basic Rorschach test to reveal the characters. Although we know them intimately, the program was gaining new audiences by the thousands each week, and the dream curse cleverly catches them up with the core roster, including their most revealing fears. It's also the first example of the show letting itself down in almost every aspect of the technical execution. This is important to fans because it forces you to make a choice: accept them for what they are or defect. Once you agree to go with it, you agree to accept that the special effects on the program are symbolic. And after that compact is made, the show is no longer bound by any attempt to render the fantastic credibly. Only then can they truly cut loose with thinking that suggests, "Hey, they accepted the dream curse. Why not take them to Hell?" Dark Shadows could only do the impossible because all effects were probably going to fall short. Not that they'd aim for that, but when that is the result, anything is possible.

In this sense, the dream curse is more a blessing than something else.

This episode hit the airwaves April 30, 1968.

I'm not certain, but I think this is the longest Daybook that I've written. I write by dictation, and I was in a particularly chatty mood that morning. The beginning of May holds an understandable sorcery for anyone on any end of the education industry.

Naturally, I'm going to be in an ebullient mood, even if it makes me collect a bunch of tangents together and call it an essay.

EPISODE 485

Barnabas knows that ultimate happiness is right around the corner because his best friends do all that they can to talk him out of it. Eric Lang: Addison Powell. (Repeat; 30 min.)

Lang relates the dream curse to Julia on the eve of The Experiment as she tries to talk him out of it. Meanwhile, Barnabas relates his instructions to Willie on the eve of The Experiment as he tries to talk him out of it. Across Collinsport, Angelique, tired of the moralizing, stabs a voodoo doll of Lang and then probably takes a long, well-deserved bubble bath.

One of the great things about Ghostbusters is its use of science to address the supernatural. It would be convenient to say that this is something that started with the novel Frankenstein, except that the process only hinted at in the book is as much alchemical as it is laboratory-grade. In exploring the dichotomy between the two methods of describing and controlling the universe, Dark Shadows generally comes down on the side of the supernatural, except when it doesn't, and it doesn't with surprising regularity. Science makes more appearances than you would think. Peter Guthrie is no witch doctor. Julia begins the show by literally seeing the supernatural through a microscope. The heroes of 1795 at least assert a preference for scientific thinking. And if scientific thinking is not always the answer, it certainly has a seat at the séance table. Julia works with Angelique to combine biochemistry and black magic to help Barnabas in 1897. The entire existence of parallel time is well-founded in vaguely articulated pseudoscientific mumbo-jumbo recited by Stokes with incredibly precise ambiguity. You know, science. Along with Cyrus Longworth and a side trip to 1840, via a chronoporting staircase well-founded in time-honored principles of total scientific illiteracy. However, Dark Shadows is under no obligation to be scientifically literate. It doesn't have to worry about Isaac Asimov clutching his pearly mutton chops as he watches it, kvetching that "It's no Space: 1999."

For Dark Shadows, science may simply be magic in lab coats, but that's not all. It's the Resistance. It's often the sole force that man has against the new world of ancient gods and monsters. Although it is carefully protected from resembling reality, it still exists to troll hoity-toity magic users and level the playing field for the rest of us. And of course, it must be mad science. Because regular science is too boring and largely exists to give everyone reasons why they can't have any fun.

Eric Lang is my kind of scientist. Just imagine him mixing it up with Rand Paul instead of Anthony Fauci. I'm sure somehow Covid would have been cured by now. Admittedly, we would all have giraffe heads grafted onto us. Which would have absolutely nothing to do with curing Covid. But I have every confidence that Eric Lang was also on the board of the Collinsport Community Playhouse and was itching to do a modified version of some Ionesco, a playwright he admired for his gritty, hard-hitting realism. After that controversial, all-nude production of Darling of the Day, he had to play it safe. Every year for a fundraiser, they would do a haunted house. Which was actually the only month out of the year that Lang would simply take down the schmattes covering everything in his home and show off his work in all its glory.

All seriousness aside, the episode crackles with more pure fun than a Chick-fil-A hijacked by RuPaul and Steve Shives, open for biz and spiking the lemonade with bourbon on a Sunday near you. It begins with Lang trying to logic his way through the dream curse, knowing that we'll be saying goodbye to Dark Shadows' most passionate showman,

Addison Powell. It's a glorious monologue that hovers somewhere between sobriety and appropriate sensationalism. As these people share nightmares, it's the closest the program comes to presenting the characters displaying their own individual horror TV series. It's as if they, themselves, are producing a meta-Dark Shadows.

Lang tries to persuade Julia that there's nothing inordinately dangerous to injecting the soul of Barnabas into the body of Adam, you know, now that all of the heads have been sawed-off, reattached, and Roger Davis still has his face. Hearing this, Julia has her doubts and says that she might prefer if Barnabas simply went back to being a vampire.

Yeah, you heard me.

Julia eventually emerges as the voice of conscience and common sense for Barnabas, you know, over a year from now. But today she has one black-stockinged leg in the bold future of 1897 and another one still in the lab, trying to chemically shrivel Barnabas into a future Don Post bestseller. Like in that episode of Next Generation where they kept aging Dr. Pulaski by taking off layer upon layer of Diana Muldaur's make-up.

I kid, I kid. Better than Crusher, sez me.

But I have to question the moral compass of anyone who would put the inevitability of a serial killing Lord of the Undead, capable of spreading a vampiric pathogen that could decimate the human race if well-shaded and unchecked, above a wacky experiment that will probably just end in nothing but a crackle, a burning scent, some shrugs, and then Lang, Julia, and Willie splitting the contents of Barnabas's wallet three ways at TGI Friday's, which, knowing what a cheap SOB he was, will barely cover the cost of the seven-layer dip and that Ultimate Megarita that is how Julia spells r-e-l-i-e-f on any day ending in 'Y.'

Why, indeed?

Shifting to the Old House, it's immediately clear that Barnabas is trying to solve his ongoing existential crisis, because there's Willie, at his side, wringing his hands and doing everything possible to discourage him from seeking happiness. Moments like these make Margaret Hamilton's Cora, from those Maxwell House ads, look like a freewheeling Dennis Hopper. Willie must have nothing to do because he just watched Julia in the previous scene and is basically repeating what she said to Lang. His namby-pamby nagging and cheek give Jonathan Frid one of his greatest and most genuine line readings. And it's the kind of moment, going by in a flash, that makes the program absolute gold. All the vampire and curse stuff is interesting if you like that sort of thing, but it's not nearly as much fun as watching this old married couple go at it for the umpteenth time. Loomis flatly states, "I don't like it."

Barnabas responds with a withering cattiness worthy of Count Petofi. He opines, "That IS a shame," sighs, and desperately tries to secure his fortune by writing a questionable letter instructing the family to hand over all of his possessions and the Old House to a "cousin from England." Yeah, like they'd ever do that.

But Willie continues his campaign of simpering instead of doing what he should, which is quickly finishing a paint-by-numbers portrait of Robert Rodan in Georgian drag to sneak onto the wall of the drawing-room as if it were yet another portrait of an ancestor that "had been there the whole time." You know, the minimal litmus test that Roger and Liz need to fork over priceless real estate to a fancy-lad stranger. Hey, if the voice of a brilliant actor coming out of a good-looking slice of human Velveeta worked for Georges Baker and Lazenby in On Her Majesty's Secret Service, why not here?

Just for a moment, I want you to picture that version of the show. Picture a Dark Shadows where the experiment worked, and Jonathan Frid must loop in the dialogue for Robert Rodan as if he'd just emerged from Boris Balinkoff's mind-transplant device. For the rest of the series.

It's a pretty good show, come to think of it. *Calling Robot Loomis!*

But all this fear over the experiment, and a preference for Barnabas to be a vampire again, has a disturbing subtext. People in abusive relationships tend to gravitate back to further abusers because a familiar love is preferable to taking a chance on a happy future. Although it's unexpected, that is a truth reflected here by both Willie and Julia.

However, Barnabas is willing to literally change his mind, so that's next in line. "Barnabas, the experiment's still free," Lang might have reminded him, before adding, "take a chance on me."

Yes, I once directed Mamma Mia. Or as I called it, "A Cry for Help." And those lambs are still decidedly screaming, Clarisse.

Barnabas is so ready for the process that he even puts on a blue bathrobe for the experiment. Like Red Sonia in that armor that I'm sure is just as protective, I assume it's for "freedom of movement," but I still feel like the old boy is being exploited.

Actually, after seeing him manfully clad in suits, capes, jabots, ascots, tights, and various kerchiefs for a year, the semiotic impact of that blue bathrobe conveys the incredibly human vulnerability of Barnabas in a way that is unparalleled across the series. Either that, or he's waiting for a Jean Shepherd narration to start describing his long-standing battle with Lang's idiosyncratic furnace as Julia once again unsuccessfully attempts to get Willie to eat meatloaf.

Well, there are no Bumpus hounds to devour the Turkey of Progress as Lang charges up the ozone of electric sex to begin the transfer. But don't think the supernatural will go down without a fight. As Lang starts to science, Willie goes to Collinwood in an act of cosmic inevitability. For the next few months of the show to happen, it's vital that Willie hand Angelique the one document she desperately needs: the letter about "Adam Collins." And it's just in time for her to get out her trusty Eric Lang Mego voodoo doll and sling the silver sentinel of science's sober sojourn of synthetic soul symbiosis study into total chaos.

And for a moment, an important moment, all of the wackiness stops. We see Barnabas, our friend and hero, screaming in a degree of pain that is suddenly and uncomfortably real. We've seen him worry. We've seen him fret. But television usually stops short of showing a character, destined to live, experiencing a pointless and sadistic agony. And Lang is experiencing it as well. Maybe we could say it's tantamount to the pain of childbirth, which is what the scene is about, but this is not that kinda pain.

This is sadism. x— it is sadism from a witch. A creature of darkness. A creature of anti-science. Someone whose existence knows only the continuum from literal hellfire to the blazing execution stake that represents human justice. How dare he be cured? More pointedly, how dare he be cured by someone other than she? In that attack, we get a full-spectrum view of the quintessential struggle for human identity. No, really. Male versus female. Science versus religion. Reason versus emotion. Fear versus informed optimism. What is at stake? Literally, the human mind and, if it exists, the soul.

No answers, except that one side seeks to use nature to control nature. One side wishes to punish the attempt to steal what was her fire, exclusively. Science will, as we will learn, win the day, but not without sacrifices. Adam will live, as will Barnabas. And no matter how big Angelique's Twinkie is, for one day at least, Eric Lang, Barnabas Collins, and Julia Hoffman had the guts to cross the streams.

This episode hit the airwaves May 3, 1968.

EPISODE 490

On the eve of Adam's creation, will the dream curse give Julia an ugly wake-up? Barnabas: Jonathan Frid. (Repeat; 30 min.)

Julia reels from the dream, and Barnabas fears what should happen if she shares it with Mrs. Johnson. Of course, Mrs. Johnson shows up, somewhat in a daze and claiming to have no dreams whatsoever. Julia is relieved after sharing the dream, and at the same time, Barnabas reassures Victoria that if she likes him, she'll love his cousin, Adam. What a coincidence that they won't be around at the same time. Meanwhile, the attempt to bring Adam to life goes somewhat haywire, resulting in both Barnabas and Adam being alive at the same time.

I often wonder if Dan Curtis found himself in a position analogous to Barnabas and Julia around this time. Do any of the three of them know the nature of the pickle they're in? The challenge facing all three is, "Once we've created the lug, then what?" He's going to struggle and shamble and then eventually go away after several months of unresolved tension. That is if it follows the model of the novel, which the whole thing does. Kind of.

This is the first case where following the literary model limits, rather than liberates, the writing staff. However, in 490, they're on the precipice, and all things are still possible. In fact, they skirt around a much more interesting storyline on the way, and things are memorably wacky before that, too.

In the cosmic meanwhile, it's so nice to see the show settle into the perverse domestic comedy of Life with Barnabas and Julia. It's even nicer to see the temporary role reversal of Barnabas hectoring Julia into action, nudging the doctor to work harder and faster. Clad in a robe for the climax, Jonathan Frid might as well be wearing a mask of cold cream and have his hair in curlers while he's at it. With the Adam experiment doomed to the failure of mixed baggery, it's in an episode of tense optimism surrounded by fatalism. Sleep gives no relief; the dream curse is now upon Julia, and that puts it one step closer to Barnabas. To what does she wake up? A plan so insane that no one would have anything to do with it unless it sat at the end of a year of compromise and terrible, seemed-like-a-good-idea-at-the-time decisions.

Doomed when waking, doomed when sleeping, the option of just stopping and living with the ugly life of a vampire doesn't occur to them. Amid this festival of fatalism — beginning with the dream curse and ending with the horrifying realization that both Adam and Barnabas are still alive — the show gives us one crucial reminder of why they're doing it at all. It's not a matter of escaping from Angelique; it's escaping to Victoria. In doing this, though, the writers set themselves up for a trap. The storyline that would have been triggered had the Adam Plan been successful is far more interesting than what we get, and it can be sensed even if this is your first time with the show.

Imagine Barnabas showing back up in another body. Arguably a more powerful one. To Victoria, a more attractive one. It's a new dawn and one that thoroughly confuses Angelique. Maybe Jonathan Frid gets a vacation. Maybe he lives but is reverted to the man he was before the experiment, so there are two Barnabi. I just know that the prospect of Barnabas re-insinuating himself into Collinwood as someone else is an intriguing potential that almost becomes realized. Maybe that's what would happen if they were to do it today. But it's vital to remember that all of these things were firsts for television… or almost–firsts. Moving on to Frankenstein is a logical step for the show, since, in our collective imaginations, that legend follows Dracula as if it were all part of the same word. The show borrows from Dracula only in the sense that both stories involve people who bite others and drink their blood. There might have been greater versatility in the storyline if they had played as fast and loose with Frankenstein. The potential of a man who doesn't exist, inhabited by the soul of a man who perhaps should not exist is the real kernel of the drama. The writers were wise to pursue that early on. The story's potential for continuing it is one of the great unrealized possibilities of the overall storyline. Yes, they revisit it, with interesting results, during parallel time. But the spark of "It's Alive" is a fleeting one.

This episode hit the airwaves May 10, 1968.

Here's a neat trick for analyzing the Dark Shadows episodes; look for installments that ping-pong or progress between the thoughts and actions of two couples. Dark Shadows episodes traditionally had about five performers, per. In many of the best, each pair of characters has a scene or two that are juxtaposed with another pair of characters. In the sort of mental exercise that you thought you would never do again after high school, step back and compare the two duos. Even if the writers never intended for them to reflect each other, it's a natural result of the creative process. However, I feel that these juxtapositions often happen on purpose, and they do wonders for the dramatic flow of the program.

EPISODE 495

When Roger hears that a new giant of a man is on the grounds, his pistol is fully loaded. Can Barnabas make the proper introductions or will Roger shoot on sight? Adam: Robert Rodan. (Repeat; 30 min.)

Adam speaks his first word: Barnabas. After a rousing soup-eating seminar, Adam becomes distraught when Barnabas leaves, so he escapes. Adam and David play, but when they rumble over David's new knife, Roger shoots Adam and probably goes home and laughs about it. Adam is wounded, but not down.

Everyone comes to Dark Shadows for the vampire. Everyone then finds their own reasons to stay. Episodes like 495 are replete with mine, and if you watch it without tearing up, we can turn this Daybook around right now and go home. I have plenty of Girls Next Door episodes I can write about, thank you. Agreed?

Isolation, misunderstandings, alienation, and all of the other pillars of my self-esteem grab the baton and share duties as grand marshal of the parade here. In fact, 495 might be the most emotionally arresting installment in the show's five-year run. Other episodes have more gripping moments, but I can think of few others that establish and sustain such poignance. Robert Rodan's sensitive and liberated performance is key, and it's no wonder that children rushing home from school now had a character with whom they could identify, and a character capable of unlocking the parental side of Barnabas they always knew was there. Not that Rodan was an ideal child and not that Barnabas was an ideal parent, as the Great Man admits in the soup scene. (And it has a Soup Scene. Even the hippest cities can't boast of a thriving soup scene, yet here ya go.) The fact that they fall short makes it all the more touching because the intention is there. Adam may be a wayward student of the spoon, but the pain we see, when he attempts to make Barnabas stay, is authentic and affectionate. Jonathan Frid similarly finds lovely and ambiguous texture in that scene, playing off Rodan for dynamics we'd rarely see again. Barnabas shows a mournful pride; he hears his name as Adam's first word and then chides himself for having unrealistic expectations based on that. Just as pointed is the pain and desperation Adam freely shows when Barnabas leaves. For many young viewers, the TV was their primary companion when adults left… if they were ever really there. The truth of that moment, shared by Sam Hall and Robert Rodan, cuts through plot, character, atmosphere, and everything else to speak directly to viewers, confronting as well as comforting. It's a biting reminder of the job Dark Shadows was fulfilling.

Hall then does something uncommon for Dark Shadows. He doubles down on it all with the other mismatched father/son pair, Roger and David. David is trying to show off a new knife, and Roger is pulling a muscle to feign interest. It's clear they're both trying, and they both know it's probably pointless. But what alternative have they? David later confides to Adam that he wishes that speaking was unnecessary since it's usually a vehicle for prying information more than connecting. Is anyone connecting in the episode? Roger even asks Barnabas to try a little harder to get along with Cassandra, as if his cousin were the petulant son of a newly married dad. David and Adam are the closest to each other, even they suffer potentially fatal misunderstandings. In classic, Frankenstein tradition, Adam's heartfelt attempts to assist are misinterpreted in ways that only well-meaning children (and recovering ones) can relate to.

One person at least tries, Barnabas. When Roger and Barnabas face down Adam (with David), the two sets of fathers and sons are matched up perfectly. We see the future play out in the present. We get how Roger got to be Roger and what David will become. Barnabas, a mild-mannered outsider (now) uses rational speech with Adam. Roger? A gun. Which he fires at Adam, anyway, even after Barnabas's technique works. The episode ends with a hint of Dumas, as do so many others (usually involving Burke Devlin). Adam ends as prone, afraid, and powerless as he begins, now rubbing his gun-shot shoulder. Given his connection to Barnabas, will they share the same pain, 'ala The Corsican Brothers? Neither Cheech nor Chong weighed in.

This episode hit the airwaves May 17, 1968.

ROBERT RODAN needs a thank you.

It was a thankless part. The next big thing after Barnabas. Grand expectations that could never be fulfilled because of the intrinsic differences. But, if you have done Dracula, then you have to do Frankenstein, and someone is going to have to play the creature. I'm not sure if Frankenstein is scary or sexy so much as sad. And sad only goes so far without other, continuing factors to propel it. My hope is that fans look beyond that... and beyond the fact that this lonely and desperate character was the focus of a storyline that began with great momentum, but, as with most Frankenstein stories, went nowhere. Then again, unless you are a keen student of literature, it can be hard to remember how most Frankenstein stories end. Something about torches and pitchforks. In that sense, the non-ending is as true to the legends as everything else on the show.

On Dark Shadows, the journey is what matters far more than the destination, and in lauding his contribution to the show, this is essential to remember. With his death, we have an opportunity to stop and remember that contribution with fresh eyes. It's ultimately inappropriate to compare Barnabas with Dracula. Yes, both are smooth and aristocratic vampires, but that's where the similarity stops. We have a much closer analog with Robert Rodan and Frankenstein's monster.

It's a strange mix that both represents these literary inspirations while moving beyond them. Few of the show's riffs, though, came as close to the source material as did Adam. So, it's safe to take a moment of license and admit that no other actor was ever given the chance to explore the world of Frankenstein's creation as Robert Rodan.

It was a gift he did not squander. The irony is that a part so broad could be charted with such sensitivity and intricacy. The thing that fascinates me about the creature is that he is, in every sense, us. Few of us feel entirely as in command and knowledgeable of our abilities and circumstances as we like to appear. We are always learning. We're always making mistakes. We are always making dangerous things out of little knowledge. Often before it's even out of the box. Robert Rodan captured the full breadth of that exploration with deftness and commitment. And in one part, he played a variety of them. From pantomime to smug, intellectualized chess mastery, Rodan showed brave command of each phase and of the many gray areas of his evolution between them. As anything based on Frankenstein would necessitate, it's a philosophical evolution. Humans grow until they die, assembled from the dead and lost parts of life experiences that are constantly forced into new service, just like Adam with his awkward limbs drafted into new battles. Few of us are graceful at it. Less so than any of us will admit.

In his attempt to grow up as quickly as he can, Adam is equally endearing and embarrassing. Rodan embodied that with the right kind of shamelessness. At a certain point, you can't worry about shame. Most compelling characters are beyond it. And most soap villains start out at dizzying heights of power that are then toppled by love. Adam started out as an endearing, oversized infant and was manipulated into abusing that heightened power as it developed. It is a painful reflection gifted to us with joy by this multifaceted actor. In a show where monsters are used to explore the learning curve of becoming Us, few did so with the forgivable kindness and heart of Robert

Rodan. He was our sad friend and most disturbingly accurate reflection. So much of that was in the writing, but so much of it was in him.

Coming up: my favorite goofy line of the series. On par with Ingrid Bergman's breathless intonation of "liverwurst" in Spellbound.

EPISODE 497

Will the gift of swanky earrings lead to new friendships or a lifetime supply of whipped carrots? Joe Haskell is about to find out! Joe: Joel Crothers. (Repeat; 30 min.)

Julia warns Mrs. Johnson not to tell David her dream, but she does so anyway. And indeed, he has the dream. Willie is his beckoner and spiders, his fear. Meanwhile, Joe informs Maggie that her new earrings are worth $15,000. When he suggests that there will be strings attached, she accuses him of being infantile. Later, Willie pressures her to become his friend when the earrings trigger her sense of vague memory about the Old House, leading her to visit.

So, Maggie thinks that Joe needs a restaurant that "serves baby food."

Equally redoubtable and reliable, Kathryn Leigh Scott sells the suggestion with a trooper's lack of self-consciousness. It's both a fabulous bit of shade and a conspicuously poorly written line for Dark Shadows. It's so awkward that I wish they had written more dialogue like it. It is equal parts completely unbelievable and totally realistic. It is an "allow myself to introduce myself" moment. Almost. Maggie is clearly ticked off and clearly needs to put Joe in his place. I think she assumes that this is the best way to do it. Either that, or she thought it was going to sound a lot better than it did when it came out of her mouth. Either way, the camera fixes on Joe's expression, which is more baffled than insulted. As well it should be. Maggie is the one sashaying around with $15,000 earrings, and Joe is either envious of the person who gave them to her or is envious of the earrings. One or the other. Probably both.

The return of Josette is a strange bit of regression for the show. If I were Barnabas, I would demand a refund from Julia. How many times does he have to take her into the shop to get brainwashed? Between Adam and a non-vampire Barnabas and a dream curse that is more neurotic than horrific, the program has run so far from Gothic romance that a gentle reminder of the show's identity doesn't hurt. It's both a good post-it of where we have been and how far we have come. There are contingents of Dark Shadows fans who dislike this storyline as if it took their lunch money and got them to write "PEN 15" on their arm. It wears out its welcome now and then, but it's also a prime example of the surprising versatility of the show's format.

In terms of equal opportunity terror, the dream curse continues to impact everyone who has ever been on the show as it makes its march toward Barnabas. Thank God it got to Mrs. Johnson. Who among us has not wondered about her nightmares? Allegedly a woman who does not dream, why would she? She lives with the all-too-real fantasy of being Harry Johnson's mother.

Her eagerness to tell David is part of the curse, yes. We get that. And the show certainly is not ageist nor overprotective when it comes to excluding David from the accursed festivities. He gets dragged in with everyone else. If I were a recent viewer of the show, it would be easy to conclude that David was the poster boy for child psychological abuse. Because he takes a lot of it. Long-time viewers know that he is tougher than he looks, however, and in an odd way, including him in the proceedings is a sign of respectful acknowledgment that kids are more than spoonfuls of jelly necessitating constant coddling. They can be terrorized by giant dream spiders along with anyone else.

John Karlen is reliably outstanding in this episode, and the script supports him extremely well. One of his great strengths is showing characters who wrestle with deeply conflicted impulses and emotions. Most actors find challenge just accurately depicting one. Karlen can create a blend of inner conflict where each emotion is distinct yet blended. His desire to protect Maggie, romantically assert himself, be a friend, avoid the wrath of Barnabas, and sidestep Joe Haskell is a heady brew. He keeps it going with clarity and energy, and the suspense her creates is more arresting than the horror elements central to the series. Karen is the episode's hidden highlight and provides one of my favorite acting moments on the series.

No one's telling HIM he needs baby food.

This episode hit the airwaves May 21, 1968.

EPISODE 525

When Roger lets slip that Vicki once was tried as a witch in 1795, Nicholas hatches a scheme to rescue Angelique with the help of black magic and hypnosis. Nicholas: Humbert Allen Astredo. (Repeat; 30 min.)

Jeff awakens from a dream where Nathan Forbes berates him as Peter Bradford. Upon waking, "Jeff" realizes that this evidence ensures that he is Peter Bradford. At Collinwood, Nicholas connects Vicki to the painting and induces Roger to explain her convictions about 1795. He realizes that she knows the location of Trask's execution tree and uses her knowledge to locate it. There, Nicholas performs a ritual to summon

Angelique. The sound of screaming indicates he may be a success.

Dark Shadows is a paranoid's delight and is sure to leave you with reflexes and impulses that will last a lifetime — an eternal gift to make a neurotic out of anyone. Vicki shows amazing fortitude and professionalism. Here she is, at her job – and living there, living at her home and work — is the witch responsible for her murder? But, you know, the witch says she isn't and is married to your boss, so you have to play along. Then, a sleazy guy with a mustache shows up, kisses hands, and claims to be her brother, which may be worse. One night, you come downstairs for your nightly brandy & bullion and catch him making weird hand gestures at a painting that looks like said witch… then he asks to "borrow it" for reasons that seem uncomfortably Kentuckian. Who borrows a painting of someone who looks like their sister? Nicholas Blair, that's who. This kind of stuff goes on there all the time. People at Collinwood, in the name of lack of evidence, lack of witnesses, or just a desire to be darn nice, end up sleeping three doors down from all manner of apocalyptic ne'er-do-wells, and they just lump it. Can you trust anyone? I'm always wary when life throws me a guest star. The Collinses. Spend enough hours watching a show about them, and you're in serious danger of taking that home and to work. Word to the wise.

525 is a joyous little core sample of the good stuff on the program. It's Jonathan Frid's day off, and the writers are determined to keep the suspense and ratings high. A wacky dream sequence with Nathan Forbes laughing maniacally is a reliable way to start any episode, corporate event, or bris. Joe must be either extremely tired of being associated with this weirdo or strangely proud because it's happening with a constancy that must make him think that Forbes is doing two sets nightly at the Blue Whale. All's well, however, because it knocks a big chunk of the Jeff Clark identity crisis out of consideration.

Quickly, we move to Nicholas sleazing around Vicki and drinking it up with Roger, finally comforting him with the company of a fellow fop. You kind of wish Burke Devlin would show up and try to intimidate Roger NOW… now that his buddy Nicholas is there. They'd just laugh at his taste in shoes until Burke skulked away to pen an angry letter to Brewster's department store in furious shame.

Roger, on cue, spills the beans about Vicki's conviction that she'd traveled to 1795 and was harassed by a witch hunter named Trask, tipping Nicholas off to the location of the Sacrificial Tree. It's easy to be a villain on Dark Shadows. It's not a job so much as a vacation. Nicholas just sits around the drawing room and drinks and leers at babes until people deliver exactly the exposition he needs, on cue. What's left? Hypnotize Vicki, go to the tree and call back Angelique. All in a day's work.

Let's praise Humbert Allen Astredo for carrying the show so effortlessly that it feels like we're watching a talented actor unselfconsciously improvise rather than some guy reciting lines and working through blocking. It's to the show's credit that they didn't simply hand over the storyline to him in perpetuity. How do you not screw up a scene? Include, Nicholas Blair. It would be enough to make the rest of the ensemble paranoid. And, I guess, they share the wealth with us.

This episode hit the airwaves July 1, 1968.

Once I hit my stride with the column, patterns began to form in my own writing. There are several "types" of Daybook columns. One of them is excessively whacky and stream-of-consciousness. Sometimes I would feel a little guilty for this. A tad too self-indulgent. But when I look at those, they are often a pretty good reflection of what the show was giving me. This particular essay really outlines the sheer number of inanities foisted upon Barnabas. It's ludicrous, and we are all the better for it.

EPISODE 530

Can Barnabas stop his ex-wife from returning from Hell before a reanimated monster kills a middle manager who reeks of tuna? Sam Evans: David Ford. (Repeat; 30 min.)

As Adam and Joe tussle in the woods, Vicki tells Barnabas that Cassandra is back and determined she learn the dream. Cassandra raises the ghost of Sam Evans to tell her, and after Barnabas squabbles with the witch, he returns home to find what may be a dead Joe Haskell tumbling out of his closet. Adam looks on in delight.

At a certain point, where is Barnabas supposed to go? At first, it seems like the Old House is the logical choice. Unless he goes out. Either place, he has women vaguely, if confusedly, throwing themselves at him as if he were the Tom Jones of the occult. That's the good news. Kind of. Especially because neither of them is Julia. Vicki shows up just as you've donned your smoking jacket, and she drops a dime on Cassandra. Bad news that the ex is back from Hell, but at least you're getting the intel early. But the dream curse is back, too. Oh, and Angelique's ghost is simultaneously around as well, calling herself Cassandra, which is all kinds of confusing, and delivering cheap perfume from the props department. I'm not sure what the bigger threat is — the dream curse or having Vicki wandering around and smelling like a dead flight attendant from a Jennings Lang movie.

It's a mixed bag at home. So, you go into the woods only to find Cassandra, probably reeking of the same perfume, pretending not to be Angelique, which is ludicrous, and the only thing to do is to declare that you'd better avoid each other — as if you were Jan and/or Marcia in a tiff over who'll be running for student government. That is, if Jan and Marcia had weird crushes on each other, which they didn't, so don't go there because Alice is listening over the sound of meatloaf sizzling in the oven and is sure to drag Julia into it, that is all anyone needs right now. And, outside, over the smell of the perfume, you could swear you could detect Joe Haskell's Hai Karate. Mixed with the KFC-drenched aroma of Adam. And there's the stench of their combat. But between the two men or the two fragrances? Maybe both.

Coming home from this olfactory nightmare, Joe falls out of the closet in the Old House drawing room — and stop snickering — while Adam leers and laughs manically from the window like some perverse Alan Funt. Which means, like Alan Funt.

As if that's not enough, you get the feeling that Sam Evans' ghost is mixed up in this. Is he delivering from a multi-level marketing scheme, too? Since that's the essence of the dream curse, probably. Which may be why Angelique was delivering perfume along with it.

It's kind of as if the Dark Shadows writers were playing an improv game, sort of topping each other while never quite completing anyone's idea, but just adding on more and more. Even a straight-faced description of the nonstop nuttiness sounds like a ten-year-old's breathless description of the action to a beleaguered dad, just coming home from a long day at happy hour. In other words, TV magic. When I think of Dark Shadows, I think of episodes like this one, because it both has everything and is at the crossroads of what the show will be. It's not great Dark Shadows, but it's far from bad, and it has a madcap sampling of everything in this era. Crazy Joe, unable to deal with the madness now calling itself "story," has become without picking up a gun. Adam. Cassandra, raising the dead. The dream curse. Barnabas, probably wondering if being a vampire were all that bad compared to what humans deal with in this day and age.

It's David Ford's last episode, and that's yet another reminder of where the show has come since the early days of red meat drama. You know, what he signed up for. Think Dan Curtis is going to apologize for the evolution in tone? No. He doubles down on Ford by making it the wackiest episode possible — without having Sam jump out of a cake with a coconut bra on. Which was probably next.

Even the details of Sam's life as a ghost are bizarre. Why does a ghost need to be wearing a trench coat? Is it raining in the afterlife? Did Maggie bury him in a raincoat because she couldn't sell it off on consignment? Did it not fit Joe? And why is Sam still blind and wearing sunglasses? Doesn't that get reset if you're a ghost? You're lucky they didn't edit in Hayden Christiansen to play a young version of you. In reality, whatever that is, Ford was allegedly too put out with it all to learn lines, and so the glasses allowed him to read off of the teleprompter without anyone noticing. David, baby, no one noticed because everyone was reading off the teleprompter, capisce?

And I wouldn't have it any other way.

In the next episode, Barnabas just decides to let Willie take the fall. Why? Probably and ultimately because Barnabas would still be writhing in his coffin, enrobed in agonized peace if he hadn't been so rudely interrupted the year before. He'd go back there, I'm certain, but have you ever tried to chain your own coffin from the inside? Of course not. No one has. It's a ridiculous question.

But is it any more ridiculous than episode 530? We all know the answer. And we wouldn't have it any other way. Farewell, David. You think things are strange NOW?

This episode hit the airwaves July 8, 1968.

I know that soap operas need to have a dizzying number of plots going on at the same time, but in this case, it's all the same plot. We need to remind ourselves that this was no accident. None were more aware of this than the people who made the show.

EPISODE 556

When Nicholas Blair announces his plan to unleash an army of satanic supermen, will Barnabas be blackmailed into the oddest job of all? Angelique: Lara Parker. (Repeat; 30 min.)

Nicholas announces his plan to rule the world. To execute it, he must have Julia Hoffman create a race just like Adam. But she is controlled by Barnabas, and so he must be controlled by his concern for Victoria, which gets manipulated by the theft of her engagement ring.

It's that time of year again when we commemorate the accidental destruction of the Collinwood set, which occurred when a cleaning went awry. Due to that, it's a special time for the show, where the action moves either to the Old House or the house by the sea, and just as the viewers are on summer vacation, it feels a bit like the show is, also. Humbert Allen Astredo and Lara Parker sport lovely tans, and even Jonathan Frid is playing Barnabas's nervousness with an easygoing air. It's almost Dark Shadows: Live at the Sands. However, it has a sense of discipline and focus that keeps the episode true to the show. The episode also features Lara Parker's first appearance as a vampire, and she makes a delightful one. She was always more than capable of playing a seductress. Now, she has to. Girl's gotta eat. And the fact that she must resort to seduction rather than use it as an occasionally amusing option is an irony that eclipses the obvious one.

The cultural influences running around in 556 are as abundant as the number of moving pieces in Nicholas' plan. But, coming out just a year after You Only Live Twice, the Bond influence, shown through Nicholas, is true CinemaScope. It's a plan only a madman could brew up — and not because it involves a proposed satanic army of reanimated corpse descendants. That's already in the Collinsport city budget. That's covered. No, it begins to fray at the edges when it relies on a scientist who doesn't know what she's really doing.

Who's controlled by an ex-vampire who wants nothing to do with any of it. See, he'll control the doctor, who'll control the production of the atom age army of supermen. But the ex-vampire will be controlled by Vicki, who'll be controlled by the first reanimated patchwork corpse man. Angelique will control them all kind of. But she's a resentful vampire who steered clear of the Vicki: 1795 storyline, so how reliable is that?

556 presents the show's most Rube Goldberg scheme, crying out for the Oom Papah brand of Danny Elfman music. Prior to this, I'd questioned Nicholas' morals, but never his sanity. Now? I fully expect him to be selling pants for fish before the week is out. The lynchpin of the whole thing is having Angelique stop trying to bite the hunky new sheriff's deputy long enough to put on a costume and terrify Vicki as a flesh and blood ghost of herself. At that point, she strongarms Vicki into giving up her engagement ring from Jeff Clark or Peter Bradford. (Candy mint, breath mint, pick one, pick both. Gotta catch'em all.) You see, Nicholas needs to give Adam the ring. And when he does, I'd say it's darned romantic looking. So, then Adam takes the ring to Barnabas to convince him that Nicholas means business. Or something like that. I had a nosebleed and passed out somewhere in the middle of describing that.

The world had been clamoring for a James Bond/Brady Bunch/Munsters crossover. Be careful what you wish for. In this case, they pull off the strangeness beautifully. Every single moment is controlled with astonishing discipline. At any point, any of this could've descended into camp. Instead, it skims millimeters above the surface, never so much as getting a droplet. It's easy to say that Dark Shadows is renowned for pulling off this kind of stunt, but in this episode, they top even themselves.

What's most important is that Nicholas Blair will return.

This episode hit the airwaves August 12, 1968.

Beyond the then-novel idea of a vampire as hero, the very first unusual/signature/subversive element to the series that I noticed was its message about the redemptive power of love. I profoundly hate talking about that, because long has done more damage to me than any other human emotion. I suspect I am not alone. Which is why Dark Shadows is wise to consistently portray it as a force that both releases people from the shadow of evil but ultimately leads to their ruin.

Are you listening, Nicolas?

EPISODE 559

Will Nicholas solve his romantic problems with Maggie by insisting that Angelique have Joe for dinner? Nicholas: Humbert Allen Astredo. (Repeat; 30 min.)

With the aid of a magic mirror and the trio of powers of hypnosis, ventriloquism, and invisibility, Nicholas fools Victoria into thinking she's been at the Old House instead of his prisoner. When she wanders in to see Jeff, he informs her that she's been missing for days. Meanwhile, Nicholas again charms Maggie, but when Joe appears, it's clear that there are rocks on the green for the devil's Don Juan. Returning to the house by the sea, he suggests to Angelique that her next victim will be Joe Haskell.

Jeez, even a smooth-talking, well-dressed, hardworking, handsome professional guy from Hell doesn't stand a chance against the eternal menace of The Old Boyfriend. It's a credit to the casting and authorship of Dark Shadows that you side with the demon on the whole thing. It's a longstanding tradition now that the show's ostensible villains are the romantic heroes, but in this case, there's nothing ostensible about it. He IS the villain.

Nonetheless, he's a villain experiencing his first love, and who can't get behind that? Maggie brings out the best in him. Humbert Allen Astredo becomes a California-bronzed Richard Benjamin onscreen with Kathryn Leigh Scott, and together, they create television's most subversive almost-couple.

There's nothing new to seeing love depicted as a transformative force. That's its job in art. It transforms the static, the pessimistic, the hopeless, and the innocent. Dark Shadows is bored with that and reliably examines what love can do for evil. Angelique is the series' longest-running experiment in that. Her story ends in the transformation that love can create. Just because she believes she begins the story as a woman in love, doesn't mean that she is. Obsessed, maybe. Jealous, certainly. If she begins the series in love with anything, it's with the idea of being someone else — primarily a Collins, wealthy and waspy. She calls that love, and it may be, but it's not romance. She just happens to find that along the way, and it's a happy irony that it's with the subject of her obsession. Even luckier? Having gotten the pleasure of burning her alive out of his system, he's eventually opened to exploring a future with the woman who condemned him to a godless, living death of savagery and solitude. As one should expect.

For Adam, love motivates him to improve himself. It also motivates him to become a serial kidnapper, but at least that gets him out of the house. Love transforms Julia Hoffman. Quentin, arguably. Certainly, Jeb. But with Nicholas, there is a genuine danger to the depiction and storyline. Not just that he's doing something dangerous — it's that the writers are.

Depending on where you're coming from. Love doesn't really transform Nicholas so much as expand his range of delights. Because of the casting of Astredo, it's hard not to root for him. Especially compared with the charming-but-bland quarterback-type presented by Joe Haskell, the program creates an immediate David-and-Goliath scenario where it's very easy to root for the diabolical Blair. Joe has spun his wheels for years… at least Nicholas wants to make a commitment. And it's not because Maggie's soul is the secret to some superweapon or something. No, he just authentically loves her. If Nicholas' charm and awareness weren't enough to make him the preferable Dr. Pepper to the predictable Coke of the good guys, now he's a guy with a sincere interest in one of the show's heroines. Because who knows what's holding up Joe? Barnabas wasn't in love with her; he was in love with someone who just looked like her. True, we don't see how Joe responded to her when he and Maggie first met. We don't see Joe infatuated. What we see is a Joe (yes, traumatized, but still) who is complacent but arguably noncommittal. Contrasted with a Nicholas, motivated for the right reasons, it makes Joe's upcoming fate even sadder. And Maggie's affection for Joe, even more so, because we know where it's headed.

As for Nicholas? Now more than ever, it's hard to root against him. And maybe we don't. We just root against his plans. Nicholas is a man who wants naughty-naughty things. But Maggie's not one of them.

This episode hit the airwaves August 15, 1968.

EPISODE 562

Joe finally learns the truth behind Collinsport's nocturnal activities. But if he's a puppet, who is the hand? Angelique or Nicholas? Joe Haskell: Joel Crothers. (Repeat; 30 min.)

Joe stumbles upon Willie, who is digging up a grave. Nicholas and Angelique divert Joe from informing the authorities, and Joe later goes to a nervous Barnabas to suggest that the police will not be involved. Joe continues to succumb to Angelique's bite, despite resisting.

Dark Shadows started out as one thing. And that one thing cannot escape what the show is becoming. The saddest example of that is the transformation of Joe Haskell. Sad because he is a wasted, maddened casualty, played with a wonderful sense of dawning horror by Joel Crothers. He and his character were once the show's rays of light. (Excluding an understandable temper and one, allowable, drunken night of soaking up beer and piddling class envy on the Collinsport Afghan.) Now, he's Angelique's blood doll, and a pitiful, disheveled one, at that. His captivation by Angelique can be written off to the supernatural, but that feels superficial. Angelique is, in every way, the anti-Maggie. Does this make her the wrong woman or the wrong woman in the right ways? Joe's desperate attraction feels tragically right. Even her comparative indifference to him is both repulsive and alluring.

Dark Shadows' early world of blackmail and revenge was built for Joe Haskell, and Joe was built to be the paragon withstanding it. He reeks of honest work, integrity, and common sense. When Willie needs a warning or Sam needs a sober ear, Joe's the guy. Vampires and demons, not so much. Dark Shadows was careful to segregate guys like Joe and Burke from the incipient sideshow. They were just not built for moments like this, and all of Collinsport is revealed to be an elaborate shell to hide what was truly brewing under the surface. Jeffrey Beaumont is designed to successfully segue back and forth between the genres. His story is, by classical definitions, a comedy. Joe's is a tragedy. When Jeffery says that "It's a strange world" he does so with bemused wonder. But when Joe Haskell says it, there is nothing more nor less than horror — at the world and his own combination of eager desire and spoon-fed ignorance. He is the doomed hero of Lovecraft, not Lynch. But David Lynch is an optimist compared to the minds behind Dark Shadows, and the fall of Joe Haskell is a prime example.

In fact, he is so alien to the newly revealed world of the supernatural in Dark Shadows that Angelique seems subtly indifferent toward him. He's a meal to her more than a man, and she takes the job because she's a pro. Not because she wants to. He's a worthy victim in only the biological sense. When they share the screen, it feels like two vastly different shows have been Frankensteined together, but that adds to the dark fascination of it. Because it's clear which is going to win, we also see which vision of the universe is stronger. Suddenly, the pedestrian world of everyday, mortal storytelling is revealed to be on the thinnest of stilts. Van Helsing doesn't stand a chance, and we knew it all along. The unseemly and fascinating part of this story is how it brazenly tells the truth about mortal life after setting it up as unimpeachable for the past two years. Joe has been played all along, and the audience — part of Joe's world all along — has been, as well.

When Barnabas returns from 1795, he immediately starts draining Vicki of blood. It's a metaphor for the show reinventing itself by feeding off its own beginnings until they cease to be relevant. Joe's victimization by Angelique is simply equal opportunity with a thousand-yard stare. And not without regrets. In 562, both Joe and Angelique seem equally horrified and enthralled at the prospect of meeting each other. Joe seems to have more of the opportunity to resist than any victim we've seen. Consequently, his eventual capitulation to bites and blackmail is all the more poignant.

This episode hit the airwaves August 20, 1968.

The trick with this one is really imagining Julia waking up on the floor of the lab looking more like she had been out on a bender than viciously attacked.

Vicious attacks aren't funny. Neither is someone suffering from a humiliating chemical addiction. And yet, just a few years ago, elements in these things were just a gosh darn laugh riot.

I am amazed at how quickly we have lost our sense of humor about once-reliable tropes. And I get a clearer and clearer idea, every day, of why they aren't funny. Certainly, the legions of the humorless are untiring in their campaign to take the fun out of everything. Their greatest victory, however, is in wearing me down to the point that I am not wholly certain why various cliches were funny in the first place. I miss the freewheeling world of political incorrectness, but now that I have been separated from it for so long, I don't recall what was so funny about it in the first place.

EPISODE 566

Barnabas becomes suspicious of Julia when she begins sleeping all day, wearing high-collared shirts, and longing for the embrace of the undead. Tom Jennings: Don Briscoe. (Repeat; 30 min.)

Julia is attacked and bitten by Tom and later denies it to Willie, who takes her to Collinwood to recover. She instructs Mrs. Johnson to leave her alone, and when the housekeeper brings her a letter from Barnabas, she tears it up. Later, Julia is summoned by Tom for the second meal of the day, and upon coming back to Collinwood, her bite marks are discovered by Barnabas.

I know that alcoholism isn't funny. And drunks aren't funny.

Having made that clear, Dark Shadows was produced before these modern opinions, and we're swimming in its pool, so get that lampshade off your head and jump in. Once you've seen the episodes enough times, which could mean just once, it becomes pretty clear that the writers often had a good time by doing an episode in drag. I don't mean that Sam Hall was wearing a dress, because I always saw him as more of a smart, designer pants-suit kinda guy, much like future TV hunk Bea Arthur. No, I simply mean that the episodes are often about something else. Usually with no conclusion. Just an opportunity to explore a situation or human moment that was fun or challenging or necessary to write about. All you have to do is re-frame a little bit of the context.

I think the reason that drinking was kind of funny for so long was that the drinkers were often in on the joke, and the joke kind of changed before, during, and after the imbibing. "Morning after" humor is a strange mix of regret, everyone agreeing to ignore the obvious after-effects, and the paradoxical pursuit of hair of the dog. In this case, the dog is Tom Jennings. Because if you look at this episode and kind of ignore the bite marks on its neck, it looks for all the world like Julia is sleeping off a hangover and everyone is either trying to deny what they know or find out what they fear. And it's not just a minor hangover. This is, in the immortal words of Robert Urich, "a full, adult-size bangaroo." It's also perfect commedia dell'arte, where the hapless servants are trying to understand the decadence of one half of the household and then cover it up to the rest. What can Mrs. Johnson possibly be thinking? She worked for Burke Devlin, so whatever it is, it can't be new.

In the midst, Barnabas is more of a fussbudget than ever. He had to put up with months of Nathan Forbes and, I'm sure, more than one night of Jeremiah in his cups, thumping around the almost-Old House while chasing maids or sneaking in doxies from the docks. In the 20th century, that level of wanton sherry consumption might pass at Collinwood, but this is his house, thank you, and young Loomis and Dr. Hoffman were hand-picked because they didn't go in for those sorts of shenanigans. That is why he wants to get to the bottom of it, even more. And Willie does everything to keep him from knowing. And Julia, knowing exactly what Barnabas is up to, tears up Barnabas's note, because it probably said, "Lay off the sauce and get back to work, you lug."

The scene where Willie and Barnabas have their confrontation in the lab is priceless, because someone has forgotten his lines, and I can't wager which one it was. But Barnabas seems so appalled at what's happened that awkward silence mixed with helpless astonishment is indistinguishable from a fully voiced response. If anything, it's more realistic. I mean, what do you say? This is an episode with no really progressive dialogue, just evasion and implication with Tom Jennings in the middle.

Tom is the bartender here, and he's worse than the clientele. Actually, that's stretching it all. Tom Jennings is a very peculiar vampire. Maybe one of the scariest, because he's the most consistently feral. Via makeup and performance, Don Briscoe emphasizes the undead and driven quality of the monster, stripping away the velveteen refinement and leaving a working-class killer underneath, and perhaps the portrayal is a commentary on class paranoia by the writers. (It's a reflection, anyway.) Barnabas can be trusted with the satanic powers of the undead; he's been to university. But a guy like Tom Jennings?

Lock up your Doctor Hoffmans! There's a Union man on the loose!

Episodes such as 566 are situational popcorn. Even when monotonous, they are character-driven delights to watch. Like any good sitcom, I know exactly what's coming and yet it always satisfies. Actually, it satisfies on a more metaphysical level even than that. Barnabas had his chance with Julia, and he ignored it. Rather than see her victimized, I almost see her avenged, and the vaguely post-coital splay and daze in which she's found by Willie and Barnabas after her two encounters says far more than what's on the page. Is Barnabas horrified because she was claimed by a vampire or by a vampire other than he?

This episode hit the airwaves August 26, 1968.

EPISODE 597

Professor Stokes stops at nothing to prove that Eve is French. But will she say oui? Eve: Marie Wallace. (Repeat; 30 min.)

Stokes warns Adam that Eve is up to no good, but to no avail. Just when he thinks he has the situation clarified, the body of Leona goes missing, as do Adam and Eve. But Stokes hints that he knows where they are.

Leave it to Universal to sell posters over movies. There are some great and Great films in their canon, but... are there? I'm speaking about the Monsters here. There are marvelous elements in those movies, yes, but did you honestly think they combined them successfully when you first watched them?

For me, only three truly grabbed me on my first viewing: The Black Cat; Abbott and Costello Meet Frankenstein; and The Bride of Frankenstein. But the Frankenfilms aren't perfect. Let's face it, other than breaking a green sweat, making threats and being professionally misunderstood, the creature has little to do.

His wife, even less. As far as being the title character of the Greatest Horror Movie Ever Made, she flies pretty casually, showing up to the plot just in time for a nightcap. She doesn't appear until the final minute or two of the movie, has no dialogue, bitterly dislikes our hero, and then gets blowed up real good.

It's a shaggy dog story, perhaps intentionally. As a gay man of the 1930s James Whale led a life necessarily fraught with as much frustration as fulfillment. I mean, look at his movies, and, don't take too long coughing up a verdict. It's no surprise that the creature waits for almost all of the film, only to find himself loathed by the girl he's been waiting for, despite her being all that glitters. Or crackles, in this case. That kind of frustrated anticipation and crestfallen hope was probably intrinsic to Whale's life. He sums it up with Bride and moves on.

It puts the Dark Shadows writers in a marvelous position. So far — of the major 'horror' works — they've tackled Dracula and Frankenstein, improving vastly on both. But here, there is nothing to improve… just explore. They pick up on Whale's thesis of frustrated desire and push it to a place much, much darker than I think is obvious. Eve doesn't just dislike Adam. As the vessel for the wickedest woman in history, she finds him to be a big green bouncy house for psychological sadism. But I think that's the safest move the show makes. Let's remove the Marie Roget element. Here's yer gender statement, pal. When a man is born, he's a gibbering id, delighted by shiny things and buttons. He's easily taken in by mustachioed sorcerers and Thayer David and is mistrustful of genteel Canadians.

When a woman is born? You got Eve. Hey, don't take it out on me. Tell it to Sam Hall. Yes, these are all stereotypes, but for whom? It's misogyny for a female audience, seeing not themselves but the kind of women they can't stand. I wonder if this is the portrayal they would have created for a largely male audience. But it wasn't, and the show, to be seen accurately, must be viewed through that lens. Yet, for modern eyes, Eve's confidence and sense of purpose are as admirable as they are questionable. It makes her the show's least predictable character. The shame of it is that it takes a possession to create that kind of volition, but without it, she'd simply be a ginger-haired Angelique.

And maybe the ultimate problem is that she's an Angelique without a purpose. They try. They really try. The real shame of Eve is that, by shoehorning in the Marie Roget element, they rob the character of discovering her sense of purpose. But Roget is so ancient and so French she lacks a context in 1968 Collinsport, despite her obsession with characters played by Roger Davis. Barnabas, Stokes, and Julia, the venerable old bachelors on the show, try to break it to Adam without devolving into a drumming circle, but he's determined to be led on an emotional snipe hunt anyway. Of course, he'll stand up for the honor of the character least worthy of it. It's another reflection of cosmic truth that makes Dark Shadows the best documentary on TV. Equally truthful is Eve's comically counterfeit lament that, as a woman, it's her lot to suffer. You know, as she holds everyone in fear and suspense. The moment is played as broadly as it's written, but there's an ugly, satiric truth to it. Eve is the one character on the show so feminine, she's practically a drag queen brought to life by the hand of Waylon Flowers. There's no denying she's a woman, but hardly helpless.

Ultimately, she grabs the Adam story, notorious for going nowhere, and takes it everywhere at once. It's an exhausting prospect and a sneak preview of where the show would go — for better and worse — for the next two and a half years. Marie Wallace is the ideal person to inaugurate the trip.

The visual depiction is so straightforward that it shouldn't work. Black dress and hose. Same thing Thayer David wore to the set. But it's her presence that is so unforgettable. Wallace relishes the joy of acting, and a successful Dark Shadows villain needn't be saddled with a causal plan. Just the kind of joy for living only actors and supervillains can appreciate.

Diabolos bless them, one and all.

This episode hit the airwaves on October 8, 1968.

EPISODE 631

Nicholas pulls out all the stops, and stakes, when he revives a vampire to ensure the resurrection of a demonic undead vixen to secure a master race for the Prince of Darkness. Harry Johnson: Craig Slocum. (Repeat; 30 min.)

Nicholas revives Tom as an agent to assist in the revival of Eve. After unsuccessfully attacking Victoria, and after being investigated by his own brother, Chris Jennings, Tom is hunted down by Barnabas who incinerates him in the sunrise.

Dark Shadows 631 could not be any manlier if it were written by Robert Bly and featured a drumming circle of Bill Malloy, Sam Evans, and Istvan. I guess I could like the episode more if you threw in Count Petofi being instructed in Zumba by the curvaceous Chuck Morgan to a tune by Jerry Reed, but other than that, this episode has reached the scientific limit for entertainment. If we experienced any more, it would have the side effects that top scientists warned pilots they would experience if they broke the sound barrier. Especially while wearing that, thank you very much. It's after Labor Day. Have some decorum, General Yeager. Have some decorum.

It's a laundry list of delight. (And just to check, has anyone here ever listed their laundry? I haven't. It's all I can do to get it into a bag.) First of all, we have not one, but two Don Briscoes, with the revival of Tom being followed hot on the hind paws of his brother, Chris. What would've happened to Chris if Tom had attacked him? Would Chris become all the more powerful? Would the werewolf part neutralize the vampire part? If someone got bit, would they only become a werewolf if they had been bitten during the full moon, or at any point in the lunar cycle? Or does he stop craving blood when he becomes a werewolf? I'm sure they've solved this in the Bloodlines portion of Second Life, but who plays that? With our luck, that's where David Henesy has been all along.

The beginning is terrific because Nicolas Blair goes to revive Tom Jennings, which he does by pulling the stake out of his heart. And he's perfectly preserved! He's just like some kind of human pen and pencil set. Except he's not human and that's neither a Ticonderoga in his chest, nor is he just glad to see us. Nicholas warned him that if he should defy him in any way, Tom would be sentenced to eternal damnation. And I guess it'll really be eternal this time. Not semi-eternal or temporarily eternal as it was the last time. The inclusion of Tom and Chris in the same episode feels akin to a kind of stunt, but I admire it, and it's the sort of muscle flexing that feels like a warm-up to the hijinks that would become routine in 1897.

An attack on Victoria leads to Barnabas finally telling her that yes, there are vampires. Now, it's not as though I'm an expert on the series who has gone for long stints writing about it every day. But you know, I would be amazed if Victoria had not gotten the memo of at least a rumor of vampires somewhere along the line. Maybe in 1795 or something? I'm pretty sure she had Barnabas's number when she came back. At least, you know, the "cousin." Anyway, it's a new actress in the part so I assume that Barnabas is filling her in as one of the most meta-acts of the series. Speaking of new actresses, it's time for my annual crush on Betsy Durkin to return. There, I said it. She's got brains and intensity and, honestly, it appears she has the capacity to understand pretty darn quickly. I'm not comparing her with anyone. Except that she looks a lot like Julia Louis Dreyfus, which is a good thing. But I'm not comparing her with anyone on the show. Or who was on the show. Wink wink. Her brief tenure is a welcome sight for me.

And maybe it's just because of novelty. Even if you have a great homeroom teacher, nothing beats a permissive substitute.

After Barnabas and Nicholas have words, it feels as if Blake Edwards took over as director. First of all, Nicholas Blair officially becomes the frustrated mirror for Barnabas. Digging up bodies. Assisted by an ineffectual redneck with a phallic name. You can almost see Nicholas thinking, "I knew I signed up for the wrong team. He gets Willie Loomis. The best I get? Harry Johnson. And a useless one, at that."

Eventually, you have, within the same 8 feet of woods, Nicholas and Harry, secretly followed by Barnabas, secretly followed by Tom Jennings. At some point, it stops being a Dark Shadows episode and becomes a Jack Davis poster for the mid-70s Buck Henry film adaptation.

Not to say that pathos doesn't enter the picture. Barnabas goes full-on Peter Cushing van Helsing when he destroys Tom Jennings, with crossed candlesticks at daybreak. And Tom has one of the most logical lines ever spoken on Dark Shadows. Barnabas stands there telling Tom how painful the sunrise is going to be, as if Tom is supposed to do something other than suffer within it, and Tom simply says, "Then don't do it to me!" And you know, he has an excellent point. But unfortunately, Barnabas is too much in the moment to ask something such as, "Do you have an alternative to suggest?"

The entire line between the dead and the undead has always been heavily blurred, at best, but there was a poignant and painful irony as Tom died, screaming "Let me live! Let me live!"

At that moment, I didn't know if he were asking to simply be allowed to continue surviving as a vampire, brought back from a second death only to be tortured back to death again in the space of a few hours, or if he were asking to legitimately live, meaning to never have been a vampire in the first place. How many vampires would ask the same thing? Because we see them speaking and displaying feelings and passions, we are never given a deep chance to contemplate the metaphysical significance of un-death. As much as they are known for drinking blood to survive, there is and must be a profoundly wrong and ultimately alienated essence to being a vampire. People long to be vampires. The hours are great. The wardrobe works. Rent is minimal. But I wonder if the real reason we identify with them is because we all, to some extent, feel separated from this concept of "living" that seems to be shared like an inside joke by everyone else. The vampire wears otherness as a badge of, if not honor, at least honesty.

Ultimately, Tom Jennings' final plea is the plea of all of us. It is a quest for Barnabas that only begins with Dr. Lang's cure.

This episode was broadcast November 25, 1968.

EPISODE 633/634

When Nicholas presents Maggie as his Satanic spouse and life force candidate, can Barnabas defeat him before his master race becomes a reality? Barnabas: Jonathan Frid. (Repeat; 30 min.)

Nicholas conducts a black rite that bonds Maggie to him. He takes her to become the life force for Eve. Barnabas, who is already horrified, is made even more so by Maggie's lovestruck loyalty to Nicholas. As the experiment begins, Maggie's pain becomes unbearable to watch. Knowing that this is his only chance to end Nicholas once and for all, Barnabas smashes the electrical equipment, killing Eve at last and sending a terrified and powerless Nicholas running. Barnabas gives pursuit with every intent to kill him, but Diabolos claims Nicholas first, as Barnabas laughs at the spectacle. Meanwhile, Maggie revives with Julia but seems to be in a haze that is connected to her time as a prisoner in the Old House. Will she remember at last? Adam escapes and charges into Collinwood, furious that his mate is no more.

This is the One Where Barnabas Smiles. I mean, really, really smiles. I won't say he goes all Whoopi Goldberg (in this episode), but he looks robustly happy when Nicholas explodes. I think it happens again in 1897 when he snookers Laura into a trap with the help of Angelique. Normally, Barnabas just looks deeply moved with sincere gratitude at those points when happiness might afflict others.

This is one of my all-time favorite Dark Shadows episodes because of how much progress it shows. Not only does the plot leap with true irreversibility, but the characters change irreversibly as well. Barnabas has two great moments of moral awakening on the show. One is at the beginning of the Adam storyline, while this one is at the end, in this episode. The arc begins when Barnabas is left alone with Jeff Clark, who is about to be mutilated to soften Adam's appearance. He frees him, although he knows it will probably squash his chances with Vicki. His moral compass is recognized for the first time since Angelique began her campaign. Yes, he continues to help evil enterprises, but a bit like Julia at that point, it is under duress or to serve a larger end. It is in this episode that this stops. He has already selected to choose good over evil, personally. But here, he goes beyond selecting good actions for himself to preventing evil being visited upon others. All told, this is a helluva journey to go on in what, for Barnabas, is about a year (not counting suspended animation) or less from when Angelique cursed him.

The cast is having a disciplined blast in this one, and the writers give them plenty of TNT. Humbert Allen Astredo must have been well-loved. His last episode begins with a satanic wedding ceremony and ends with him being consumed by hellfire. In between, he induces coronaries, gloats, wins, loses, and finds that his powers have been sapped. He does almost everything an actor can do in a four-hour play yet pulls it off in 23 minutes. Meanwhile, Kathryn Leigh Scott plays both an icy, occult loyalist and a spell-struck Josette as the whammy leaves her. She looks as if she's having a ball as well, and she works in two kinds of menace. Her Kool-Aid drunken loyalty to Nicholas motivates Barnabas by making him equally jealous and mortified.

The man of the hour, however, is Jonathan Frid. Barnabas has spent months in hesitant apprehension. He wrung his hands so much; I'm amazed he graduated from the show with any fingerprints left. However, here he gets to indulge in inner conflict that turns into passionate action. Months of a story finally explodes into seconds of resolution, and Frid seems more refreshed and energetic than he has in months.

The production is wrapping up sweeps and approaching final exams and Christmas break, making it a perfect time to introduce a more family-oriented story (with Amy and Chris) and lay the grounds for the next big thing Quentin Collins.

This episode was broadcast November 27, 1968.

EPISODE 660

Barnabas may be able to defy the centuries to save Victoria, but can he defy Julia? Julia: Grayson Hall. (Repeat; 30 min.)

Spurred by a photo that Quentin had David plant, Barnabas is convinced that he should go back in time and save Victoria Winters from being hanged as a witch. Stokes and Julia voice doubts, but the appearance of graves from the past convince him that he must proceed.

Finding purpose. It's an onus for everyone. For Barnabas, even more so, and the sheer amount of Dark Shadows makes it more than possible for him to explore that question, it makes it essential. At a certain point, what else are you going to do with these people for hundreds of hours? They can't drink brandy and talk about a pen forever.

For the first time, we really see Barnabas contending with living in the past and present at once. At least, for the first time since his arrival and conversion. Just because he's no longer a supernatural man doesn't mean he's immune to feeling the effects of the supernatural. The show opened the time travel can o'worms when Barnabas was first unleashed. Unusual time travel, but time travel, nonetheless. We are all time travelers in a very similar sense, just on a different scale. One of the reasons the show resonates is that the past is always living with us and living us whether we like it or not. Conventional wisdom tells us not to focus on that. It's pointless. But Barnabas has no choice, and here he's confronted with a chance to do something about it. Will it change him? No. It will change others, and changing others for the better, rather than the worse, is perhaps one small way he can make cosmic amends. With Nicholas Blair out of the way, Barnabas is on the other side of intimidation. After he smashes the equipment to revive Eve, we see a different character. While the past thirty or so episodes have been a warmup, now Barnabas at his best and fullest is striding onto the field. It's an appropriately timed emerging since it's in the service of taking the baton from the retiring protagonist. Fitting that it should happen in 1796, the year he left his home and the year she finally found hers — both in a life after death after life.

The show rarely deals in parallelism and metaphor, but it reaches for something beautifully sophisticated here. Julia takes on the role of parent, telling Barnabas again and again he can't will himself through time. Similarly, Barnabas tells the children they can't go to Boston. David becomes a strange conscience for Barnabas when he complains that adults get to do as they please, only to be told it only seems this way. But this clearly sticks with Barnabas as he realizes that he does have free will and that living a life where it is inhibited is to live the life of an intimidated child. He's not even going to be intimidated by his own past, as we see when he comes as close as possible to outing himself to Stokes, only to be stopped by Julia, coughing commensurate with a sitcom character in a ham-fisted coverup.

This begins a story that both stands independently, as a primetime episode, and connects the beginning of the series to its eventual resolution. Victoria has come looking for a purpose, and Barnabas will end by finding his. In between, they meet. 630 comes roughly halfway through the series. No episode nor arc could be more fitting.

This episode was broadcast January 3, 1969.

EPISODE 665

Everything's at stake when Barnabas ends his trip to 1795 by saying goodbye to Vicki... and hello to sending Angelique back to Hell in a fiery flambé of just desserts. Barnabas Collins: Jonathan Frid. (Repeat; 30 min.)

Angelique gloats that Vicki will be revived from torpor only to awaken in a coffin, unable to escape. Barnabas, hearing of this, wryly retorts by having a torch-wielding Ben burn her alive. Barnabas then sees Vicki off to her future with Peter Bradford, at peace and happy that she is simply alive. Unable to will himself back to 1968, Barnabas reasons that he must return to the 20th century the way he reached it the first time: in his coffin. As he starts his descent into suspended animation and ensures his coffinback and tray table are in their full, upright, and locked positions while his carrion luggage is stowed under the sepulcher in front of him, Nathan Forbes seemingly stakes him.

The challenge with Dark Shadows — on both sides of the screen — was and is monotony. Soap operas fill the most hours possible with the least amount of story that they can. People may only tune in once a week. Certainly, the key demographic, housewives, were taxed with myriad distractions throughout the day. In many ways, it is "anti-storytelling." The virtue here is not economy nor even detail, but the believability that comes with intense, regular familiarity. That's what makes them feel so strangely realistic. But sometimes even soap operas have to abandon that tidal rhythm and begrudgingly let one world end and another world begin.

Welcome to Terra Nova. Dark Shadows has six milestone moments that define its arc, and this is the third, marking the middle of the series in both its episode run and emotional journey. Of course, they return to 1795 for it. This is, figuratively, where it all began. There is more going on in these 24 minutes of television than in 24 entire episodes of the average show. And that's because, perhaps, there isn't. That's what you get when you finally enjoy the payoff for nearly 450 episodes, giving Barnabas about as much cathartic satisfaction and growth as he's going to be allowed.

It's an invitation to appreciate the five-act structure of the series. If everything before Barnabas is Act One, then this ends Act Two. 665 bookends a story that conceptually begins in 1795 for both Vicky and Barnabas. It ends there, as well. If the two characters are strange mirrors of each other, orphans out of their native eras, the most crucial parts of their lives begin and end in the overlap: 1795. Twice, at least.

The first act of Dark Shadows introduces Victoria. The second introduces Barnabas and focuses on their interaction, with 1795 as a fulcrum for both of them. For him, the arc actually begins with her first trip to 1795. It also ends in the most appropriate yet unlikely of places: in her second trip to 1795. (During his second journey there, as well.) After Vicky finally departs with Peter Bradford (to no doubt die of dysentery on the western frontier, which was probably New Hampshire), we look at the other unstuck time traveler, Barnabas, perhaps to see what kind of humanizing effect she had on him. He once again has to say goodbye to a woman he ostensibly loves, but this time, it is willingly. That is a Brobdingnagian leap for a man from his era. Few have suffered as much as he has in the pursuit of love, and his newfound sense of easy confidence evidences one of his greatest transformations.

Although fate again thrusts him to 1795, Barnabas begins the conclusion of Act Three in 1897. It's as if he keeps returning for a reset, like some sort of perverse variation on Groundhog Day. With differences. In 665, he returns to his point of origin to demonstrate emotional mastery. At the end of 1897, he returns to see that he is the master of nothing. Forces far larger than he make a mockery, and perhaps even a Macarena, of his well-earned autonomy. And why does this happen? Why is it important? Is it to ridicule what he has accomplished? Perhaps. But perhaps some of it alleviates him of responsibility. Yes, absolutely, he is captain of his own ship and master of his own maturity. Yeah, yeah we get it. And that's just ducky. However, too much reliance on that mentality can lead to total devastation if forces genuinely beyond your control have conflicting plans. That takes us into Act Four, where Barnabas becomes even more of a storm- tossed ship, first as a Lambchoptic puppet, composed of a sock seemingly worn by the robust actor William Conrad over a week in August. It concludes in Gerard's Siege of Collinwood in 1970, demonstrating to Barnabas that while he may have control of himself, he has no control beyond. So, 1840's Act Five is a chance to reconcile self-control while accepting that it has human limits. What's left? The necessity of trust. He chooses to trust Angelique as much as he trusts Julia and overcomes his most tragic flaw— a resistance to forgive. Primarily, himself. Of course, forgiveness is easy to muster when you and the other person have hundreds of years to evolve after the inciting incident. His reward? Angelique, shot and killed. And, you know, that's a thing. I think we can all admit it. And she is shot by a Trask, seeking revenge for the death of a father he didn't even know. This proves that carrying a grudge, at some point, is more of a hobby than a righteous cause. That's what it was for Barnabas. It's certainly what it had become for Angelique, and it's over the course of the 1840 storyline that we see her realize it and give it up.

And that's the story of Dark Shadows.

Episode 665 shows Angelique at the opposite end of her own forgiveness spectrum. We can buy a certain amount of infuriated jealousy. But at this point, Josette is dead. So, that's out of the way. Cross that one off the to-do list. Naomi is dead.

Nathan Forbes is finally in a dance belt. You know, everyone is pretty miserable. So, you would think that Angelique's work is done. But, like Sammy topping music with trick shooting and celebrity impressions at the Coconut Grove, she has to murder Vicki. Twice. Hanging, of course, because, you know, tradition. And then she has to plan on reviving her inside a coffin to die all over again. Why? I guess because Barnabas loves the gal or something. But the fact that Vicki's running off with Roger Davis should be punishment enough for Barnabas. It's not like he has a shot. No, here, she is drunk on evil to an extent that would have shamed Herbert Lom in a later Clouseau movie.

Perhaps Angelique has to be that evil, mechanically, because they want to reverse engineer this whole thing to justify the incredible, Fantasy Island moment when Barnabas opens the door so that Ben Stokes, who's been waiting with a torch for Christ-knows-how-long, can light her up. It's a great moment. Despite our love for Angelique, there's nevertheless something satisfying in it.

Because we know she'll be back. She's just gonna go to Hell for a little while and then show up in 1897… with a considerably improved attitude I might add. They all know this by now. I mean, I'm surprised that Barnabas didn't pack a lunch for her, like Charley's wife handing him a sandwich on her endless MTA of iniquity. It's not really an execution. It's just calling the Uber a little early.

That moment, and the sentimental moments between Barnabas and Ben later on, are necessary reminders about this hero. We met him as a lone agent out-of-time, defined by the friends who can never truly understand him. As unflagging as Julia and Willie are, they are constant reminders that he is not home. Not really. In 665, we are warmed and saddened to learn why. There is something truly grounding about this stranger, normally stranded in a strange land, in the company of his best friend. Someone that no one in the 20th century, save Vicki, knows. It puts his character into context, and it puts his heroism into context, and it puts his loneliness into context.

And maybe that's ultimately why 1795 is such a nexus. Ben Stokes. As life becomes increasingly monstrous, Ben rises to the challenge with ever-greater humanity. He's both a servant, like Vicki, and an occasionally ruthless man-of-action — with a heart the size of Canada — like Barnabas.

Maybe 1795 isn't home. Maybe Collinwood and the Old House are not home. Maybe Ben Stokes is home.

Seen like that, I understand why Barnabas feels so alone without him.

This episode was broadcast January 10, 1969.

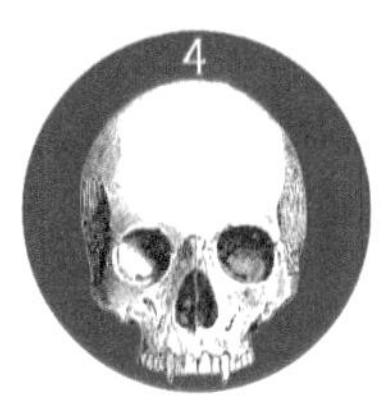

1969
ABYSS

All things bright and beautiful are in the offing.

Yes, yes, Victoria is going away. And at just about the halfway point. Dark Shadows is in constant transition, so it's very hard to plant a flag, die on a hill, and say that "this is it." Which I love to do, anyway. Like the "real life" that is a pale reflection of the truth of Dark Shadows, the only "it" is change. And yet there is such a thing as distance from the destination, and as we get closer and closer, essentials become apparent. Barnabas has been more than the leading man for some time; he's been the troubled and doubt-ridden hero. But we can ignore that uncomfortable truth as long as Vicki is around. Barnabas is the kidnapping, brainwashing, Collinsport-strangling heavy. Right? Yes. And FDR was allegedly complicit in our lack of preparation for the Pearl Harbor attack. Your point is?

He's still one of history's greatest heroes. So was Roosevelt.

Omelets and broken eggs, gentle reader. Grab a fork. Barnabas has a brother to meet and redeem in the fantastic future of 1897.

EPISODE 688

When David begins writing stories about men with strange urges and unusual hair, is he of a certain age or just possessed by the occult? Ned Stuart: Roger Davis. (Repeat; 30 min.)

Ned Stuart arrives at Collinwood seeking information on Chris Jennings, an old acquaintance of whom he is strongly antipathetic. David, manipulated by Quentin's song, writes a story of a man who becomes a wolf. He then goes to the mausoleum to open the door that protects Chris.

The real phantoms in Dark Shadows are the metaphorical phantom limbs represented by absent, missing, or neglectful family members. At times, they seem to outnumber the characters who show up, and their influence quietly resonates throughout the series. I wish I could attribute this to the revealing, emotional wounds of the author. Because it was ongoingly crafted by committee, this is a frustrating impossibility. But it may have an even greater significance considering how many people and perspectives were involved in the production. It may — may — *be something shared and important about the community behind Dark Shadows. Everything works at the home of Collinwood, except for what they claim to hold dear: family.*

Victoria is looking for parents. Carolyn is missing a father. David is missing a mother. Barnabas, a fiancé. And then there are those who try to take the place of those absent — or who find themselves cast in those parts. Julia, for instance, who is neither Josette nor Ben, is ultimately Jeremiah. Part of him, anyway, as far as Barnabas is concerned.

In 688, missing family and surrogate family permeate the action. They're present on both ends, and only at the climax do they threaten to collide. Ned is avenging his sister, a woman robbed from his life by a catatonia resulting from witnessing Chris' transformation. On his part, Chris is an acid to family wherever he goes, if inadvertently. By turns he is absent, missing, and neglectful. He shows up in Collinsport after his twin brother dies, making him a living reminder of missing family. His cousin Joe is on his way out. He's rarely in his sister's life. It may be for her own good, but she has no idea.

So, between a grieving Ned and a both grieving and grief-infecting Chris, we get David by way of Quentin. One, arguably driven by paternal neglect, one driven by a curse ultimately resulting from abandoning a pregnant wife, and by default, becoming a neglectful parent. Dark Shadows can be a harsh, Victorian noir universe. It doesn't care about what you know and didn't know. Or what you meant to do. It cares about what you did. And whatever you do, don't do it to a gypsy. This entire strain of family misery can be traced to a gypsy curse, and that was triggered by a Collins: Quentin, a man whose spirit is now becoming David's father figure. It's the ghost of a man, responsible for a son's death, becoming an almost fatherless boy's puppet master, and striving to eliminate the last descendent-recipient of the curse his actions initiated — Chris Jennings, a man with no idea he's a Collins.

The figure of the gypsy spikes briefly on Dark Shadows, but the significance is quietly seismic. Although they cause intense misery for Quentin and others, they do so in defense of family. They represent absolute familial dedication, and, between Petofi and Quentin, they do not care for bachelors. They may not have a home, but they have hearts as strong and impenetrable as iron when it comes to their relatives. Not only do they menace the Collins family, but they also shame them by implication.

Compared to the Rakosi tribe, Collinwood is like the Golden Corral of clan cannibalism. It's little but bile and betrayal, and most parents would secretly sell the kids for the right offer. It's classic WASP culture, where family often results from antiseptic obligation rather than the earthier drives of passion or good, and old-fashioned religious guilt.

If the writers and crew share anything, it's a well-represented WASP background. Dark Shadows talks about a lot of things, but the fallout from a WASP upbringing is one of them. Even with an Irish name and a paucity of a religious life, few are as WASP-y as the Collinses. It's a tart commentary on an entire swath of America that's usually taken for granted or not spoken of. Maybe because of the illusion of uniquity. Maybe because repression prevents it, and repression and codes of silence are two hallmarks of WASP behavior. The suggestion is that within the bedrock of what we think of as the American aristocracy is a fundamental untrustworthiness. What should you be able to trust? Family. What should always be there? Family. Yet, in Collinsport, your emotional wellbeing and, for some, very life expectancy can be measured in the degrees of separation between you and the founders.

Whether they knew it or not, the writers are revealing and perhaps exorcizing the demons of a culture that claims to have none. In this case, the secret that keeps getting out is symbolic of the Cosmic WASP's cultural nightmare — a werewolf. Hirsute. The ultimately familial animal, existing in packs. Lying under the skin. Literally, a dog. Driven by guttural impulses. A creature with late night stirrings that make brunch impossible. The very symbol of impurity, and you can fill in the blanks for any non-WASP group that may be sparking today's round of protestant paranoia.

No matter how long since they've moved into Collinwood, that family may never run out of things to unpack.

This episode was broadcast February 12, 1969.

EPISODE 693

When Julia recruits a seductive occultist to exorcize Collinwood, will the vengeful spirit of Quentin Collins meet his match? Timothy Stokes: Thayer David. (Repeat. 30 min.)

Chris wrestles with leaving until Julia tells him about the haunting of Collinwood and David's possession. He is further shocked to learn that he may be a person of interest to the spirit. Meanwhile, Stokes manipulates David into confirming the haunting. He conducts an exorcism of the house as David screams for him not to and must be restrained. The professor seems triumphant. However, as Stokes maintains a vigil that night, Quentin appears in the mirror and taunts him with his failure.

Even though he's not in every scene, and even though the "star" of the episode is Professor Stokes, the real lynchpin to 693 is Chris Jennings. Not so much for what he does, but for what he almost does, namely, get the hell out of Dodge. When Donald Briscoe's Jennings finds out that David is possessed, his stunned reaction is quietly authentic. In the jaded world of theatre insiders, werewolves are not known for their muted representation of dramatic truth, but Jennings is really struck by how deep this situation runs. He's been a Lycan for years. He's responsible for Sabrina's catatonia and hairstyle. Sees pentagrams on foreheads. It's not a life devoid of the fantastic. And even he is thrown by this one.

This is one of the few episodes of the horror series to contain actual horror rather than the mere symbols of horror. Chris has consigned his young sister to live in a house with a boy whose relatives believe to be possessed. Moreover, so does their — and his — doctor. And the doctor further believes that he is somehow important to the possessing entity on a level she can't pin down. Maybe it's true. Or maybe they've got a wicker man on the other side of Widow's Hill. Either way, there is no safe option among the people you once thought were the only safe option. A werewolf is a monster, and because monsters are special effects, they are rarely, legitimately scary. The horror factor in a werewolf movie has little to do with the werewolf. It's with the amnesia of the human within. As much as you fear for the safety of those around you, you're also grateful for them. They see what you can't. They can restrain or even destroy you when the time comes. They are the last line of defense when you go mad. But what if they end up being mad themselves? Worse yet, what if they don't, but just sound like it?

As abstract as Chris is, he is still us when we started watching the series. He's an outsider to Collinsport. Unlike Chris, we've gotten used to the town. We're hard to shock, as are the Collinses. It takes a real-world surrogate to make us step back and appreciate just how jarring the situation is. Outside the house, Chris, a visitor, tries to leave. Within the house, another visitor — Quentin — is such an unwanted guest that the Collinses have to call in an exterminator: Stokes.

Never again will Stokes be given such an arc, largely because the defeat he suffers is humiliating on a level tantamount to his arrogance. Because of his charm, that's an easy fact to lose in the sandpile of 1,225 episodes. Fortunately, he doesn't take his crystal ball and go home. He advises. Time travels, himself. However, compared to the build-up he's been given, Stokes never delivers like he tries to, here. Nor is he given the chance. Perhaps he doesn't even give himself the chance. Where is he at the final climax of the Leviathan arc? I don't recall. Where is he when Gerard reaches a fever pitch? Allegedly out of the country, but if I learned that he just put on a fake mustache and waited the whole thing out at the Blue Whale, I couldn't blame him. Under other circumstances, looking in the mirror and seeing David Selby staring back would be a delight, but not cackling madly.

Stokes' first and last major defeat has been coming since we met him, and Gordon Russell's dynamic and gritty script both roots and elevates the professor as both all-business and there to do nothing but take care of same. He smokes like a noir detective. He roars at David after snapping a symbolic pencil of him, making himself more viscerally threatening than Quentin has ever been. And thus, more of a match for the silent giant. Stokes lays traps but lays off the epigrams and witticisms. The bon vivant mask discarded at last, perhaps it was just a tool to bring him close enough to Collinwood to fight a danger he always knew was in residence. And then there's the exorcism, which has an immediate sense of emotional violence that defines horror. It's a perilously uncomfortable situation, and that's the kind of authentic fear I referenced.

If it were merely Stokes conducting an uncharacteristically Abrahamic ceremony with his characteristic panache, the whole thing would be just TV. And if it were David writhing and screaming, I'd write it off as Desperate Bid for Attention #538. Putting them together is a deeply unpleasant alchemy, and it makes Quentin vaguely more sympathetic. As nasty as Quentin has been, there's something unsettling-yet-necessary about seeing Stokes press David while deliberately withdrawing his warmth and sympathy to the point of humiliating him with a lie. By the time the exorcism happens, David's raving response has an immediate panic to it that seems a little too real. Is David afraid that Quentin will retaliate or afraid that Quentin will once more leave him alone and defenseless amongst these increasingly angry adults? Either way, he seems like a victim of abuse from all sides and his helpless, hapless agony during the ceremony blends with Thayer David's thunder to make this one of the show's most disturbing installments.

Quentin's returns, and by now, our responses are a carefully programmed ambiguity. I mean, of course he's going to return. He's the next threat and he has yet to say a word. And of course, it was too easy. While I, like all red-blooded Americans, would be happy to watch an extended scene of Thayer David sitting in a chair (which was Warhol title, I think), I also know that Selby is cosmically obligated to get him out of it. Stokes, nervously smoking away, has a seediness here. He's a man all too happy to terrorize a kid. Quentin? Oddly triumphant in his reassurance to Stokes that his skills are meaningless. Could this be intentional on Russell's part for the short-and-long term planning of the show? Stokes must be defeated for us to more fully understand Quentin's powers… and to catalyze Barnabas's trip into the past. But Quentin is our next hero. And by showing him taunting a character who was, at least in this episode, an occasionally self-important bully who made a child scream (if for the best reasons)? It's hard not to start liking him already.

Maybe that's the real reason behind Quentin's laughter.

Sometimes he's better than the people he haunts.

This episode was broadcast February 19, 1969.

EPISODE 696

When Quentin claims Collinwood as his posthumous digs, why does Maggie need to be mind controlled for the closing? Quentin: David Selby. (Repeat; 30 minutes.)

David has vanished from the old house, with only the phone he used to contact Quentin as the clue. Amy, at Collinwood, is again under Quentin's control, and lures Maggie there. Barnabas is fearless in pursuit where he finds Maggie again possessed by spirits from a past she never lived.

Unless you're expecting a vampire, which is a pretty logical desire, this is what you're probably looking for if you're tuning in to Dark Shadows for the first time. But you didn't get this episode. Let me guess, you wound up watching an episode about Jason McGuire, lyrically alluding with criminal intent, instead? You liked him well enough, and he made a good villain, but wasn't there supposed to be a monster or Cousin Itt in this one? Maybe a were-bat? Musical number? Can David at least get a pet snake? No? How about some dachshunds? They're kinda creepy.

Maybe it was an episode about Liz Stoddard. I bet she spent twenty minutes talking about how she was slowly going to die. And you're sitting there, thinking, "If this is what the show is like, I may beat you to the grave, even if I die of natural causes at a ripe old age." God forbid, it was a Worthington Hall episode. Is it the one where Charity is having second thoughts or the one where Tim Shaw is quietly resentful?

It pays to love such episodes. In the words of Emerson, "If a man's measure of happiness is one of the many Adam episodes, then he is likely to die a blissful man." Seriously, finding peace with filler builds patience and character. 696, on the other hand, is pure entertainment. As I'm often fond of saying around these parts, it's a great episode to begin screening the series for someone.

From the get-go it grabs your attention like few episodes, and we know by implication (and by having seen a show, any show, and thus innately understanding the rules of television fiction) who are the heroes and what the problem is. Maggie is screaming for Barnabas that David is missing. And the fact that a weird, antique phone has shown up as a curious calling card in the boy's bedroom is all of the evidence they need. Who is Barnabas? Who cares? He's the hero. Obviously. Who is Maggie? Again, who cares? She is invested in the well-being of someone else. There's only one place where the answer might reside. Collinwood. And in a bizarre inversion of the way the series begins, Collinwood is the haunted house, and The Old House is the bastion of safety.

Upon watching this, I have no doubt that Herb and Marilyn Shapiro of Tampa, FL, to whom Collinsport realtors showed the ramshackle Old House in 1965, are in a furious argument right now because dammit, Herb, if she told you once, she told you one million times, it's better to have the worst house in a good neighborhood. And you passed it up, saying "well, it's no Collinwood. Let's look into some manufactured housing ."

And then Barnabas comes along, renovates it, and doesn't even have the decency to flip it. No, he's just going to live there and hold cosplay events. And given that he's intermittently a vampire, it's probably going to be for a century or two.

Then, the rest of the episode is spent with Barnabas exploring Collinwood with Willie Loomis, and beyond being the title of his future series on the learning channel, that also gives this odd couple the chance to explore exactly what you want to see someone explore on a show called Dark Shadows: A Haunted House. When the lights don't come on, Willie has misgivings, but Barnabas further establishes that he is the protagonist by claiming that they don't need lights. At that point, he whips out a flashlight with a beam so incredibly focused that it creates that crisply defined white circle on a dark wall usually reserved for the animated opening credits of an Inspector Clouseau movie. There is a divine perfection to that moment, because it is not a response to cliché. It is the real deal from which all the later clichés will spring. Barnabas then reassures Willie that they are safe because he doesn't sense the presence of spirits.

Maybe Barnabas noticed that Roger cleaned out the bar before they evacuated because Quentin's spirit is in full control of Collinwood and his power may be spreading towards the Old House. Of course, he hasn't managed to put the cable bill into his name. That's fine, but what's with all the pay-per-view wrestling specials?

All kidding aside, this is a rare moment when we see a villain in unchallenged control rather than just stirring the cauldron and implying a whole bunch. I suppose Quentin kind of has what he wants, but no matter how many times I see this stretch of the series, his obsession with killing David because he is heartbroken over Jamison is just... weird. It's hard to remember because it may not make a lot of sense. And why does it take him so long? I suppose because he has to be released from the room first or something, but why should some wood paneling stop him when he can conjure music out of the air, appear and vanish at will, enslave another ghost, cause poison to materialize, and use the phone? No, he doesn't make an army of zombies rise as will Gerard, but then again, he doesn't have to.

I have long theorized that this is not the ghost of Quentin. That Quentin never died. Instead, it's another mask of Judah Zachary and the so-called skeleton belongs to anyone. But what if the ghost of Quentin were waiting for someone to come along? Someone with some kind of edge with time travel. Someone who could help change the timeline.

Perhaps the ghost initially tried some sort of spectral working from beyond the grave and accidentally sent Victoria Winters back to 1795. Josette and Sara may not be crazy about the past, but they are at least at some kind of peace over it. They are focused almost entirely on influencing the present. Quentin only seems to want to influence the present. Perhaps he knows that the right person can change the timeline and save him from this particular fate. Instead of giving advice and guidance to the living, he is hoping that one of the living can give advice and guidance to his 1897 self.

Heightening Quentin's power and heightening the mystery surrounding it are essential tent poles for Sam Hall to plant and raise as we are headed into the show's longest flashback. It's going to be nearly a year of wild adventure, and although nothing on the show perhaps compared to the indomitable evil and rousing adventure of the past body of episodes, nothing could prepare audiences for how he would deliver on the promise of installments like this.

This episode hit the airwaves February 24, 1969.

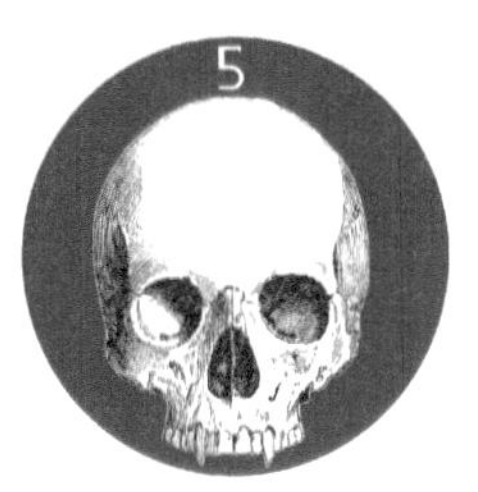

1897
REALM OF
THE WILD MAN

"Night has fallen over the Great House of Collinwood..."

This is simply the show at its finest. It is the best of the story thus far, retold with the full confidence of what they can accomplish. Barnabas Collins leaps back in time to learn the secret of a ghost who has seized Collinwood and threatens the death of its only heir. In doing so, he meets a dashing, impossibly wise scoundrel who makes Han Solo look like a Mormon. That's Quentin Collins, and his fall and rise will resemble what Barnabas has experienced, himself. Can he save this caddish mirror? Gypsies, witches, returning fire demons, hypnotized assassins, yet more ghosts, music hall strumpets, religious hypocrites, a charismatic sorcerer, and Louis Edmonds's astounding mustache all stand in his way. Now more than ever, the bat must soar to new heights.

EPISODE 717

Can Rachel Drummond recruit Barnabas to confront the danger of the tower room before it consumes her? Barnabas: Jonathan Frid. (Repeat; 30 min.)

Judith discovers that a madwoman named Jenny lives in the tower room. Rachel Drummond, sensing danger, goes to Barnabas for help. As their mutual attraction grows, he vows to investigate the strange happenings at Collinwood.

Da plane, da plane, and welcome to the briar patch.

Traditionally, this is the one where I am supposed to talk about crazy Jenny and Marie Wallace's bold, uninhibited performance because this episode really establishes the character... beautifully. Not only do we see her at her nearly-most-histrionic, but we see range in both Jenny and Wallace. Neither character nor actress is one-note, and for such an extreme character, kicking off with that means to establish the potential for suspense any time she is on screen. Indeed, Jenny is an authentic wild card, and we're never allowed to get ahead of her. Not only that, she's a poetic one. Her intelligence tells us scads about Quentin and his tastes, once we learn that she is his wife, and it makes her both a worthy opponent and a victim who's fallen from the highest of mental towers. Oh, and she has a musical number, which reveals a predictably rich voice for Wallace, a stage vet who never did featured singing in musicals. It's exactly the character debut you'd want, both quintessentially "Jenny" and teasingly unpredictable.

But I don't want to talk about that, so you'll find no mention of it here.

The secret rockstar of this episode is Barnabas and the side of him we see emerging. He even has swagger to his melancholy. For all of the high stakes and tension of Mission: 1897, he's having the time of his life. How much of this seems real to him? We are still in the pilot stages for a Dark Shadows that is essentially its own spinoff. In 1897, the show distills and refines itself, and then reinvents the recipe with that clarified formula. It's not just Dark Shadows, it's Dark Shadows that knows it's Dark Shadows… what that means, what that allows, and does so without a lazy sense of privilege. The star, Barnabas, is getting the same rebooted treatment. Barnabas is like a successful nightclub act that's finally getting two shows nightly at Caesars and isn't wasting a moment. He has almost a giddy sense of confidence that redefines the character without erasing his essence.

1897 is the perfect place to bring out his best, and he has to be wondering why the hell he had to wake up in the Day-Glo cereal box of post-Camelot 1967 instead of here. 1897… the Future! Just enough advances from his native time to crackle with new wiring, which probably shocked Dirk Wilkins across the drawing room more than once when he installed it. And just enough proximity to his own era to still know how to dress for dinner and pen a decent thank-you letter. Everyone is kind of a variation on what he already knows, but with a bit more transparency, and wait, here comes Maggie, I mean Josette, I mean Rachel, and by Rachel, I mean eventually Kitty, and by that, I mean Josette. Ah to hell with it. It's Kathryn Leigh Scott and we're darned glad to see her, too. And this character seems to be open to dating. He's got gypsies instead of Willie, and they're twice as wise and on a familiar level of untrustworthy. Plus, they're superstitious, requiring him to waste less time making threats. They know the score. I was going to say that the downside is no Julia, but after a week or so without her nagging, spying, moralizing, and guilting, I'll just say, plus, there's no Julia. She may be a friend, but, as I said, he's on vacation. And instead of pretending he's on a secret mission, he really is on a secret mission. The worst that happens is that he gets stuck there. Oh, don't throw me in the briar patch. And maybe the timeline gets changed a little bit.

So what? Big deal.

Outside of 1795, he's a time tourist. And this is the Presidential Suite, baby. e's got the Old House. He's got Maggie more than he ever had her before. He's got lackeys. And everyone enjoys a good, poetic turn of phrase rather than just staring at him like they're going to beat him up in back of the Blue Whale and take his lunch money. But on what is basically his big date with Rachel, he is smoother than caramel cognac. And the old dog knows it. It's like a Hammer production of James Bond. His scenes with Rachel have dialogue that's practically musical.

"There's nothing childish about attempted murder."

"Here at Collinwood, old hates don't die. They lie in wait for the innocent and the unsuspecting."

"I've lived through danger before."

"No one is quite what they seem, except me, of course."

"Such a lovely hand. Why would anyone want to harm you?"

Cornier than Kansas on the 4th of July. And they work. Every syllable, sincere. That's the secret. Rather than a nightmare of endless terror, it's Barnabas's ultimate dream, complete with kisses from The Josette character for his evilsmashing bravado. It's a beautiful moment, and it underlines what 1897 is, measuring his fall with the Leviathans and long struggle to rebuild. Which he does.

The only things missing are Mr. Roarke and Tattoo greeting Barnabas as he departs from a seaplane next to Scatman Crothers, Steve Lawrence, and Marion Ross, explaining for the audience the fantasy he and the island staff are about to fulfill.

Come to think of it, it may be my fantasy, too.

This episode was broadcast March 25, 1969.

EPISODE 725

A lugubrious luau breaks out at Collinwood! When Quentin's a zombie, Jamison is Quentin, and Trask is back, will Barnabas say aloha? Gregory Trask: Jerry Lacy. (Repeat; 30 min.)

As Quentin continues to both inhabit Jamison's body and writhe around in a graveyard, Gregory Trask arrives to recruit Jamison. He sets about conducting an excruciating exorcism as Barnabas looks on, helpless to stop the craven clergyman.

Enter Gregory Trask. This is where the 1897 storyline kind of runs off the rails... now and then. Like the 1795 storyline, 1897 contains more filler upon actual viewings than in memory. Yes, Trask's a great villain, and there are volumes to say about Clan Trask, but that's counterbalanced by long patches of episodes that take up so much time, it makes me wonder if the character had dirt on Dan Curtis.

But I'm obligated to like the Trasks in their steadfastness as Collins antagonists. I'm about a decade behind on my Big Finish listening, but have they done much with the Trask family per se? That's the parallel story to the Collins chronicles. It's interesting to ponder the DS story from their perspective. A Lovecraftian hotbed of aristocratic menace!

OVERHEARD....

Yeah, Greg, you gotta go see what's happening at that house they walled up your gramps in. You know, where your dad disappeared. Well, okay, the OTHER house on the estate. You know, they have a vampire up there. And a witch. That's fine, but around kids? Quentin's back. Carl's still dating showgirls. They're hiring all of your ex-employees. Oh, and Quentin's now in the kid's body. No, not like that. Well, after he had the boy almost desecrate the corpse of Gabriel's old widow, all bets were off. Where's Quentin? He's a zombie. Maybe it has to do with all the gypsies they're harboring. Yeah, it's a real normal house up there. You know, your dad built a mortuary out of nothing and did pro bono work as an attorney. Your granddad came to this godforsaken town when the Collins family was keeping occultists on the payroll. Maybe it was to help the syphilitic sailor they thought was a dandy marriage prospect. He was married, but did that matter to them? No. Hell, they were marrying off their sons to island girls that the uncle would sleep with on his own. Now Greg, you're an educator and a pastor. They have two kids up there, looked after by some trampy maid. Kids, Greg. Yeah, they're half gypsy, but let's let that go. Their mom? They locked her up in a tower because that's how they treat the sick. She's running around with a knife, and do they call the cops? Of course not. I say it's self-defense. You have to help that poor woman. Help the kids, too.

Inaccurate, but the truth usually is.

Meanwhile, back in reality, Barnabas is having a hell of a night. Judith, the voice of reason, has Jamison locked up in the drawing room and screaming. She thinks nothing odd about him being alone in the room with a grown man who keeps sticking his head out and saying, "Not yet. Give me just a few more minutes," before ducking back in for more terrified cries of fear and pain.

Fortunately, Barnabas comes from an age of advanced and sophisticated corporal child-rearing. If any character in literature is capable of dealing with the middle ground between modern common sense and old school, birch branch pedagogy, it's the man who did wonders with Willie Loomis by way of his instructive cane.

This is what makes Quentin look civilized.

It's the fourth anniversary of the Daybook, written as my third week in corona captivity begins. I got into all of this eight years ago due to nearly two months of self-imposed isolation as I watched all of Dark Shadows in just a few weeks. If anything, this all feels strangely familiar. My only advice, since you insisted, is to keep Dark Shadows on at all times. I mean it. They are the much-needed set of extra voices, rooms, and locations desperately required right now.

They are home. And their home is ours. Be well.

This episode was broadcast April 4, 1969.

EPISODE 727

When Trask takes advantage of the Collinses' generosity, will Barnabas take advantage of his Charity? Charity Trask: Nancy Barrett. (Repeat. 30 min.)

Quentin, revived, is distressed to find no one in the tower room. He and Barnabas dislike Trask, who's now staying at Collinwood, but Quentin mistrusts his cousin from England more. Later, Trask's daughter arrives and knows Rachel. The latter later reveals to Barnabas that she was once forced to work for Trask, who abused her when she was younger. Barnabas retaliates by biting the younger Trask.

There's a great moment in this episode early on. Trask is in the drawing room, praying to, literally, the high heavens, full-force, and Barnabas walks into the foyer from outside. He hears the religious ecstasy roiling within the drawing room. He knows who it is. And he knows what all of that implies. At no point has anyone in history said, "Oh, good, a Trask is here; our troubles are over."

You know, as if his mission wasn't difficult enough. It was just a year or so ago, kind of, that he was having to wall a Trask up. That should have fixed it. How could an ostensibly celibate guy have such a legacy, and seemingly do so from behind a wall of bricks? Yes, he could have had his kids beforehand, but it's not as interesting to contemplate.

I don't know what it is about a really forcefully uttered prayer by a guy in a long black coat and mutton chops, but it is a portent of doom like few others. Jonathan Frid captures the only rational response. It's not so broad as to ruin the day of theology enthusiasts, but it definitely lets us know that he's not hearing a blissfully gentle cover of "Moon River," either. And Barnabas's expression subtly conveys the rarest quintessence of an understated, "Oh, shit," that simply commands that I use the word, for none other suffices. Of course, like any irresponsible critic, I read into these things what I want to, and in this case, as he's processing bellicose and Biblical booming from beyond the door, I wonder if Barnabas is asking himself, "Should I hang up my coat, stroll in, and engage in thoughtful banter, redolent of implicated knowledge and planned counter-strikes, or should I simply hoist my cane aloft and beat the bullying bastard into 1898 before he can screw up the storyline any more?"

Banter wins.

Later, Quentin enters, strangely compliant to Trask until he's alone with Barnabas. In that scene, we see both Quentin's strength and the weakness Barnabas must overcome. For a moment, we see them collaborate against a common enemy. Quentin, however, assuming everyone is as opportunistic as he is, turns his suspicions with wearying inevitability toward Barnabas, cueing our hero to again show the patience of one of the saints embarrassed by Trask's allegiance. It's frustrating, but it illustrates the size of the challenge confronting Barnabas and again outlines the overall arc of Quentin's story, indicating that it's only the beginning. In structure and complexity, it is an arc that may very well be the show's greatest narrative triumph, necessitating nine or so months to tell.

Mechanically, Barnabas and Quentin have very different story arcs, not only in particulars, but in the gears of the storytelling, itself. Clearly, Barnabas has the longer story in a number of episodes. But he also has a longer arc in terms of sweep and span of life. Barnabas's story is not about what his origin does to transform him, it's about what it leads him to do with his life. Quentin's story is shorter, especially in that everything interesting possible is knit up in his origin and immediate aftermath. No wonder Quentin seemed wasted after 1897; what else could they do with him? His story is about going from boyhood to manhood. Barnabas's story is about going from being a man to, ironically, a god. A master of time, space, and the very plasma of life. He would sometimes reject his godhood. Sometimes embrace it. Quentin can never use his condition to any advantage. Barnabas's true curse was that he could.

Beyond that, the episode putters along perfunctorily. It's another episode in Trask recruits, this time letting us know that Rachel was his prisoner and that his daughter loves the power to say 'no,' as much as he does. Well, Barnabas has other plans.

Unable to crush him immediately, and suspended by Rachel's fright, Barnabas lets it go. Well, other eras of Barnabas would let it go. But the 1897 Barnabas is Silver Age to the point that I'm amazed Willie Loomis didn't become a talking dog sidekick. Which would have been great. Like, you know a spaniel. I digress. THIS Barnabas might not punch Trask's lights out, but he can at least bite his daughter and hold her in his sway as spy and saboteur. Besides, biting and controlling Nancy Barrett is a legitimate part of the cyclical story that the show is developing.

She's the only dependable Trask I know. Hallelujah!
This episode was broadcast April 8, 1969.

EPISODE 727 (Take 2)

When a scheming clergyman demands that Collinwood praise the Lord, will Quentin pass the ammunition? Gregory Trask: Jerry Lacy. (Repeat. 30 min.)

Barnabas and Quentin spar over the location of an escaped Jamison. Trask arrives and threatens a terrified Rachel Drummond, who liberated herself from his abusive school after being punished for a teenaged tryst. Barnabas attacks Trask's daughter at the end of the episode.

Doubles! Twins! Reflections! And a terrible school.

The story of Worthington Hall revealed in this episode is a story of stunning cruelty, and the audience experience of enduring its master, Gregory Trask, until the very end of the 1897 storyline is excruciating. But it is a pain shared by Barnabas and Quentin. By all rights, either had the moral sanction to drag him to the Old House and have Magda turn him into goulash. But they don't. Why?

Quentin is already in transformation when he returns to Collinwood for this story; he just doesn't entirely know it. The guilt of abandoning Jenny may not have him wringing his hands, but his desire to keep her isolated from his life is not the attitude of a devil-may-care cad. A true cad would disavow that there was anything to hide. Quentin at least has the conscience to want to deceive. So, regarding Trask, he's playing by more rules than he might have once disobeyed. Even if he's just trying to stay in Judith's good graces, that's at least an acknowledgement of consequences. Additionally, the man was just a zombie and spends time in this episode pondering why and how. Quentin's most monstrous moments are when he has no mind at all and must hear reports of what he did while his conscious mind was out. It will be the same thing as when he is the werewolf, and this is a foreshadowing of that. If Barnabas's secret is one of urges kept under wraps, Quentin's is deeper and more existential. When Barnabas seizes upon his capacity for evil, it's because he is choosing not to be good. Quentin, however, is slowly learning to choose goodness, but has something so "cursed" within him that a monstrousness manifests itself whether he tries to make a choice or not. The lesson of Barnabas is that some have free will that is excruciating to exercise. The message of Quentin is far more 20th century. Free will is irrelevant. We ARE the monsters. Our crimes are done unconsciously. In both cases, he's revealed as such by a curse. Because I think "revealed" is more appropriate than "transformed." Quentin, by abandoning his family, dies to them. But he comes back. His damage, however, continues, despite his rebirth. The second curse simply makes him aware of what he is... and what he does... just by being himself. It's not really a curse, then. It's a window. His struggle, after the painting is finished, resides in being an evil man who must choose not to be. The painting becomes his gift to see himself whenever he wishes. It's a constant reminder.

Barnabas is a good man finally mastering the choice to invoke evil. (And not choking Trask on the spot, here, is a tough choice for him to make.) He is Quentin's mirror in this sense, and in this episode, both men address the same mysteries with information the other lacks. Being two sides of the same metaphorical man, they naturally mistrust each other. Only through tragedy and courage will they learn to trust and confide in one another. If 1897 is about anything, it's about virtue and vice learning to acknowledge that each has an invaluable element of the other within it. Vice gets things done and can do so with a sense of judiciousness. Virtue does more when it can admit that its representatives need the liberties of vice to fight the villainous.

Trask exists as a counter to both. His grandfather had good intentions wrapped in a toxicity he couldn't see. Gregory is a toxic man who is wrapped in the cloak of good intent, knows it's only a cloak, and doesn't seem to care who else sees it. Because they're not going to take the risks associated with calling him on it. If the Emperor with the new "clothes" were an intentional exhibitionist, he'd be Gregory Trask. Both Quentin and Trask learn that they are fundamentally evil people. But Trask likes it. He's Quentin's dark future, where the Cad of Collinwood has gamed the system to a point above reproach. He even resembles a dystopic Quentin from Earth 3. Sideburns. Long coats. A charisma. And a hypnotic sense of lust. Quentin eyes the ladies, but Trask practically carries them away to a mental seraglio. As he leers at his own daughter and savors his power to punish Rachel for smooching with someone other than him, we begin to give Quentin a break. Quentin is simply a chauvinist. Trask is a misogynist. The difference is demonstrated by watching the two men in contrast.

And here's Barnabas, navigating between the two and realizing he might not be so bad, either. He's in his social milieu and has enough of the hang of the vampire thing that he doesn't have to use it. I'm sure he wanted to when Trask asked him to leave the drawing room. But that would have called attention to himself, and this is a long game. Instead, he plants a spy with Charity and gets on with the larger work. His first mission is to free himself from the irony engine that is 1897. Yes, Trask and Quentin are two ends of a perverse spectrum. Just as Barnabas and Quentin are dark reflections, Quentin — especially as a ghost — and Trask are dark siblings. Both invaded Collinwood when least expected, attracted by the promise of power, and both have designs on the estate's heirs, David and Jamison. The coincidence could not have escaped Barnabas's attention. He's been fighting to free the present from the past. Quentin and Trask plot to direct the future from the seat of the present. All Barnabas has to do is stop them.

This episode waged a one-show-war against crime in the streets on April 8, 1969.

EPISODE 730

Quentin and Jamison delve into the world of occult chicanery while Edward learns that the past can be a real mother! Laura Collins: Diana Millay. (Repeat; 30 min.)

As Quentin uses occult influence to prevent Gregory Trask from taking Jamison, Laura uses Nora to insinuate herself into the house. This disrupts plans both good and bad, and Edward is stunned and incensed at her return.

Laura arrives in a brazen move by the show, shouting back to the primary supernatural threat from the show prior to Barnabas... which means prior to most viewership. Diana Millay gives a shockingly relaxed, modern performance as the returning

Laura. She brims with confidence as a character and as an actor. Arriving at the worst and best time, Laura's proto- reemergence is classic 1897. The story arc is the show's first shot at Dickens, and nothing screams Dickens like terrible timing. (Ask any high school student with an essay due on Bleak House.) Children, about to be sent off to an unthinkably cruel boarding school, meet their long-missing mother in the nick of time. But does she offer a more diabolical form of escape?

No wonder the record and sky-high ratings were reserved for this storyline. If the 1795 storyline were written for housewives, allowing them to be Vicki (out of place and glamorously persecuted), Josette (except no one else sees it, the blind fools), and Angelique (and hear her roar), this was aimed more at the demographic running home from school. It's written for kids in front of the TV, and it's talking about weird parental dynamics openly and from their point of view. This kind of depiction of liberal parent vs. stern appeals to any child with a disciplinarian in the roost… or who wishes there were someone who cared enough to be one. It provides fantasies across that spectrum. And it really layers the truths because it's not black and white. Yes, we know that Edward is ultimately on the right end of the spectrum. He just has no idea what's really going on at Worthington Hall. Quentin is also on the right end of the spectrum. Yes, the man wants what's best for Jamison. He just can't overcome the fact that he's the uncle who educates before he schools, and while this is fun, it's not sustainable. And then there's Laura. Who's all about love and fire.

To what degree does Laura actually care for the kids (she did abandon them, after all), and to what degree is she trying to satisfy an evil fire god? Yes! I don't think they are mutually exclusive for her. And the kids (on the show and as viewers) get a little of everything. Laura is about indulgent passion for her kids. Quentin is about indulgent fun. Edward indulges with structure. He actually cares more than either of the others, because it's more than a convenience, and yet he lacks the tools to demonstrate it in any way that Jamison and Nora can appreciate.

The clever thing in the episode is how Louis Edmonds' performance shows that dichotomy. When Nora is terrified of the face in the fireplace, Edward is determined to erase that fear. He attempts it terribly, but he tries. The show then takes us to the conversations that the children don't see, yet concern them. Say what you will about Edward, but he puts his full passion into raising the children. He stayed at his post when the trainees -- Quentin and Laura -- ran (off to Alexandria). That's why Quentin only snipes at him.

With 730, Dark Shadows becomes an increasingly masculine show, and I don't mean that in some two-fisted, brutal, five o'clock shadow-sporting, Bud-swilling, Rowdy Roddy McDowell sense. Yes, men cause a lot of the problems on the show, but often as dupes and doofi and people who think with more romance than reason. But they often have soulful vulnerabilities or elements of amusing self-contradiction that add a puckish dimension to the depiction of men. Only in people like Gregory Trask and John Yaeger do we see purely lustful evil after this point.

And some of this is by contrast. A year ago, Vicki and Carolyn and Julia were all wringing their hands about the Life and Death of Peter Bradford, and, well, okay. Vicki had just returned to see a man torn apart like a dog toy in the jaws of two jealous and competing females. Our hero was powerless in Angelique's shadow. It was still Vicki's show, and we all just live in it. But with her story vaguely resolved, it belongs to Jonathan Frid. The beautiful thing about both Frid and Barnabas is that they don't seem to want it. There's no preening and scene stealing. Just as Barnabas serves the family, Frid seems to serve the show.

In the service of THIS episode, we have to recognize the entire ensemble. David Henesy is the respectable skeptic not predisposed to believe Nora's ravings about their returned mother. David Selby effortlessly sells the rapport with Jamison that demonstrates why the later haunting will be inevitable. Diana Millay is the ultimate Weekend Mom, and a believable one. And then, there's Louis Edmonds.

Good gravy, talk about service to the show. There is no such thing as a wasted Louis Edmonds scene, and that's never been truer than with Edward Collins. Roger may have the most of his episodes. Joshua has the most mythic importance. Parallel Time has those fabulous scarves. Brutus is named "Brutus" and sports a pointy beard, which is its own reward. But Edward Collins is his most prized creation as an actor. Relentlessly stiff, yet never predictable, he's the spirit of late- Victorian zest and progress. Hilariously so. In this episode, he says both "chicanery" and "humbug," so there you go. I was so excited, I contacted Wallace, who lamented that balloons didn't drop from the ceiling. Edward is the prime Victorian male archetype, which is a polite way of saying, "well-written stereotype." At the same time, he always has the capacity for surprise. When Edward reveals or discovers a new layer of himself, such as when he becomes Edward Collins: Vampire Slayer, I have no choice but to buy it because Edmonds completely justifies whatever the writers cook up.

And just wait for the transformation Count Petofi unleashes! Edward's inner life of meek subservience says everything about Edward's almost fetishistic adherence to obligation, social codes, and the safety of a rigid limit of options. The man has more structure than a Stephen Sondheim song. And he's every bit as witty and refreshing. Just watch the fun Edmonds has and you, too, will start giggling in precisely the manner that would merit a severe upbraiding from Edward. Perhaps a strong reprimand. A searing indictment is not out of the question. There's a likelihood of a thorough caning from an experienced hand. And, inevitably, a healthful diet rich in salubrious roughage.

Hail roughage! Hail Edward Collins, its high priest!

And, whatever you do, be grateful for Louis God Bless 'Em Edmonds!

This episode hit the airwaves April 11, 1969.

DIANA MILLAY — her passing has a poignance to it on many levels. For many fans, Dark Shadows was a part of their lives since its first episodes went on the air. It was a contemporary show rather than a piece of another generation's nostalgia. As one of the first cast members, only thirty-one when she took the part, it is a wistful reminder that the show is on a steady course to becoming an animal that lives completely in memory.

As Laura Collins, she followed Burke Devlin as a feared and much-talked-about piece of the recent past that refuses to be done with the Collins family. Is she a reminder of past sins? Given Roger's cold and distant nature, it's easy to assume that she is the victim of some sort, there to rescue David from a parental love so vacant that Liz is compelled to order carry-out in the form of Victoria Winters. Instead, she adds to Roger's complexity when we find that she is the show's first real female villain, causing us to think twice about who he was. Not only that, but she sets the stage as the first, real "outsider" female, creating a motif that balances Vicki. Vicki is also an outsider, but one who seeks only meaning and identity. Like Angelique after her, she represents the danger of women from the larger world. Laura allows us to appreciate the positive nature of the women on the show we've so far met. A primarily female audience was given a band of surrogate sisters, and now they and we have to close ranks against the interloper.

As that, her greatest legacy was as the first supernatural villain on the show. Ghosts are fine, but can they truly stack up against a living creature with an agenda? Not in the drama department. The introduction of Laura is the program's first, long-running risk into the personified paranormal. Yes, there was the ghost of Josette, but she's expected in a spooky house and exists at this point as a special effect more than a truly interactive character. For all of the credit given to Jonathan Frid as the show's first great supernatural foe, Laura has him beat. Not only that but as a type of monster with no heritage nor blueprint. I'm still not sure what a Phoenix is, but Millay certainly was. The cool confidence of her performance successfully charted that new frontier for the show and made safe every choice they tried afterward.

Interview after interview gave Millay the platform to describe the joy of helping to create that character. She identified strongly with the mystical, alluring creature, both lustfully of this earth and empowered by primal forces beyond time. In her hands, the novel nature of the threat was an invitation for ownership and creativity. That self-assuredness cemented a character that is as credible as it as fantastic, and Millay gives Laura a set of missions that should contradict each other, but don't. She is ancient but contemporary, tied to the past of Roger, his ancestors, and countless fathers before. But she is decidedly contemporary, also, existing on her own with no need for the Collins material resources or status. Yes, she needs something, but it's the most unjustly ignored element of the Collins wealth: David.

Millay relishes her performance like few on the show, and like the concept of the Phoenix itself, is a study in contradiction and balance. She convinces us that she is a loving mother and a ruthless force of hellish consumption. Few performers can maintain both of those impressions, but Millay had to and did. She was impossible to pigeonhole as someone with only one dimension. Thanks to the delicate nature of her acting, we experienced David's twin senses of total fear and total need. She had to bring both of those elements out in David Henesy so that we could experience genuine sympathy toward his plight from her first moments until the end. I'm still undecided about the fate he faced beyond the flame. It's a totally irrational curiosity, but Millay's dedicated sincerity is impossible to ignore.

The adage in performance is that every character is the hero in their own eyes. With Diana Millay, we never doubt it. When she returns as the character, it's a harder sale to pitch, but she manages to do so again... with a twist. Now, undeniably a villain, Millay repeats her mission with a more colorful bent for unapologetic evil. She's no longer an unopposed god among mortals. The presence of Angelique, Barnabas, and even seasoned occultist Quentin gives her a reason to revel in her plans rather than coyly allude to them. It's yet another dimension to a character of teasingly allusive possibilities.

Millay delighted in her identification with the role, often insisting that she had worlds in common with her. As a cast member dedicated to mysticism, going so far as to write several books on the subject, she was both an ensemble member and a committed fan of the show's subject matter. She was an actor, reveler, and even thematic ambassador. Of course, she wrote about the supernatural. Of course, she wrote and performed motivational lectures. Put the two together and you have Laura, and the Phoenix, and Millay and the ebullient sense of mischief that made us believe that Collinsport was a world of possibility for everything that followed.

EPISODE 732

When Laura uses the power of the Phoenix to torture Quentin, will Barnabas's new bride-to-be throw a wet blanket on her plans? Angelique: Lara Parker. (Repeat; 30 min.)

Laura reveals that she has returned from her death in Alexandria, and she seeks revenge on Quentin, who abandoned her to pagan priests and their altar. Angelique agrees to help Quentin if Barnabas will introduce her to his family as his fiancée. This thrills Rachel Drummond, as you can imagine. Meanwhile, Quentin learns that Laura's survival is contingent on a flame in a small pot remaining lit. He's determined to snuff it.

Quentin dies a lot. Given what he deals with in the average week, I don't blame him. But it's not by (his) design. No, on top of everything else, crazy spouses and fire goddesses top off the day by killing him. Fate made the wrong guy into the family vampire, although he fits a little better into the coffin than Quentin. Not that he's having a good week either, and of course, Angelique is at the heart of it. Only she could combine gifting Quentin with the spark of divine life and ruining date night for Barnabas. The moment when she reveals herself to Rachel as the next Mrs. Barnabas Collins is as deliciously sadistic as the series at its cattiest. The execution hovers right — *right* — on the edge of farce, and were the genre any closer to real life, it would be. The horror expressed by Jonathan Frid (mixed with all-around mortification at the whole thing) is perhaps the most honest moment of acting in the series. I say, "perhaps the most," because the most goes to Kathryn Leigh Scott in the same scene as she gets the news.

Most Kathryn Leigh Scott characters live to suffer. Somehow, she can pull it all off with a strange strength and integrity. I never get the idea that she's a victim because, as an actress, she thrives on the promise of action. In her reaction, there is confusion, pain, and then, just as the camera fades out, a hint of knowing umbrage blended with a tad of revenge. For most actors, it would be the first choice, and once you go there, what else is left? By reserving it for just a vanishing quantum of frames, Scott maintains the potential for the character to go anywhere. Lara Parker's decadent cruelty, Jonathan Frid's tightly disciplined displays of controlled humiliation, and Kathryn Leigh Scott's subtly and deliberately controlled emotional gamut make for a master class, and it all takes place between that scene's last line and the following fadeout.

And that's why we watch Dark Shadows. One of the reasons, anyway.

Knowing Angelique's purpose here, which is only understood after 1897 ends, her actions at the beginning are all the more intriguing. And it's a long, long game. Potentially decades-long and layers deep. As the storyline wraps up, we learn that Angelique is there On His Majesty's Satanic Service under a special agreement that she land a man without her powers. Instead, she must rely on good, old-fashioned guilt and blackmail. At this point, her plot may or may not be many men deep, and perhaps repeated. It's Barnabas, first, just to get rid of Rachel. Then, it's Quentin, but just to remind Barnabas that Q's face is on the record album cover, too. Then, she looks all the more selfless when she "works hard" to cure Barnabas of her curse, which, if you've seen the entire series, you know that she can do with nary a nose twitch. But she gets to be the martyr here by stretching it out. So, how long does Angelique's plan go? At least the next seventy years, and then back another 130 or so. If we ignore the hints that 1840 Angelique is in direct continuity following 1795 Angelique. But just ignore that. Imagine.

Very occasionally, Dark Shadows boils itself down to something very simple. And if a Major Plot Event gets in the way of a convenient interpretation, fall back on the defense of "poetic truth." This isn't history and it's not science and sometimes even the writers got confused. But there was a consistency of intent. That's what shines through and matters as much as anything. The idea of Angelique's Long Game of Redemption (and staying on Earth, where the hours are better than in Hell, and the English chefs stay in England) ties parts of the room together. And if we imagine that she's only feigning unfamiliarity with the timeline in 1840, it explains the character and her evolving choices with an eerie sense of strategy. Now that we have the advantage of seeing the entire series before us at once in streaming and on dvd, we can look down on it as would a satellite. Small plot events and occasionally contradictory lines become the tiniest pieces of geography. They become invisible when seen beside sprawling continents and mighty oceans. It's a stunning view, and Angelique's machinations in this episode hint at that.

This episode hit the airwaves April 15, 1969.

EPISODE 738

When Dirk Wilkins works in the Ra, Laura comes back for more. But Quentin is Set to douse her flame for good. Dirk: Roger Davis. (Repeat; 30 min.)

Dirk instinctively recites a magical incantation that brings Laura back from the brink of death. She confronts Quentin, who has to deal with the strong emotions of Jamison, who has become very dedicated to his mother. Barnabas does a hilarious double-take upon entering Collinwood and seeing his former aunt alive and well.

Technically, this is about Laura demonstrating her powers by returning from the brink of death — thanks to Roger Davis and his mustache, the eternal reasons for the season. But that's not what leaped out to me. Yes, it's a fun episode, full of the arch moments, preening, and catty revelations that make 1897 great again. That's why I chose it. That's the experience I thought I would have, and it didn't disappoint in those regards. But I didn't realize I would tear up. 1795 is the story of how a boring man became an interesting one... but in an often-boring way. 1897 is about how an interesting man became a boring one, but in an always interesting way. When does Quentin's transformation, his REAL transformation, start? As well it should, it starts with Jamison. He's the end of the journey, with a resonance that rings in Quentin's ears long after death. He's also a completely modern man-in-the-making. He's the bridge between the world of gas lamps and gas guzzlers. The works of Lara Parker, author, notwithstanding, we know dashedly little about Jamison. But we can tell a lot about him by who loves him, teaches him, and sticks up for him.

Of course, it's Quentin. And if Jamison is the Victorian era's ambassador to the age of modernism, then Quentin is the ambassador to Jamison. You can see the culture buckling through the eyes of Quentin. In a world of rules and strictures, Quentin's every breath is an act of defiance. It's a shame that, when he arrives in the modern world, the man is too scared to enjoy it. He was, perhaps, too much of the antithesis to Edward. But Jamison can be something more than either of the men alone, and I think Quentin knows that. Edward's too far gone, and so is Quentin. Carl doesn't count, and Judith, literally, doesn't have a vote in the matter.

This comes into focus with the twinkle-eyed sincerity of his shameless manipulation of the boy. If Jamison came in from school, terrified over dreams, Edward would have sent him straight back with no sympathy. Quentin understands. And when Jamison has qualms over waking a servant to make him tea, Quentin has no stake in the hierarchy (except, perhaps, being in good with the boss when he finds himself in old age). He explains to Jamison that he'll be at the top and needs to get used to the idea. Edward might have shamed him with the lesson; Quentin inspires. He does that out of expediency and love. David Selby's miraculous range comes through once more, suggesting that Dark Shadows was a vehicle built for over two years just to accommodate his talent. Because he's both totally serious and completely opportunistic. Maybe it's one and the same for Quentin.

Maybe he doesn't need to lie to get what he wants. He just wants things he rarely has to lie about, because everyone knows he's a bottom-feeding scoundrel with the tastes of a hedonist. It's when Quentin wants something loftier that we have to wonder. In 738, there is a benevolent purity to the con. Like so many before and after him, Quentin knows he's doomed, himself, and fights for a better Collins. That's the transformation that's been building in the show since the 1795 storyline. Barnabas is infected by the outside influence of foreign magic and rejects it. Quentin is saturated with it so far, he's forgotten who he was prior. It's the threat of Laura that initiates his thoughts of the man he can be with it, however.

Appropriate that Barnabas enters to see her just as she's really spreading her plume. If Quentin becomes his second brother-not-brother, it fits that the same catalyst for the alien and occult also infected his first brother-not- brother, Jeremiah. He escaped Laura twice. There is something patterned about dark haired, baritone, Collins men (and Roger) finding their downfall in blonde women (sometimes wearing wigs) with penchants for magic. Somebody write a dissertation already, I'd do it here, but I got two shows in Vegas tonight.

Laura has encountered the Barnabas bullet twice. She and he are almost as linked as he and Angelique, except here, he's simply an adversary, and it's a way for him to get a perspective on an "Angelique-type" from the outside. Ironic that they should miss each other in the 1960s by only a few weeks. It's the great issue of the Marvel Comics/Dark Shadows What If? that never happened.

This episode hit the airwaves April 23, 1969.

EPISODE 743

When Laura programs Jenny to become the ultimate assassin, will Barnabas and Quentin put their differences aside to combine forces? Barnabas: Jonathan Frid. (Repeat; 30 minutes.)

Barnabas tricks his way into obtaining Quentin's Book of the Dead. It's a successful gambit, perfectly timed to reveal that Laura Collins is actually Laura Stockbridge Collins, a returning fire demon from his youth. Quentin must trust Barnabas when considering his mysterious cousin against the obviously more destructive forces around him.

It should have been a matter of one world ending and another world beginning. Simple, right? There was a point when it happened before. The show shifted focus, officially. A story about Victoria changed to one where Barnabas was no longer this really interesting side character. He was the character. Where? Perhaps right before 1795 or during. During is a good choice because it starts out as Vicki's story, but she has to be forced into a witch trial just to give her something to do. No, it's officially Barnabas's story. It introduces Angelique as the catalyst for his change. If she got the story moving, it's no wonder that the show should finally resolve itself when she resolves herself.

Batons pass hands in marathons, and sometimes they come back. Dark Shadows specializes in cycles that vary based on what's happened in between. Even the structure of the show is a cyclical ritual. Recap. Title and theme. Narration. Resolve the recap. Add less information than it feels at the time. Unresolved crisis. Credits.

In between all of that is where lives change, and 743 is what could and should have been the fulcrum from Barnabas to Quentin because it contains the moment any self-respecting fan is waiting for from the moment they hear the heroes on Dark Shadows didn't stop with Barnabas. There was this other guy,

Quentin. And for a time, they are both the heroes of the show and yet are constantly pitted against each other. Terrified mistrust is the one beloved and shared virtue tying all Collinses together across the centuries. It's no wonder that Barnabas doesn't save time by simply being honest with Quentin. Honesty bruises the gin, and the writers are going to need it if they have to unite these guys.

Seeing them unite to deal with Laura is uniquely satisfying, and Jonathan Frid and David Selby maintain the tension with admirable gamesmanship. Bringing back Laura Collins was one of the show's truest masterstrokes. She becomes a thread taking us from long before the appearance of Barnabas to a point even more distant in the past than his origin, and then into the fantastic future of 1897. I'm not sure what this does to critics of the program... prove its delightfully substantive complexity or give them ammo to cry, "Codswallop!" (By the way, that's not asking for opinions. It's a test with a right answer and a wrong one.)

Laura is kind of the linchpin of this. The thing that stops Quentin's story from becoming the dominant one for the rest of the series is that it pretty much resolves itself in 1897. It's extremely satisfying, but it's brief. The story of Barnabas runs through the entire series. However, it's fun to look at how the cycle changes itself, however briefly, and if only to comment on the Barnabas story. Both stories involve men who cheat. Both stories involve women who are cheated on, Josette and Jenny, respectively. Both stories involve a magic user who inspires the cheating. But Quentin's story is far more cynical. Even though the man in it is more of a cad at the beginning, he also has much more destructive women surrounding him. Chicken or ovum? Angelique legitimately loves Barnabas. I think it's pretty clear that Laura has very little interest in Quentin except as an excuse to get her to Alexandria. Josette is a victim in all of this, but she is only used against Barnabas to induce guilt, anxiety, and two, at first, drive him to choosing Angelique. Laura, however, is an engine of pure destruction, which is, of course, the job of fire. Angelique is more of an elemental figure of nature, and thus, is more driven by natural urges in and around procreation and the emotional attachments associated with it. She uses Josette, with a lot of cruelty, but it is to either get Barnabas or punish him for not attending that particular Sadie Hawkins dance. On the other hand, Laura positively weaponizes Jenny as an assassin, pure and simple.

I'm sure the program examines Laura's motives, but I'm not sure they really matter. Just as Quentin is a passion driven mirror for Barnabas, allowing us to appreciate the latter's contemplative nuance, Laura's destructive nature is the perfect foil for Angelique. Angelique's evolving heroism is perhaps the most truly interesting part of the 1897 storyline, and by seeing her in relief to Laura, it's easy to begin viewing her as the more sympathetic figure.

Quentin's storyline is ultimately less tragic in the Greek sense, but it somehow feels sadder. He is surrounded by no one who seems to really love him. Jenny is crazy, so whatever she feels is going to change in about five seconds, disqualifying it from serious consideration. And Laura is a nightmare who never really loved him. However, both Josette and Angelique genuinely love Barnabas, and this makes us continue to care about him as a vulnerable figure, because he is presented as intrinsically lovable. Why? He is ultimately a good man, and his seeming flaws, which are his conscience-based indecision and the rash action he takes to compensate, finally show themselves as virtues. No, they are not necessarily part of the masculine archetype, but that's the point. Barnabas is an extremely feminine thinker in a world surrounded by women. Quentin shows what you get with an excess of masculine thinking. He is lust and he is action. You know, everything that a man is supposed to be. So unlike Barnabas. But it only makes Quentin a magnet for women to exercise their wrath for wrath's sake. And it also manifested itself in the nature of his curse: he is revealed as the savage, lone wolf who never finds a pack.

If the largely feminine audience always liked Barnabas, but could never quite identify why, the presence of Quentin defines it by implication. It's the show saying, "OK, now here is a traditional man with the traditional psychological traits of a man. Yeah, he's a lot of fun, but he also winds up sad and alone. look at Barnabas. Not really the traditional masculine figure at all. And he ends up being all the better for it."

Television at this time was beginning to explore these redefined models of manhood in characters like Spock. but Spock's decisions seem to originate somewhere between the cultural requirements of being a Vulcan and actual biological predeterminism, also associated with being a Vulcan. Barnabas comes about it simply by thinking a little differently. In many ways, he exhibits the sort of masculine representation that we would see in someone like Hawkeye Pierce, so someone get him a martini.

Seeing Barnabas and Quentin working together on magical workings in this episode, we begin to enjoy the synergy possible when the two men combine to take power back from a strictly vengeful figure like Laura. Audiences, desiring both men, briefly had their beefcake and got it to bite their necks, too. This was on the mind of the zeitgeist, echoing the most psychologically insightful episode of Star Trek, "The Enemy Within." With that, author Richard Matheson concluded that the balanced masculine psyche required both the Barnabas side and the Quentin side. Dark Shadows has a slower burn, and eventually, and subtly, champions the feminine thinker over the masculine one. I would imagine that this is certainly a more appealing conclusion for a largely feminine audience, many of whom were dreading the daily return of their mid-century modern nightmares of husbands who would be coming home every day shortly after the show's closing credits would roll. But it's also excellent modeling for boys watching the show, and somewhere, deep in the minds of mothers, there had to be more than one who quietly valued that positive modeling.

You know, sort of. If you ignore countless moral failings and the potential for supernatural violence. But those are aspects of Barnabas's personality that he doesn't want. It's telling that he should return to women again and again to eliminate those abilities.

Because they probably aren't worth it. Not really.
This episode hit the airwaves on April 30, 1969.

EPISODE 755

For once, Beth has to explain to Quentin why his clothes are shredded; will Dirk's surveillance mission on Barnabas be as revealing? Laura: Diana Millay. (Repeat; 30 min.)

In and around Quentin staggering in from the lycanthropic night before and learning that he transformed, Laura confirms her suspicions about Barnabas... by burning his home and having Dirk watch him phase out of the room.

"Gee, Lois, I never see Barnabas and Clark around at the same time."

Which is pretty much the long and the long of it, since it takes Laura most of the episode to ask. The very brief money shot of the installment is when Beth tells Quentin what he'd been up to the night before, the night of his first transformation. It goes about as you would expect, he's horrified beyond belief, but he must believe it anyway, because how else will David Selby explain the condition of his clothes to Ohrbach's loss prevention department? Had Quentin been a scientist, like his avuncular namesake, he might have looked upon the situation somewhat differently, but Quentin is good at being a scoundrel, not scholar. It could be for the best. He prides himself on projecting very specific appearances at all times, not just for social propriety, but to escape the strictures of social propriety without anyone noticing. The real horror of a werewolf story lives with the man who can't control what he becomes. For anyone who says the wrong thing without thinking, no matter the given circumstances, this is an understandable nightmare. For Quentin, that nightmare is just beginning. At one point in the episode, Laura cracks wise to Beth about being familiar with Quentin staggering in from a night on the town as the cock crows. In some ways, Magda's curse will be even more enduring because the image of Quentin vaguely passed out in the drawing room, clothes in shredded disarray, is probably more familiar to early risers than Quentin pressed and dressed. Barnabas has a constant secret to hide. Quentin has a brief transformation. Thus, less to see, less to explain, less to elicit the concerns of others, and ultimately, a longer lifespan.

Laura might care to differ, and her campaign to out Barnabas makes her the Irwin Allen of such matters. Telling Dirk to casually reveal a mirror or crucifix is way too subtle. Why do that when you can magically set his house on fire, forcing him to dematerialize in front of a window? It's too bad she's not in love with him, because it's precisely the kind of scheme into which Lois would drag Jimmy. And I'm thankful. The show has evolved into the Silver Age comic it was meant to be. If the expected dematerialization and secret wall panel don't seal it, what will? And it's clear why they must introduce Petofi. Barnabas is a superhero on a mission, but he's still squaring off against (enhanced) soap opera villainesses.

Laura qualifies, and as those go, Diana Millay remains great fun. She has the uniquely brittle approach of a self-conscious social climber afraid someone will find out she's not up to snuff. Angelique simply doesn't care what others think — in quite the same way. Perhaps that's a function of Lara Parker actually coming from blue blood stock, but it's an approach to a somewhat similar role that still differentiates them. On Millay's part, that bleeds into Laura's character. Angelique might one-up someone on the way to a more crucial goal, but for Laura, especially in an episode like this, the one-upmanship is the goal. She observes that her performance as a concerned mother is just that, a performance. It's clear that she's perhaps the most ruthless villain on the show, there to burn children alive, sustain her existence, and move on. Mother of the year, folks!

Come to think of it, maybe we don't need Petofi so soon, after all.

What, what am I saying?

This episode hit the airwaves May 16, 1969.

EPISODE 759

With Angelique destroyed, Barnabas stands alone in the last stand against a pagan fire god...or does he? Barnabas: Jonathan Frid. (Repeat; 30 min.)

After Angelique vanishes from Laura's attack, Barnabas awakens to learn that she knows his secret. He attacks Dirk, placing him under vampiric control, taking him from Laura. She learns this after gloating over her knowledge of Barnabas and the recollection of her relationship with him when she tortured his uncle in the 1700s. Going upstairs to gather Jamison, she finds that he is a decoy of stuffed pillows and that Angelique is alive and ready for action. Barnabas smiles broadly as Laura's world crumbles.

Robert Cobert? You have the day off. Sometimes, like weddings and coronations, there is only one man to compose the proper music. In the case of 759, that one man is Mike Post and Pete Carpenter. This episode lunges from the coffin, grabs art by the collar, and demands it. The only things missing are a jerry-rigged cabbage cannon, Sandor being drugged to the point where he's not afraid to fly, and Barnabas lighting a cigar while loving it when a plan comes together. I suspect he even had Magda paint a red, diagonal stripe up the side of his coffin while he worked as a soldier of fortune in the LA underground. Make no mistake; this great episode of Dark Shadows does not look like an installment of The A-Team. It makes a great episode of The

A-Team look like an installment of Dark Shadows. Get it straight.

With Jonathan Frid and Lara Parker, this much fun just can't be legal. And what a way to kick off summer vacation for the kids. If I had been a ten-year-old fan of the original run when this episode hit, you'd have needed a diamond- edged spatula to pry me off the ceiling. You may need one now. Outside of the sentimental moments of the bonding and friendship and alienation and loneliness that defined the series, storytelling like this defines why Dark Shadows is so watchable.

Like that time when he reveals the fate of Dirk Wilkins. And just stares at Laura as she finally realizes that she has no monopoly on mind control. Nor on a cruel disregard for the "sanctity" of human life.

To me, these moments — are the absolute apex of Barnabas before his second fall and subsequent rise as the battle-scarred, weary hero of 1840. He is so accustomed to being one step behind. Reacting only. Making decisions based on desperation and panic. 1897 — specifically, this part of 1897 — is his most heartening and endearing phase. Not only does he outwit Laura, but he does so while acknowledging their long, mutual history. She savors the fact that she has him in her power and has done so since he was a child. A little boy in love. Powerless to save his uncle from a doomed relationship. Creating the pattern that would make Jeremiah's union with Josette just… plausible… enough. Barnabas always had to suspect that Angelique's spell wasn't the only thing driving his uncle.

The pleasure of his revenge is the pleasure of playing a game better than its ostensible master. Laura's talents are for misdirection, a cultivated knack for being underestimated, and zero care for the lives of humans as she pursues her goals. Burn a kid. Release the worst in Dirk. She is the occult equivalent of Trask. There is no line between malicious madness and religious faith. Angelique may be a creature of the occult, but Barnabas is her higher power. Satan is just how she gets there. With Laura and Ra, it's impossible to determine if she harms in service of Ra or if service to Ra excuses her bloodlust. Either way, Barnabas has seen too many people get the Ra deal, including Roger, Victoria, and David if he asked around upon his release.

Although they don't celebrate victory with fist bumping and curling up in front of the latest episode of

Fireplace we still get a true sense of how Barnabas and Angelique are an inevitable couple. This is a multi-phasic collaboration of totally unnecessary set-ups and knockdowns designed not only to defeat Laura, but to humiliate her in a final blow for humanity. To send her back to the Egyptian underworld with no uncertainty that she is a ham-fisted amateur in the occult cruelty department and will never be better than second-rate. Laura's an immortal. Maybe a demigod. So, there's no true getting rid of her, and corporeal dissolution isn't going to teach the lesson she needs. Laura needs the closest they can get to a prom night-sized bucket of pig's blood, and that's what she gets. It's the kind of vengeful pedagogy that Barnabas can't teach alone. He needs Angelique's reassuring edge to overcome both his self-doubt and the distracting need to jump to Magda and Sandor as the next thing on his to-do list. Fortunately, he has Angelique in his corner at last, which is right where she wants him. Perhaps his eventual show of confidence in her in 1840 is his way of saying thanks. There are more ways to answer, "I love you" than saying, "I know."

How much does an imperfect man need to pay just to squeeze his way into purgatory? For Barnabas Collins, is it ever quite enough? Roger will get away with it. Whatever "it" is. Saint Joe Haskell, certainly. Poor guy. But no matter what Barnabas does, it may never be enough. There will always be new clauses to curses and further Trasks awaiting him in any decade.

It's a troubling story if that's the point. And it may be. But the point is not for Barnabas. It's for us. Like everything on this show of outsiders, it's to remind us, fellow outsiders, that we're not alone. To reassure us of this when life throws us a

Trask, life will also throw us a Roger Davis as our new familiar. Neither state is permanent. And that's the good news. The only thing permanent is our potential for greatness. When he is later knocked down by the Leviathans, Parallel Time, and Gerard, it has increased resonance because we remember, even when he may not, what he has within him.

But for now? All of that matters for the series and none of that matters for the present. The only thing that counts in this moment is that Barnabas really, authentically smiles for the second of two times in the series. It's a great smile.

The plan has come together. And that is just as much fun as it sounds.

This episode hit the airwaves May 22, 1969.

One of the great gifts of Dark Shadows is its ability to secret its most endearing elements amidst the flashier ones. I tune in for Barnabas and Quentin, but who delights me (and moves me) as much, if not more? Louis Edmonds.

EPISODE 761

When Edward gains proof of the evil of the supernatural, will he become Collinsport's last, best hope for victory? Edward Collins: Louis Edmonds. (Repeat; 30 min.)

Barnabas rescues the children by teleporting in, which causes the flames to die out. Edward, now having realized that Laura was a creature of the supernatural, vows to protect

Collinwood from the occult. He'd better hurry, because Quentin and Evan have a Satan to summon!

With Laura dead, and that part of the series' auto- remake out of the way, Mission: 1897 really flies off into new territory. Quentin's transformation has begun. (So has Magda's.) It's a sobering transformation, so at least they keep him good and sauced, which is always entertaining. But equally entertaining and surprisingly mature is the evolution that goes largely unnoticed: Edward, played with comic exaggeration and human texture by the reliably underestimated Louis Edmonds. And he evolves in more ways than one. He's one of my favorite characters in the series, the very picture of a Victorian straight man. But let's not limit him to that. In just this episode alone, he heals and matures in surprising ways and galvanizes into something beautifully ludicrous and completely understandable...

Edward Collins — Monster Hunter.

It's the evolution of Joshua, who lived for denial, and a rebuke toward Roger, who lived for willful ignorance. In between, with all of the insanity endured for a hundred years, you'd think that one Collins would grow a little backbone, believe what's clearly going on, and grab the stake & hammer. In Edward, they do. And for a post-Dickensian cartoon, Edward is a surprisingly modern man. He's a single father, now for reals, and his warmth toward his children is wholly authentic and heartwarming. Quentin, it seems, never robbed him of a wife because he never really had one. With that new perspective, of course, he must mend the family. Now that Judith has the wealth and Trask is amassing the power, all of the external sources of Edward's anticipated identity vanished in months. What's left but to be a genuine mensh? His relationships are all he has, and he's no longer the forbidding iceberg. He's Roger and Liz's grandpa-in-waiting.

More than that, all of the forces he once saw as corrupting to that sense of John Harvey Kellogg propriety are, well, not that important. He's now the Lovecraft hero who decides to strike back. That journey will take him to Barnabas. I think he has it in for Barnabas because Barnabas shames him by implication. He's the guy who didn't settle down. But he's disciplined, unlike Quentin, concerned for others, unlike Carl, and warm, unlike Edward. He even macks on the KLS character with appropriately hygienic restraint. Barnabas is living the Edwardian bachelor dream, then proceeds to go full- on superhero. Did Edward save his kids? No, Barnabas did. Edward will have to kill Barnabas to become him. The fact that he's a vampire is the berries in the sloe gin. This is secretly the story of Edward Collins becoming the best of the twentieth century as Quentin retreats from being the worst of it.

And there's the mustache, too.

This episode hit the airwaves May 26, 1969.

It's always time for a Harry Johnson joke. If I've said it before, I will repeat it until the entire class can recite it by rote. In the words of St. Mel of Brooks, the point of it all is to "rise beneath vulgarity."

EPISODE 764

What's in the cards? Can Barnabas stop Quentin, or will an ultimate assassin bring a new shadow of death to Collinsport? Tim: Don Briscoe. (Repeat; 30 min.)

Barnabas attempts to learn the identity of the werewolf as he tracks down the silversmith who made the amulet of protection that will one day be found in the 1960s. Evan tests

Tim's programming as an assassin and Beth, reluctant to out Quentin to Barnabas, has the choice removed when he bites her.

As the episode ends, Barnabas again bites someone to place them under his control, reminding viewers that he uses his abilities to strategic ends as much as to feed. Would he have been this cavalier in the 1960s? He's used this advantage twice in the space of a week or so. As much as I feel sorry for Beth, who ends up being a pawn of Quentin, Barnabas, AND Petofi, it's nice to see her current, new master so confidently on a mission. It's an increasing level of chutzpah. Would he have had it a year before, meaning seventy-one years ahead? Perhaps. Back then in the future, he recalls how he will be chasing Adam around with a gun. But certainly not in 1967, as he slyly swaps blood slides and works to revive the mind of Josette. Prior still? In 1795, his reactions are almost entirely reactive and based on following or defiling the codes of the day. Like the two-blooded, red-fisted heroes before and after him, this time, Barnabas Collins makes his own rules. This time, it's personal. This time, he's bringing his Vigoda.

He also tells a young Abe Vigoda that he'll have a bright future. Kind of. I mean, I wish. In a beautiful nod to continuity, young Ezra Braithwaite (played by Edward Marshall, whose Harry Johnson popped up in episode 669) reappears for the very first time to make the pentagram that he'll die for in episode 685. If that makes sense. By the late 1960s, the fully developed Ezra was played by future nighttime TV hunk Abe Vigoda. Even though Vigoda is not in this episode, he's a well-crafted minor character in the DSU and Vigoda gives a touching performance. But he's not in this one. (So, sue me.) However, Edward Marshall is, and he's good, too.

The rest of the episode (that's not about Barnabas trying to beat the fleas off of Quentin) is devoted to Humbert Allen Astredo and Don Briscoe starring in the first remake of The Manchurian Candidate. This is where 1897's hellzapoppin approach to storytelling starts to consume itself with too many ideas thrown around too frenetically. You can feel the generous creativity oozing from every corner of the show, but perhaps there is so much going on that you increase the opportunity for a bad idea to slip through. Dark Shadows is known for, um, borrowing? Is that the right word? It seeks inspiration from many sources, reprocessing them for a different era and audience, and with the depth and dynamism of a soap, it arguably does some of them a service. But most of these are pretty old, or, in the Case of the Leviathanly Lifted Lovecraft, at least FELT pretty old. But the very liberal borrowing from the recent film and novel of The Manchurian Candidate is the strangest "quoting" ever executed by the writing staff. A guy gets a whammy to play cards until a specific card triggers the urge to kill. Same thing. It even feels stranger because it's that rare case of the show taking a modern story that verges on science fiction and plunging it into the past. Dark Shadows defined itself by going in the opposite direction and confronting contemporary characters with the dangers of costume dramas. In the case of the Tim Shaw storyline, it accomplishes the plot objective, but with too much winking. When a quoted idea, whether for the sake of satire or not, exists to be recognized more than to be revised and reconsidered, it's not a shining moment.

I mention it here not to bury Dark Shadows, but to praise it. Out of 450 hours of storylines, it may be the one fumbled misstep regarding the issue of storytelling-by- pastiche, constituting the smallest fraction of the show's screen time. Exceptions do prove rules.

This episode aired the hit the airwaves May 29, 1969.

EPISODE 765

As Barnabas pumps Beth for information, will Magda pump Quentin full of silver bullets? She's locked, loaded, and ready to say "I'm sorry" six times in a row. Quentin Collins: Alex Stevens. (Repeat; 30 min.)

With a wolf on the prowl, Barnabas knows that Beth holds the key to its secret. Barnabas bites her, and she informs him that the wolf is Quentin, and that Quentin has a legacy he doesn't even know about: two children. Magda, rife with remorse, hunts the wolf, as the wolf stalks the estate. Finally, Magda shoots the wolf, but fatally?

It would be inaccurate and hyperbolic of me to say this episode is "pure action," so I will. For Dark Shadows, this is pure action. And if Dark Shadows action has a name (other than Thayer David), it's Alex Stevens. We owe him a lot. He performs several spectacular falls in this one, on par with his astoundingly Marvel Comics explosion through the Evans Cottage window earlier in the series. His greatest stunt may have involved padding on the floor, but I didn't see it, and the sudden reality of it is stunning. On the attack, the werewolf leaps over the railing on the second story landing in the foyer, lands, and keeps going. If you own an ankle, you realize what an impressive stunt this is, simply in its blunt relatability. It's a straightforward moment, and it may be the most magical sight on the show.

Because special effects are clearly unreal, even at their most realistic, they are inherently devoid of wonder. The great Ray Harryhausen may be a magnificent artist and technician, but magician, he ain't. Even when his work defined 'state of the art,' the herky-jerky movement and weirdness of scale immediately told you to start using euphemisms like "heightened" later on lest you be harassed by his devotees.

Magic is different. Magic shows the impossible as possible and leaves as the only conclusion: this happened. At that point, apologies to the makeup crew, Stevens could have gotten away with no appliances at all. Just a t-shirt that said, "werewolf," and we'd be sold. It's a moment of sudden wonder, and suddenly, from the floor up, Collinwood stops being symbolic of anything and becomes a real place.

It taped today, but it played on Friday, May 30, and I think that's a symbolic day. It's a good day to bring in a werewolf at his most exciting. And I hope the choice was strategic. This was, for many, the last day of school for three glorious months. In the past few days, Jonathan Frid and David Selby had recorded their contributions to the album, Original Music From Dark Shadows, which would become a massive hit in that year of massive hits. Viewmaster reels were steady sellers. It was the year of the Barnabas Collins Dark Shadows Board Game. And this one, action-packed, exposition-packed installment slammed the locker door on school for the best part of the best year of the best show that millions of kids had ever seen. It was the last day they had to run home from anywhere to see it, and the writers ensured that the marathon mattered. It certainly feels as if there is more screen time for Stevens than on any other episode of the program.

Dark Shadows may have very well been at its zenith. Ratings and demographics were measured differently then, and so I can't state anything definitively about who was watching. My instinct tells me that, given the items for sale and the significance of the day, this may be one of the most- enjoyed episodes of the entire series. It was certainly the most meaningful for a nation of kids. I don't need anthropological data to back me up on that.

A great episode? Certainly. Mature? Thank goodness, no. You have bats. Beth, with a vampire's dream of an endless neck, bitten and controlled. Barnabas learns of Quentin's curse, the children, and finally, what he's doing in 1897 at all. The last part is the vegetables of the episode, but at least there's cheese sauce. The enlightenment of Barnabas Collins has been coming for months and months, and you know the writers are planning something big when they finally plug in the light bulb over his head. Now, equipped with as much of the truth as anyone knows, the adventure of 1897 should be concluding. Barnabas should be climbing into his coffin for the voyage home.

Of course, a certain Count is about to hear that a certain body part is waiting for him in Collinsport. And if stuntman Alex Stevens is magic, the Count is sorcery.

This episode hit the airwaves on May 30, 1969.

EPISODE 771

When Carl brings home his shocking true love, everyone at Collinwood needs to take a shot... probably of penicillin. Carl Collins: John Karlen. (Repeat; 30 min.)

As Barnabas and Beth plan to find the undead Dirk Wilkins to distract Edward, Carl interrupts with his vulgar, cockney fiancée, the alleged medium and music hall embarrassment, Pansy Faye. Her display of second sight ends with an accusation that one of the Collinses will be knit up in Dirk's death. Later, Barnabas returns to the Old House where he finds her bitten and collapsed.

Dark Shadows is about as self-contained as a pair of fishnets on the opening day of a Pritikin camp, and that makes it murder to introduce to prospective viewers. No, this one isn't self-contained, but it comes very close, beginning with vampire-on-vampire suspense and ending in the murder of a character we meet just a few minutes before. It's a hilarious little jewel that is inarguably pure comedy, as Jonathan Frid gets the easy job and big payoffs of doing astonished take after take. The heavy lifting is done by an especially histrionic John Karlen and then Kay Frye, as his Alfred Doolittle of a fiancée, the psychic medium, Pansy Faye. Barnabas is at the height of his swashbuckling best, with Beth at his side, as he plots to foil Edward by revealing Dirk as the local vampire (this week.) With cosmic inevitability, the endeavor is halted mid-bat-pole by Carl, blithering of saltwater taffy and true love. It's a great summation of a universe that encourages heroism and then mocks us with its ridiculousness.

Think you're going to help the community while your social equals look on in disgusted apathy? Don't worry. The community you're there to help will soon arrive to make the effort look pointless.

Class envy is an ugly thing, and envy isn't even the right word. Envy goes from the bottom-up. From the top- down? See: Collins, Judith. Pansy Faye is exactly the sort of figure designed, like a Xenomorph by a Predator, for her to hunt. You can almost hear the thermographic scan kick in when she catches sight of the crassly cacophonic strumpet. The episode does a funny thing when they meet because it allows you to see the conflict from both perspectives at once. Judith is a snobbish and intolerant prig, and it's in response to a boorish sense of entitlement. The one that completely betrays the promise of humble, respectful good values that the working class claim when it wants to be offended into getting something.

Unless a Vanderbilt were tuning in, no viewer then or now knows what it's like to be a Collins just three generations away from Joshua. But Pansy Faye's brash idiocy, with the gibbering Carl as ambassador, kind of inspires everyone to feel like a Collins, and it's a subtle lesson in taste and etiquette for anyone willing to peek into the mirror. We've been spoiled by Vicki's example to see female outsiders to Clan Collins as possessing a purity of spirit often lacking by the decadently corrupt residents. But that changes, too.

If you've seen the series before, you know that Pansy Faye's spirit possesses Charity Trask, largely because it gave Nancy Barrett something interesting to do. That, and Dan Curtis was suffering under a curse that compelled him to make America listen to I Wanna Dance with You to an extent that almost — almost — makes us long for London Bridge. Under the Barrett administration, the United States of Pansy changes as drastically as it can without ushering in a new character. Was this planned? Was this a response to the writers honing the part for a familiar actress' strengths? I have no idea, and the "why" is irrelevant.

She warms and humanizes as a character, and we can credit death for that. Go down as Kay Frye, come up as Nancy Barrett. Gain a lot of nuance on the way.

It's not the only place this happens in the series. On Dark Shadows, death isn't an end; it's just a cue for transformation. The show takes the esoteric, gatekeeping mumbo-jumbo surrounding the Transformative Nature of Death and makes it literal enough that the rest of us unenlightened slobs might get some practical use out of it. Every culture kills its youth to one extent or another in the form of liminal rituals like hazing and walkabouts, where the prior identity is removed, a form of symbolic death is imposed, and an adult magically pops out the other end. This is a constant theme of Dark Shadows, starting with Liz Stoddard more-or-less killing her youthful, married identity and cocooning for a couple of decades before emerging in that smart red dress she wears to bail Carolyn outta the can. Vicki passes through death, kind of, in 1795. Adam is nothing without the death certificate he brings with him when he applies for fast food jobs. Quentin, of course. Only in Collinsport does Avis rent more coffins than cars. But the king, predictably, is Barnabas, who dies with a greater regularity than South Park's Kenny.

Each time he rises, which is arguably at the crack of dusk every night, he transforms. Sometimes wiser. Sometimes more impulsive. Inevitably, a tad on the hungry side. Even if we only count his transitions between humanity and parahumanity, that's still six ping-pongs between the worlds. On a strictly symbolic level, he simply has that much learning to do. For Barnabas, the story of Dark Shadows isn't Dracula; it's Groundhog Day. We see that down to the various rituals of renovating the Old House and agreeing with Joan Bennett that, yeah, the resemblance to that portrait sure is weird, and now, I need the keys to the Old House because Lowe's is delivering, like, a metric ton of backsplash tiles, and if I'm not there when they arrive, they'll take them back and restock them, and I'll have to send the gypsies to Logansport to straighten it out, and I think we know how that'll go.

On a show that constantly remakes itself in varied cycles, this is the most primal of all, and it often smells exactly like you might think. On Dark Shadows, transformation isn't a mandate, but it is a fact. Sometimes, as with Pansy Faye, it's the result of a terribly unfunny practical joke. Sometimes, it's a punishment. Sometimes, it makes no sense at all. Often, I don't even see the characters learn from it. They don't need to. Not as long as we learn the lessons. Sometimes, that lesson is to value the changes, like we see with Pansy Faye. Sometimes, the lesson is to hold fast to what hasn't changed. With Barnabas, it's a matter of knowing the difference.

Viewers may have already just won this episode on June 9, 1969.

EPISODE 780

Can Barnabas stop Carl from bringing about the end of Collinwood before Trask brings about the end of Barnabas? Quentin: David Selby. (Repeat; 30 min.)

Carl alerts Trask to the threat of Barnabas. The vampire, now allied with a Quentin who knows and accepts his secret, removes the evidence of his coffin before going on to kill Carl to save the future. Trask confronts Barnabas, and the two men await the telling dawn.

Sam Hall. Such an ear for dramatic dialogue. Properly theatrical yet always true. His plots are modulated with a pace as organic as the human heartbeat. Characters, distinct. Payoffs, rich. Yet always unpredictable. As much as I admire the exquisite writing of Gordon Russell, Sam Hall is the undisputed Master of Collinwood, and his best scripts expand beyond the needs of writing Dark Shadows and take on a storytelling voice that has the resonance of art. Immediate, yes. Written briskly and under incredible demands to produce, produce, produce. Rather than excuse his work, these facts make it all the more remarkable. In episode 780, his skill for economy melds seamlessly with the language of the characters, the substance of their climactic exchanges, and the propulsive risk inherent in the story. Put simply, he is a poet who gets out of his own way.

The "star" of the episode is the brutal and brisk execution of Carl Collins. Carl's fears and desires are understandable and considering the threat of learning that a strange relative is a ravenous, undead engine of murder, not necessarily unwarranted. We let Carl's prior extremity and histrionics too easily overtake the fact that at last, his panic is justified. In killing Carl, Barnabas trades the life of one Collins for many. If Barnabas goes, so do Quentin and David and who knows who else. It's time. It's time for this story to step outside the pleasant slow burn of the soap opera model, own up to its own stakes, and make things happen. Quentin accepts Barnabas for who he is, Carl is an understandable casualty of brass tacks, and Trask faces down Barnabas with a bold fidelity to his faith.

It's a four-man powerhouse of storytelling. Each character evolves and takes chances that define and redefine themselves. Barnabas reclaims the feral sense of strategy that established him on his release in 1967, but with values in line with something larger than addressing his immediate pain and loss. He even dares Trask to saddle him with Carl's murder. A rousing gesture, but an irrelevant one because Trask, justified in his hunt, has him dead to rights, despite the paucity of eyewitness evidence. When Barnabas shrinks from his cross, there is no more proof that matters. Those fine points of who-didn't-see-what are all words, words, words under the reality of the Damoclean sunrise.

Quentin does his part as well, and this episode is a microcosmic portrait of both his overall journey and what makes him the series' second protagonist — yet he never loses his essential gift for guile. He goes from melancholic repose with his companion music to smugly condescending to Trask's self-serving sense of justice. From there, he sets aside fear to see Barnabas for the man within the monster, and even collaborates to cover Carl's death with a fittingly unsentimental show of theatrical relish, not just enacting the con, but reveling in it.

Jonathan Frid, David Selby, Jerry Lacy, and John Karlen (in his final turn as Carl, his most unusual character) all seem to know that this is an episode of substance and almost rambunctious, driven meaning for the characters. Like the writing that inflames the installment, there is a confidence in their acting. Each man, undistracted, performs with the honest solidity of performers who know their characters and take them to inevitable destinations. That sense of inevitability is not an end, Carl excluded, but a beginning. Each man has a mandate to reveal his ultimate essence, and what results is like a series of Rorschach blots that unfold with the recognizable universality of a tarot deck.

Three years after filming began, 770 was captured on that soundstage. Dark Shadows has gone from a take of ambiguity and anxiety in a darkly domestic expanse to a tight chamber piece where each player defines himself with finality and yet, above all, possibility. Always possibility.

Except for Carl.

This episode rolled up its sleeves June 20, 1969.

EPISODE 817

With David's life in the balance over two centuries, Quentin learns that he lacks the one thing Petofi is determined to master: Time. David Collins: David Henesy. (Repeat; 30 min.)

Petofi allows Quentin to visit Barnabas in his coffin, and learns that the road to 1969 might be more challenging than he thought. Beth breaks from tending to David, now astrally trapped in Jamison's body, to serve Barnabas until Petofi shows her a vision of her vampiric future.

Somewhere in the wilderness, as seen on a backlot, a note is scrawled...

Please, Robert Bly, put away the drum and step away from the fire with that drink. Who can see it's a pousse cafe in a Yeti mug, anyway? No one is impressed. Sure, right, we all think it's mead. Now please go away before Jordan Peterson hears us and wakes up!

Yes, we're going to talk about manliness, as is my wont, but not your kind. We shall have no deep feelings shared nor bonding acknowledged, thank you. Because that's all a bit much. Manhood is the opposite of flatulence. He who smell't it is most certainly incapable of having dealt it.

Go back and read that last sentence in Count Petofi's voice. Yes, you hear the music, too.

Manhood. Whatever that means. This really is a core reason why I love Dark Shadows. Wallace and I have been in the midst of assembling the Daybook Book in fits and starts, and I frequently inundate him with new title ideas. Today's question: "How to Love Dark Shadows." More accurately, it might be: "Why I Love Dark Shadows." Episode 817 is a good place to start.

As Wallace once wrote, "Dark Shadows doesn't tell a story. It accumulates one." If there is any real story to the show, it's ours… the viewers'. Dark Shadows is a tough show to watch. It's an even tougher show to "get." It takes time away from our lives. Yet it becomes a genuine companion, ever- changing. And we can't help but be changed by it.

So, what is it... this Dark Shadows? You know the answer. It's okay, we're amongst friends.

Dark Shadows is Barnabas Collins. Thus, transitively speaking, he is what changes us. Knowing him. Watching the arc of his second life... maybe even his Sansar. Feeling the pressure to make decisions burst into full-on choice. This daily immersion slowly wears away the import of our world and replaces it with his.

817 is so beautifully resonant because it lets us step back and look at Barnabas and Quentin as the pure friends we always wanted them to be. Every Gilgamesh needs an Enkidu. That was a lesson in manhood for me when I first saw it. These things, if they are to have value, must be unexamined. They can only be acknowledged through silence. Ergo, I must write an essay about it. What's more, Dark Shadows lets us ponder the power of the soap opera format to build that friendship in real-time, from a place of intense distrust. Its success both sneaks up on us and seems like the most natural thing in the underworld. Quentin approaches Barnabas in the coffin, and the respect and affection they share are effortless. David Selby does most of the heavy lifting in the scene. It's some of his best work because it's so relaxed, attentive, focused, and authentically kind. In the midst of a ludicrous situation which sneezes squarely in the soup of "write what you know," he is like the very real stone in a Zen sand garden.

Later, when Quentin compares notes with Beth, also having returned from Petofi's, their conversation about the supernatural is stunningly casual-yet-intense. They are beyond romance and beyond the bodice-ripping hullabaloo that encapsulates how we met them. They are, maybe, friends, but colleagues-in-wartime, first. My, how things have changed in four months. And who was the agent of those changes? Barnabas, by action and by example, goes from being a stranger in his own hometown to the Jackie Daytona that everyone needs-but-never-knew-it. Beth needs a concerned mentor with no ulterior motives. Quentin needs a (literally) Edwardian hand of structure with no judgment. Selby's Quentin is increasingly aware that, no matter how much Barnabas divulges about the future, there is something darker that he's not being told. A few months ago, Quentin would have seized on the existence of such a secret. Now, we get the sense that he's somewhat relieved at being sheltered from it. It's a world all too eager to talk about ugly truths, and as 1897 goes on, it does so with less comical hysteria and more wistful acceptance. This is an episode where a twelve-year-old boy asks a woman what it feels like to die.

They've all been awakened from their sleep by Barnabas Collins. And so have we. Dark Shadows, for once, talks about what matters at the most primal level… how the ritual changes us. Its characters become us and we become the characters. Down to Beth watching herself become a vampire on a suspiciously television-like box in Petofi's chambers. It's the only show that matters.

This episode took to the air on August 12, 1969.

EPISODE 834

When Count Petofi appropriates Charles' studio for a clandestine rendezvous with Edward, Charles is puzzled to learn that a beautiful portrait of Amanda Harris might ruin the mood. Petofi: Thayer David. (Repeat; 30 min.)

Charles Tate discovers the secret of his own power, and Petofi monopolizes his home to meet Edward and expose his knowledge of Barnabas as the vampire. Barnabas ventures forward in time, via the I Ching, to interview Quentin's ghost about how he died.

Nothing defines swagger like Jonathan Frid, Thayer David, Grayson Hall, and Louis Edmonds, and 834's I Ching wands glisten with a palpable mist of their testosterone. I have no idea how a show like this, with an episode like this, could be called a soap opera. "Supernatural drama" is more like it. Or maybe just, "Dark Shadows," because at this point, it defines itself. The swagger begins, though, with Roger Davis. And a bit before.

The writers swagger, having established Charles Delaware Tate as the most powerful being in the universe. I would say more powerful even than Petofi. If the Count were that powerful, he would have given the abilities to himself. Tate is the perfect man for the job, however, because he is one of the people in the Dark Shadows universe least likely to want it. If Petofi has to choose a vessel for the power, let it be Tate. Roger Davis responds to the task with his most cerebral performance on the show. Most Davis characters are situational pugilists, dealing with very direct conflicts with high stakes and little time. Tate, however, is a man saddled with the ultimate existential realization of his chosen profession, art. It's safe to live by manifesting imagination if that manifestation is only two-dimensional. But the responsibility that he realizes here is beyond the infinite. Can he change a math equation? Would that make buildings rise or fall? Can he change the shape of a continent? Or eliminate the stars with a splash of black paint? Is he experiencing the ultimate liberation of an artist or the ultimate prohibition? Roger Davis captures this complexity with the deliberate economy of a Go master. No small feat.

Petofi, of course, is Living Swagger, forging names and appropriating art studios to trap Edward. Edward returns the swag by both embracing and dismissing bohemianism. And then staying even after he realizes it's a trap. It's the perfect embodiment of mechanized, Victorian thinking and propriety. When his worst enemy, Count Petofi, drops a dime on Barnabas, Edward should suspect that something is up. But Edward thinks like a reptile, with only a few up and down switches that give him very limited modes of very binary thinking. That only enhances his confrontation with the former Fenn-Gibbon, because Petofi is nothing but operational contradictions.

Best of all in this is Barnabas. Because he doesn't have the power cosmic. He's not the living embodiment of Victorian ideology. Early in the episode, he realizes that he must figure out how Quentin is going to die and how to stop it. Frid's own actor's terror here comes to the rescue, as always. It gives him a marvelously petrified millisecond of indecisive horror. Unlike any other TV hero of the era, he's not a master detective. Barnabas Collins is largely the master of finding himself in the wrong place at the wrong time, making him more akin to the heroes of Easy Rider and Little Big Man than Mannix. Nevertheless, he must summon the inner Mannix and solve the problem in the most ludicrous way possible, by projecting his soul temporarily through time to his awaiting body so that he can chat with a lethal ghost who never talked, get him to discuss his own death, and then return to 1897 with the news. It's ridiculous anti-thinking, tantamount to solving a Rubik's Cube by switching around the stickers. It smacks of desperation.

It works.

Desperation births a strange willpower, and Barnabas may not be a master detective, but he's no slouch at risking everything on insane ventures. It's one of the benefits of being a living corpse who's suffered every conceivable tragedy. The schemes he executes, especially in this era, work because of sheer chutzpah and the bravery one can only achieve through abject terror. At this point, the audience isn't tuning in to feel afraid, but rather to see what someone else can do when fear is all they know… and fear for the right reasons.

This episode hit the airwaves September 4, 1969.

EPISODE 842

Count Petofi and Angelique face the one force no occult power can overcome. But what could it be? Julia Hoffman: Grayson Hall. (Repeat; 30 min.)

Julia realizes that her force of will cannot only propel her through time but also makes her immune to the machinations of Count Petofi. Surviving a point-blank shot, she responds by recruiting Angelique to best the Count. Later, Charles Delaware Tate fully understands the extent of his powers by creating life from art.

The Dark Shadows that I want, the Dark Shadows I remember, and the Dark Shadows I get are three distinctly different shows. I want an Edward Albee version of Doc Savage with vampires, and no one is sensible enough to make that. The Dark Shadows I remember is an endlessly engaging, unfinished symphony of surprise as Barnabas wanders toward episodes that I was told were too expensive to show. The Dark Shadows I get is a sustained note of comforting monotony spiked with fleeting moments of delight and wonder. There are moments when I shout to no one, "Red alert! There's the imagination and delight and risk!"

When Dark Shadows is good, I mean very good, it crisscrosses the best of American character drama with tales of profound, speculative fantasy. It can be the equal of great theater and exceeds the brainiest science fiction. I say things like that, but when it comes to proving it, I'm often bereft. I usually have to tell people that, you know, there are 1,225 episodes, and if you just watch it, that will appear, like some kind of theatrical magic eye poster. And I could never do those; it's perverse to ask it of others. Which, of course, I love doing.

Still, the pleasure of writing the Daybook is to become Khan in the Mutara sector, bolting from his chair and announcing, "There she is! There she is!" And 842 needs to hop up on a pedestal and pose for that moment, because, well... there she is. It may be all of that or it may be all of that only in the context of the other 1,224 installments. I'm not sure that anything in Dark Shadows is what I'd like it to be. Is anything a self-contained example of itself? You simply have to judge for yourself after watching it, and if you do that, by the end, even the most die-hard critic of the show has at least seen it. Does it amount to anything? Not my problem.

It's not a payoff episode in terms of resolving storylines, but it nevertheless answers questions the show has begged, which is a horror no-no, and depicts characters actually talking about their relationships, aspirations, and surprises. A secret to acting is that a performer can build a career on making decisions, discoveries, and disclosures. Taking a note from that, 842 propels itself with a marvelously satisfying sequence of all three.

It may never top its beginning, as Julia suffers a fatal bullet wound from a diabolical trap... set by Petofi to force Barnabas to be her unwitting murderer. Such inventive sadism. In a Republic serial, it would all have been resolved with some kind of cheat that in no way matched the set-up. But Gordon Russell is too crafty for that. Why cheat when you can explore the existential extent of your own wackadoodle time travel conceit? That's what they do, and in doing so the show uses its exhausting length to investigate all of those bizarre implications no other medium could afford. Time travel through an I Ching trance is patently silly (unlike the dignity of a flux capacitor or vaporizing equalizer) until you really explore it to such an extent that it somehow legitimizes itself. Julia is there, but only through the force of will that symbolizes the spirit with which these characters soldier on through 950 hours of contrived terror and unlikely romance. These characters keep trudging on because they have to. You know, like we do in life. And Julia, more human than any of them, summons a friendship that dwarfs love and simply goes there. In doing so, she is a woman beyond time and may be the most powerful character in the Dark Shadows universe. Moving among cursed titans of cosmic powers and immortality, she is more immortal than any of them, immune even to the powers of the great Petofi. Now, she is a god, and instead of being driven mad with power, she represents all of us base creatures of limited time and matter by doing her frickin' job. Finally, one of us is thrust into the fray and she spends her time finally talking sense to these giants. Getting them on the same team. Pointing out that there are stakes beyond what they want in the impulsive right now. And she gets Angelique — Angelique on the side of truth, justice, and the Collinsport way.

That's how you thrash curses and send sorcerers running. That's how you mix it up with monsters. Faulkner declined to accept the end of man, and when I see Julia Hoffman straighten her spine and go to work, I understand why.

That's why Dark Shadows matters.

This episode was broadcast September 16, 1969.

EPISODE 856

When Quentin awakens in Petofi's body, will Magda think to pry him out in time? Quentin: Thayer David. (Repeat; 30 min.)

Petofi switches bodies with Quentin to travel through time, and Quentin is unable to convince Magda and Beth that he is not the Count.

We've seen it before, the old Petofi body switcheroo. First Jamison, just for a laugh, and then Quentin, to travel in time. In at least two places — the other being when Angelique makes a shadow decoy in the mirror to fool Laura — the writers have the confidence and savvy (or maybe luck) to set up secondary payoffs to what seem like small story mechanics and surprise us. 1897 is such a generous storyline that we get these seeds planted not just weeks, but entire meteorological seasons, in advance. In this case, it leads to two of the most interesting performances on the series and sheds light on the pluses and minuses of the characterization of Quentin Collins.

As Ben Stokes, Thayer David blended strength and vulnerability with surprise and nuance. As Quentin Collins, trapped in Petofi's body, David adds another layer to the alternating realizations of advantage and privation... intelligence. Quentin is a bright man, used to being in control of his immediate circumstances. If the 1897 storyline is about Quentin growing up (literally going from ghost to man), then to do so when deprived of his familiar talents, he's got to rely on underdeveloped strengths. Is Quentin intelligent? Yes, quite so. He is perhaps not as academically advanced as Barnabas, but he excels at observation and processing, which are not always his vampiric cousin's strengths. Do we see this? Up to now, not as much as we should. Quentin has height, looks, and limitless charm on which he can rely to get him out of most problems. Not only are these "muscles" stronger than his mind, they usually lead to results that are a lot more fun. Well, that fun is Petofi's to be had as he kidnaps Quentin's body and sticks our hero in the family truckster. As this storyline goes on, Quentin's evolution is clear. The character is haunted by Petofi's terrorist actions within his shape, learning of the privilege he took for granted and honing his humanity by relying on contemplativeness and compassion in the place of sex appeal. Never before or since has a character on Dark Shadows evolved so thoroughly, believably, and dramatically. He is cursed by the gods on a level that goes beyond the Shakespearean and into the amphitheaters of the Ancient Greeks. Quentin is a man who has everything, ignores that fact, and instead lusts for everything he doesn't need. If his stint as the packless wolf began the lesson, this seals it.

Heightening this with both a wild theatricality and a strange subtlety is David Selby's performance as Count Petofi. I was about to write that he makes a marvelous Bond villain, showing us who Quentin would have been if the writers hadn't cared about making him anything other than a total, blackhearted bastard. As those guys go, this is one of the most charismatic portrayals I've seen on screens great or small. Then it struck me. I know what Selby's doing, accidentally or not. He's showing us the man Quentin would have been in middle age if he had learned none of the lessons forced on him by fate and the writers' room. This Petofi'ized version of Quentin has everything he could have ever wanted and is revoltingly smug about it. The sickening truth is that absolute power cannot corrupt the alread corrupted; it just serves as an admirable compliment. In the moral balance, the "real" Quentin's lesson is even more haunting. He is humbled. He learns. He becomes a better man. And perhaps as such, he is alone and empty for nearly a century. I say that passing no more judgment on it than does the show. It is simply a fact for him. Virtue is no guarantee of joy, and there is no ruder awakening for a man like Quentin Collins when vice has lost its luster as well. He becomes twice the moralist that his brother is, a fraction as happy, and unable to go back once he's seen there's a better way to treat the world. And we wonder why he goes mad.

This episode hit the airwaves October 6, 1969.

EPISODE 871

As Angelique explains how she made Barnabas a new man, Charles Delaware Tate reluctantly shows Count Petofi the proper way to '69. Count Petofi: David Selby. (Repeat; 30 min.)

Kitty Soames manifests the spirit of Josette to such an extent that she and Barnabas seem nearly reunited, and it feels so good, perhaps because Barnabas understood. But what? That, Angelique explains when she tells Quentin how she faked Barnabas's staking by creating a duplicate of him while she cured the other of her own curse. Meanwhile, Petofi forces Charles Delaware Tate to throw the I Ching wands, and the 49th hexagram at last appears, taking the artist into visions of 1969.

Petofi now knows how to transport himself there, and he roars with triumphant anticipation of his destiny in the future.

871 makes me appreciate just how elaborate Dark Shadows actually is. It also makes me wish the rest of the show were more like 871. There is not one frame of subtlety to be found. Even if the line delivery is occasionally muted, the writing is not, and it makes me appreciate Sam Hall and Gordon Russell all the more. The episode's writer, Violet Welles, was their amanuensis — Barnabas taught me that word — and by just inhaling the creative fumes coming off their conversations and creations, she may be the show's best writer and secret weapon.

And she doesn't have time for nuance. Sometimes, God love 'em, Sam and Gordon had the other characters in prior episodes suck the wind out of the series with talk-talk-talk.

That's what happens when you fill ten weeks of programming with ten hours of actual plot. Because, perhaps, she had fewer shots at being produced, Violet Welles is a writer who's got a lot to accomplish, thank you. And if anyone opens their mouth around here, it had better be to advance the plot or FINALLY explain what in Sam Hall is going on over at the Old Mill at this time of night.

This episode is almost all payoffs. Sam and Gordon were wrapping up 1897, the show's finest hours of entertainment and imagination, with a length of nearly 175 episodes. That's almost the duration of the entire series before Barnabas was introduced. They (and the other writers) must have been led staggering out of their office to this "day off." I can see interns putting little capes on them like James Brown's pit crew helping the equally spent legend off stage at the end of a concert. They were probably led to typewriters elsewhere to keep working on House of Dark Shadows' latest draft.

This isn't the last episode of 1897, but it's awfully close. Might as well be. Violet's assignment must have been a bittersweet compliment. To get that far, and then hand it over to someone else? Was there envy? Pride for a colleague? Relief? All of those things are probably too interesting. It was probably just business. It's very easy to gaze at art on a deeper level than the artist ever did. "Theatre," I was told, "is art. Television is a piece of furniture."

That was a truism within the TV business, itself. For Sam, Gordon, and company, it was more than likely another day at a good gig, one that fans liked far more than they did. And how can we not with 871? It begins by rooting us in the core mythos and giving our hero what he's wanted since we met him: Josette. Yes, okay, she's supposed to marry Edward, but, well, Edward's no Jeremiah. And, yes, she's having flashforwards to being Kitty again. That's pork chops and applesauce compared to barriers that Barnabas has faced before, including sending his soul backward by nearly a century to be intentionally trapped in a sealed coffin. But even the few lines of happiness we see are an emotional banquet we've wanted for nearly five hundred episodes. Barnabas isn't the only one who's been waiting.

The big news follows right after, which is the narrative of how Angelique both cured Barnabas of vampirism and arranged for him to be staked without causing him actual harm. It's a monologued montage that deserves a Lalo Schifrin score, and Lara Parker walks away with it. Unusual for Dark Shadows, it includes flashback pieces featuring the actors who are, themselves, in the narration. Normally, DS takes us behind the magician's curtain very early on. We're on Team Monster. In this case, we've been sitting in the audience with the rest of Collinsport.

It's a whackadoodle plan involving a Doppelgänger created by doubling Barnabas in a mirror — literally through the looking glass. It's a nutzo piece of fantasy fluff, but it works because Lara Parker sells it with her trademark, passionate sincerity. That, and when I hear New Age people who pitch the woo to me, their descriptions of what they do are always vague. When I ask them to break it down, they castigate me for expecting something like a scrying mirror to behave like a household appliance. Jeez. Sah-ree. Somehow, the dreamlike logic of Angelique's plan makes as much, if not more, sense. It's like something narrated by my subconscious as I slip into sleep and has a sense of realism that is undeniably true because it makes a very specific type of credible nonsense. That, and it's a technique they used on Laura Collins months earlier, giving it verisimilitude without letting us know it's Chekhov's Doppelganger. It's a strangely cruel plan. I'm never confident about the peaceful passing of the staked double, and every time I watch The Prestige, The Great Danton's cruel sacrifice reminds me of this. No wonder Barnabas is relatively unfazed by things like his upcoming trip to 1796. At this point, he's been several types of dead, and that's his least-troublesome set of experiences of late. And his is only in the first half of the episode, mind you.

Petofi has had it with hanging around Collinwood. The Old Mill is clammy, it's fun to be David Selby, and the future awaits. When he gets Delaware Tate to throw the wands, he gets instant results as to which-way-to-1969. It's amazing what a competent stooge can accomplish after suffering years bungling incompetents. (Just ask Barnabas after he put Carolyn on the staff.) In an episode where Barnabas experiences the most romantic fulfillment, he's had in three timelines and Angelique describes the most amazing occult caper in Dark Shadows history, leave it to David Selby to walk away with the ending. As Petofi, future bound and claiming that nothing will stop him, Selby brings a maniacally grand sense of emotional oomph that makes the Ring Cycle feel as important as the "Chicken Tonight" jingle. There are moments in drama so, let's face it, shamelessly overwrought that they cannot be resisted, only embraced. Most mortal actors would have mugged their way through it with shamed insincerity, bellowing to Just Get It Over With. But Selby is a poet with a native sense of integrity and wonder. His loyalty to storytelling is too great and too real, and he nails the unadulterated joy of pure evil with a zestful energy I've rarely seen. In that moment, he is a living Marvel Comic book, reason, emotion, and passion completely bound together.

And to the credit of both Selby and the originator of the role, we somehow don't feel as if Thayer David is upstaged. On this particular stage, it is a spiritual collaboration of beautiful and perfect unity. These men were as opposite as the Trylon and Persiphere, and in Count Petofi, with the tight poetry of Violet Welles, there is suddenly no difference at all.

This episode hit the airwaves October 27, 1969.

EPISODE 885

When Barnabas finds himself back in the 1790s, can he turn his greatest defeat into victory? Barnabas Collins: Jonathan Frid. (Repeat; 30 min.)

As Kitty vanishes into a portrait of Josette, Barnabas loses consciousness and awakens in 1795 on the eve of Josette's suicide. He is determined to change history, confronting Angelique with honesty and a compassionate plea for mercy. She betrays him yet again and shows Josette a vision of herself as a vampire high atop Widows Hill.

I used to think that this was all about Judah Zachery. It's vaguely convenient to imagine him puppet-mastering the whole thing to emotionally decimate the Collins family. As Saint Ming would say, he likes to play with things a little before annihilation. The Zachery Codex is awfully elegant, and it makes for some USDA prime smarty-pantsism. The longer I am with Dark Shadows, the more comfortable I am saying that these grand theories are just those. Maybe they are accurate. Certainly, if it helps you read the show, then subscribe to them by all means. Subscribe to enough of them and then McMahon may show up with a check. Let's just hope it's not his bar tab.

(By the way, I miss entertainment. Is it the 70s again? I'm ready for it to be the 70s again.)

However, just because a grand theory works for a lot of things, it doesn't mean that it explains everything. The moral arc taken by Barnabas Collins could be seen as his torture, but it's a spectacularly risky and unsuccessful one. After all, although it is emotionally ruinous, it leads to his ultimate success as an ethical man. It could be that some other source is influencing the narrative. For a long time, I couldn't really figure out who it was.

Now, I do. Sarah.

Just because she's a child doesn't mean that she lacks the ability or gumption to manipulate as many spectral workings as possible. Perhaps this entire story is a contest of will between the two of them. Because, when properly motivated, there are few things more unstoppable than a determined kid. What would motivate Sarah to take on Judah Zachary?

Well, his one-time protégé, Angelique, may have strayed from her master, but he still trained her. Imagine that you die and suddenly see the full narrative that drove your life and demise? Not only that, but if Sarah thought his student was bad news, the teacher was practically Newsmax.

But in death, Sarah realizes that she has a living agent, which is more than can be said for most of the regulars on The Love Boat. Her red right hand to punish Judah is her immortal brother. She knows Barnabas' strengths, and more than that, she knows his failings. She knows that he is a raw element that must be tempered and honed before he can be properly deployed in battle. And, as with anyone who takes on transforming Poppin Fresh from an unbaked doughboy into a rock-hard brick of weaponized melba toast, ready to scrape the roof of evil's mouth, there will be pain.

And it could be a combination of the two things. With Judah becoming increasingly aware of this inconvenient Vampire and his tough, grizzled, eight-year-old girl of a ringside Burgess Meredith, he puts more and more obstacles in the path. Looking at episode 855, it might be the result of the manipulation of Sarah. Or it might be the result of the manipulation of Judah

Zachary. Or it could be the two of them going at it. Maybe Judah rips Josette into the past, and Sarah sends Barnabas after her. Or perhaps Sara has set the whole thing up to test her brother's character.

The episode is a hidden treasure. Soon, the series will turn into a sequence of hidden treasures. Every episode will be a reward for having watched all of the others. But right now, this exists like the Time Trap sequence around the 660s. It's a seemingly superfluous gift that exists more as an example of the show's Hellzapoppin exuberance than as a piece of mechanical storytelling necessity. It feels like it's their way of saying, "and here's a special something for being a loyal viewer." After all, the show doesn't exactly specialize in two or three episode "very special events." We've been trained to expect this kind of side trip to last for months. In fact, Dark Shadows is the only show I know of where the special sequences contain fewer episodes than the average storyline, rather than more now.

It's Barnabas at his most tender and heroic. When he

At this point, they don't even really bother with a time travel mechanism. Basically, don't stand too close to a portrait of Josette while there's a fire going in the fireplace. Similarly, don't look at someone who is standing too close to a portrait of Josette while there's a fire going in the fireplace. It's just science. And that's not what you came here for. But if it is, give me a minute and I'll put on a lab coat and Dr. Lang's surgical chaps.

Still, this is part of the plot of the overall series, and if you want the benefits of any kind of overarching story themes, you have to put on an apron with me, grab a hammer, and bang away at these things in the rationalization forge. The fact that there is no seeming time travel mechanism is the entire point. It's a wonderful mystery that invests us in interpreting the story. If we realize that part of the Leviathans' plan is to both put the whammy on Barnabas AND hold, and let me see if I remember this correctly, the ghost of Josette as hostage (as a backup), then perhaps this was orchestrated by them to remind Barnabas of the intensity of his feelings for her. Maybe it was Sarah's doing, to remind Barnabas of the stakes underlying his ongoing crusades. Or, you know, "Judah Zachary," because it's pretty convenient to blame him for everything from the destruction of Collinwood in 1970 to some of those sweaters they made David Henesy wear toward the end of the series.

It's an immensely gratifying episode. It's almost like seeing Barnabas at his high school reunion, vowing to undo everything he did to that bathroom stall in the science building when he was a sophomore. It's one of the most authentic examples the series gives us of his evolution. Literally, a side-by-side portrait. You know, if one of the sides is hundreds of episodes prior. He is making the decisions we wanted to see him make In the first place. And he's making the decisions that we suspected he was capable of back then. And tells Angelique that he can only give her his gratitude, he is being honest. By 1840, that would be enough for her. So in a sense, it is as much of a trial for her as it is for him. His mistake is in seeing her as the woman who saved his life in 1897. Yes, people can change. But not yet. This moment of her embittered selfishness doesn't make us hate her as much as it makes us pity her, and it adds a depth to the ultimate forgiveness that she will show him in their final voyage.

As he made plans with Kitty in 1897, we have never seen him happier or more confident or more fulfilled. This adds a harrowing context to the impersonal turn towards a larger evil that he will take in the next few episodes.

So, why? Why do they do this to him? If not the characters in the series, then the actual people making it?

Every time I think I know every kind of crazy there is, I meet an entirely new kind of crazy. And that's how we learn. For Barnabas, a man with a tenuous relationship with reality at best, every time he thinks that the universe is finally reflecting his opinion of what it should be, it pile-drives him into reality. And he must climb the steps of Mount Morality once again. But he is not a video game character, continually leveling up. If the real subtitle of the show is The Continuing Education of Barnabas Collins, his cycle of ethical awareness followed by cynical downfalls gives him greater and more nuanced understandings of humanity with each turn. Because it's not just his story. It's our story as we venture out of the idealism of the Enlightenment and into being enlightened.

The difference finally reveals itself in 1840. Up to the fall ,we are about to see, his heroism has been driven toward redressing who he was in the past, trying to bring the modern world into alignment with the aspirations of his era of origin. Everything he does is about repairing the past. Because the past is safe. The past is a known quantity.

What he has yet to attempt is building a bridge to the future unknown. That's what his final arc, after this and after the Leviathans, will teach him to do. It's based more on accepting what is rather than what should be and guiding that with a courage that comes from saying, "I don't know." Because to say that requires Barnabas to let go of his greatest fear: himself.

And he does. And good for him. And I would like to think, good for Sarah.

This episode was broadcast Nov. 14, 1969.

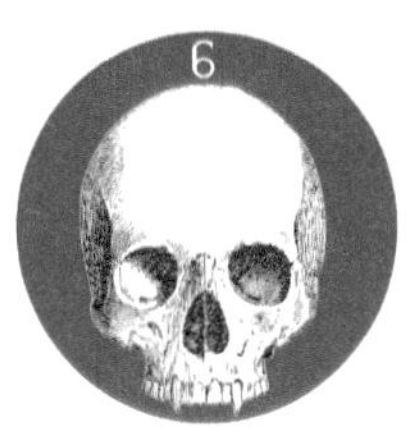

1970
DARK NIGHT OF THE SOUL

"Night has fallen over the Great House of Collinwood..."

We were leaving the 1960's with the moon landing on the horizon. And although John F. Kennedy, his brother, and Martin Luther King had been taken from us, NASA's lunar achievement was going to be a disproportionately noble response by Team Humanity. And then, The Manson murders. It's no surprise that our next adventure plunges its golden boy into hell. Barnabas goes from babyface to heel to as he's recruited into a cult led by a charismatic twenty-something of a primordial snake-god. It's a storyline so unexpected that the phantom villain from the show's first year has to rise from a grave he never occupied to warn everyone that Chicken Little was right. David knew it all along.

It's easy to look at Star Trek and see the 1960s. It's a little harder with Dark Shadows, which is ironic since it actually takes place in the 1960s. Sometimes. Dark Shadows was seemingly concerned with reprocessing boring classics, so we didn't have to read them and pretend they were as much fun as a Remo Williams novel. However, the events of their era could not help but find their way into the stories. Nowhere is it more evident than here.

EPISODE 933

Quentin and Amanda have crossed the decades to reunite, but can they cross Hell, itself? Amanda: Donna McKechnie. (Repeat; 30 min.)

Quentin and Amanda navigate through hell, never allowed to touch, as they prove their love through twisted ankles and giant spiders. Paul Stoddard sits in a faux fugue at Chez Stokes until he encounters his doom at the hands of the Prime Leviathan in the professor's rumpus room. As he dies, Amanda seemingly pitches over a bridge in the underworld.

While 933 wouldn't air for three weeks or so into January, it was still the first episode shot as a new decade began. Violet Welles, who often refereed during plot arc exploration with Russell and Hall, shows the wit and gravitas of the best of those two writers, and this installment is a grand example. The show was standing atop the magical year of 1969. This was, in many ways, one of the last hurrahs of that intense madhouse of creativity and fun that began with Barnabas's mercy mission to 1796 and ended with the rise of the Leviathans — with the 1897 spinoff in between. Was 933 seen as a beginning or an end? It was both and neither. A film was in the works, and I suspect that Parallel Time was being talked about. They had freedom to jettison two great characters because so much was possible, but to see them both (well, almost both) go in one installment is a brash choice, nonetheless. Paul Stoddard, the most important non-character of the series, barely establishes himself before serving as one of the cruelest sacrifices to the Leviathans. Wasteful? Perhaps, but I see it as a gutsy statement of where the show was willing to take audiences. If they can kill the entire reason the house was a crypt in the first place, nothing was too precious to be above becoming canon and cannon fodder. There is a lot of "new" upon our return from 1897 and killing Paul

Stoddard both re-centers the story on essential characters (and a re-emerging heroic Barnabas) and opens up room for the character of Jeb. The Dark Shadows canvas may be broad, but it still benefits from a tad of elegance. The reappearance of Amanda Harris can be seen as a non sequitur, given how little impact it ultimately has on the story.

They may have had bigger plans for the character; it feels that way. Donna McKechnie certainly has a breathtaking beauty and integrity, like a Brundlefly fusion of Kathryn Leigh Scott and Alexandra Moltke. Never let it be said that Dan Curtis didn't have a type. I can see the reluctance to jettison her as an actress, however, Stephen Sondheim's landmark musical, Company, would open in late April, and McKechnie was a key player. Doing both could not be an option, and so Amanda had to go.

I'm not sure anyone on the show ever received as mythical a sendoff. Sy Tomashoff must be congratulated. Building all of Collinsport in something the size and width of a small bowling alley was tough enough. Putting in what at least appear to be multiple levels of Hell, a chasm into an abyss, and the pit of a giant spider, also? It's a creative masterstroke by the entire production team. Is it "Hollywood"? No. But if you focus on that kind of realism, it's like getting a box of doughnuts and only seeing holes. They took a world of hand-wringing over the kitchen table and put the pits of Hades in its place. Both David Selby and Donna McKechnie are key to selling the dramatic truth of the show's wildest setting, and their trip through the underworld is an example of the program's creative ambition and generosity toward the audience. I can only imagine being a kid and connecting the dots.

The program's been dabbling with a hellish sub-dimension for some time. How close were they to Diablos' office? Could they have wandered in? Was the interior of the Leviathan altar overhead? Was it hollow inside? Were there batpoles? How closely connected could these things have been? And did they stand a chance of bumping into the transformed

Jeb, shambling toward Professor Stokes' place through the servants' corridors? How did Nicholas keep that tan down there? Because it was a good one.

Not too long to think about it. The show typically moves sequentially in the episodes, but in what feels like a warmup for cinematic storytelling, 933 employs crosscutting between two concurrent narratives and does a sophisticated job at letting each build the tension of the other. The mini-climaxes and (often literal) cliffhangers have a precision that Hollywood often lacks. The Last Jedi comes to mind as a film that mangled the same attempt.

But let's face it — the Walt Disney Company is no Dan Curtis Productions.

I mean it.

This episode was broadcast January 21, 1970.

EPISODE 936

Carolyn goes from funeral to fun when her eulogy attracts the most eligible bachelor in Collinsport! Jeb: Christopher Pennock. (Repeat; 30 min.)

Paul is dead, Jeb is born, Roger is antsy, and Barnabas isn't feeling too well himself.

Why Barnabas? Why did they choose him? I'm sure there's a more literal explanation, but a lot of it had to do with the fact that he was on TV, and that's free publicity. Snake cults don't run on love and good intentions. I assume Barnabas's propensity for immortality is what led him to manage the Leviathan project. Oberon and Haza probably mentioned something else from his resume at the interview. They should have negotiated with Mr. Best and had Quentin transferred from his job cutting lemons at the High Hat Lounge. Neither Barnabas nor Quentin shows a lot of management potential, but Quentin routinely caters Jeb's lunch with his fist. They could have actually held Amanda Harris hostage, threatening a further, extreme coiffure. Josette was only good until a séance would come along. Given that it's Collinsport, a séance is pretty much guaranteed with greater promptness and regularity than the bus to Logansport. But Barnabas is their guy.

Right now, it's like he got drunk and joined the Shriners without realizing what a demand it would place on his schedule. Barnabas comes off like a mid-century Catholic school administrator who's been to a post-Vatican II educational convention and has to tell the brothers to stick to time-outs instead of running them down with Buicks as proscribed in the Book of Leviathan. David, even hypnotized David, needs discipline, but Jeb's going a tad far. Bill Malloy would probably just have keel-hauled the boy, but ocean travel mellows a man. In all seriousness, if Jeb's attack on David does anything, it allows Barnabas to display his sense of decency at the outrageous attack. Now that Jeb is aboard, Barnabas no longer has to sub as villain, and he makes up for it in this episode, putting out fires where he can.

Neither of the Collinwood 1701-D staff (David and Carolyn) have an easy time of it in this one. Carolyn now permanently thinks of her better qualities as Stoddardian, and I can't blame her. David's no doubt looking into restaurant management opportunities in Panama, although I imagine pedestrian dangers are even more severe than in Collinsport. Roger suspects foul play, but #1 Dad may be too late on that one. Overall, it's a bad day for parenting at Collinwood when Roger is the responsible one. Liz is too busy pouring herself a congratulatory Campari and Yoo Hoo for attending a funeral that's not hers. Parenting has always been problematically demonstrated at Collinwood and the rest of the series evidence that as Liz and Roger become increasingly distant. Excluding a few warm moments coming up, this sequence is a turning point in the kids' erosion of trust in their parents. Of course, the story is shifting violently toward Barnabas's journey rather than domestic travails so there's not as much time, but Carolyn and David will pay various prices when Gerard attacks. The show can only pretend that this is a loving home for so long. The absent parent is always the preferred one for the kids, even when they're trying to burn the kids alive. Dark Shadows has always been about sins of the past. With Laura gone, Roger steps up as much as he can, but that's limited by the fact that life at Collinwood got complicated when his ex-wife flamed on and grew stranger from there.

I know this episode is "about" Carolyn, Jeb, and Carolyn & Jeb — and about Barnabas's futile attempts to unsmoke the cigarette of snake-cultery. But I'm wondering more and more, "Where is Roger Collins?" In this arc, he's taken into Quentin's confidence and fights "on the team" more than he ever has. But even as he ostensibly participates, it's not to an impressive degree. But what's he going to do, issue a catty memo? Again, perspective splits between production and story. As far as production is concerned, Roger's days as a villain are played out. He has to stay because of his plot function regarding David, a successful mini-heartthrob and story catalyst. Roger and Liz also make good civilians to remain vaguely threatened, vaguely unaware, and vaguely available to hear and deliver exposition. But with only +/- 6 parts to spread around per episode, the increasingly supernatural ensemble edges out the mortals.

But within the Dark Shadows universe, itself, what explains it? After you've seen your grandfather's brother come back from the grave and try to kill ~~Burke Devlin's~~ your son, you don't have to touch that hot stove twice. Roger's participation dwindles drastically after early 1969 when Barnabas leaves for the 1890s. Gone on business for the beginning of the Leviathan arc. Gone again for Gerard's haunting. In fact, Roger will not be seen after episode 979. For the character, that's only six more episodes and the show still has nearly a year and a quarter left. A key reason that Dark Shadows feels less and less like Dark Shadows right now and onward? Well, Kitten, you're looking at it. Liz doesn't fare much better. She has fewer than 30 episodes left, although she is the first character we see at Main Time Collinwood and will be one of the very last. If the show (as we know it, on 1198) feels like Dark Shadows in its final moments, that's it.

Because we're influenced about what makes up the series by when we enter it, for most of us, this makes the latter section of the show feel alien to us. This is purely subjective, however. Start your viewing later, and Roger and Liz are strangers on a series belonging to Barnabas and Julia, those heads of the family are absent for nearly 20% of it — nearly 25% if we discount the pre-Barnabas segment.

This transition is all the more dramatic as Christopher Pennock is finding the character. He's discussed being uncertain about his sure footing as he began as Jeb, but the character is written with the same ALL CAPS WITH WHICH HE ACTS HIM. Where is subtlety in bringing to life a primordial snake god man-messiah? You tell me. Storm and Selby, the other high-water marks on the hottie hunk scale, had the benefit of not speaking for their first months. So, not only did they get comfortable with the ensemble, but their speaking roles were entirely new characters. Few have had to do so much so quickly, and Pennock acquits himself with high style.

This episode was broadcast January 26, 1970.

CHRISTOPHER PENNOCK was, in the most Marvel of manners, an Ultimate Being. He was impossible in every sense... impossibly talented, neurotic, loving, tempestuous, honest, intelligent, and necessarily profane. We lost him today. He had been suffering for some time. Depending on his mood, Pennock might have joked that he had been suffering for his entire life ... when he wasn't busy living it to a degree that would have shamed the most boisterous krewe on Fat Tuesday.

The "next hottie" to find himself on the program after Jonathan Frid and David Selby, Pennock was no himbo. He kept himself honest with constant doubt. He was worried that his rough beginning as Jeb Hawkes made for a poor introduction to the ensemble. In truth, he handled the awkward hipster snake god with a sincerity that encapsulated the idea of a dark messiah who was more delinquent than demon. It was the first of many parts that allowed him to contribute irony as well as integrity.

Beyond being a solid, east coast, red meat performer worthy of his Actor's Studio affiliation, Pennock was an author, artist, and spiritual explorer who clearly saw the ludicrousness of what he was doing and committed to it full force... perhaps somewhat because of it. He found the total joy of John Yaeger's compass for evil. He loved Gabriel's sour wit and loved the character's tearful pique as he revealed his true motives to the father he murdered. To the detriment of his career, Pennock's taste for the idiosyncratic made him impossible to injection mold as Leading Man #7. But as the show entered its post-1897 malaise, Pennock brightened every scene he was in with a unique blend of commitment and knowing humor toward himself. He was only newly brought it, detached from the legacy of the show's early mythos, and he was here to make the most of it.

At its essence, theatre is about the struggle to make necessary changes after learning uncomfortable truths. Ladies and gentlemen, Chris Pennock. Growing up resisting the repression of the east coast's bluest WASP blood, he was a much-needed anarchist against rigid conformity. From interviews, it's also clear that his anarchy was in the pursuit of something better. He was frank with all of us. When the conch shell of The @ButtockPennock blew the clarion raspberry, we heard of life's triumphs and tragedies with relentless candor on social media. Often in secret code. I think my first interaction with him was over a stated intention to end it all. He had a forlorn dignity about it, and I couldn't bring myself to argue with him. What could you do?

Later, I was lucky enough to participate in a dinner/interview with him where he eagerly talked for hours about the end of the world, severe depression, his post-coital encounter with a well-meaning transvestite, and then finished it off with a staring contest (for an audio podcast) that he let me win. It was a great night. I was never more nervous nor more at ease.

It's hard to imagine a festival without his Falstaffian presence.

I'm not sure he's really gone from the mortal world... in the same sense that I'm not sure he was ever fully mired by it.

He had the unmistakable crackle of bodhisattva as much as man, and the uncompromising humor and affection that surrounded him at his best prove my point. In his passionate extremes, he achieved a wild and pained balance. If matters became too dour, an ironic observation would rip forth with a master's timing. And he was just as capable of deeply human kindness and insight. He genuinely existed with one foot on earth and one foot someplace else entirely.

Both places are the better because of it.

EPISODE 941

Jeb's romantic evening with Carolyn is interrupted by the surprise appearance of Quentin's fist. But will Maggie pay the price? Quentin: David Selby. (Repeat; 30 min.)

Quentin rescues Carolyn from Jeb with successful fisticuffs. Before Barnabas can whisk Carolyn away to seclusion and safety, Jeb kidnaps Maggie, suspecting that she is Barnabas's weakness. As Barnabas threatens to summon Oberon, Jeb laughs, knowing that Maggie is laid out in a mausoleum.

There are a lot of audiences for the program, and between satisfying all of them, the show also has to be true to its own, unique mythology. Dark Shadows is both all continuity and flees from continuity whenever it can at this point. I don't think there's any greater corner into which they painted themselves than the one with mutton chops and a cool, gray coat called Quentin. It's not just David who remembers him as a ghost; Liz does, too. I like how they acknowledge that in this episode, and I also understand why they dropped it pretty quickly — or why the Collinses are a pretty forgiving, gullible family. The writers have to because it's a conversation that goes nowhere. The characters have to because they'd have no relatives otherwise. Mrs. Johnson has leftovers, and if another "cousin from England" doesn't show up pronto, that ambrosia salad will get to a point where even Willie wouldn't eat it after a bender at the 'Whale.

Quentin's reluctance to re-engage Liz is a character moment that you might miss if you blink, but it's enough to perform its function on the show. If it weren't for the Leviathan arc, they might be able to devote more screen time to Quentin's Return by making it the sole story. But that might require bringing back a villain from 1897, like Petofi, and who wants to see that? (Except everyone.) However, that's running in place, and to the show's credit, they moved forward to book a third hottie on to the program. It not only kept the show fresh, it also

— and I'm just theorizing this — kept Dan Curtis from being a victim to anyone's success. There has to be a line for a producer between working for ratings and working for the source of your ratings. Just as no one suspected that Barnabas would be such a hit, no one suspected that Quentin would, either, and arguably to a greater merchandising degree. As much fun as 1969 was, 1970 would be about topping it, and retreading 1897 so soon was a path they wisely avoided — and at a cost. Barnabas and Quentin are kept around because to not do so would have been suicide, but now often at the service of Chris Pennock and James Storm. The most strangely sexless arc is the one in between Jeb and Gerard — 1970 PT— in which there was no hottie. Yes, Quentin is dashing in a Ron Burgundy sense, but he's also a loudmouthed, clueless, overreacting bully. Cyrus may be sympathetic, but he's hardly an alpha. And Yaeger? The mustache and wig don't have the Goulet magic they might have hoped.

Before any of that, 941 presents a moment of 1897- style action that is always a cherry in the show's fruit cocktail for me. The fight scene between Jeb and Quentin is a last hurrah that might as well have taken place on Cestus III so that the Metrons would release Collinwood from their grasp. Quentin introduces Jeb to his biscuit hooks in his best and most Quentinesque modern costume, and the whole thing feels like a sly reassurance from Dan Curtis. The man can and will release the kraken at the drop of a putter, so tune in. With enough patience, Dark Shadows is any show you need it to be. Soap opera? Of course. Character farce? When you least expect it. Musical? Oh, they go there. Horror? You bet. Science fiction? The time travel and dimensional leaps qualify. And prime- time action? That, too. It may even have a dash of Brady Bunch. 941 has a strangely and endearingly adolescent ending, as if they sensed what their prominent adolescent audience might do. Barnabas threatens to call Principal Oberon on Jeb and Jeb responds by making fun of Barnabas for having a crush on Maggie.

It's a strangely sweet and innocent ending for an episode that begins with — and let's take the schmatte off it— Quentin preventing a rape. I don't know if that is supposed to be mentioned or not, but Jeb slips Carolyn a mickey, and it's not for a good night's sleep. Now, Dan's biggest problem is over how he redeems the guy. I'm not sure he worries too much about it or if he lets the story take care of it. That, and the culture of 1970. I'm not rushing to get out my hankie, but watching it in 2019, I wonder if they'd introduce that character choice at all or, if they did, if Jeb would be seen as eventually redeemable in any way. It also helps to humanize Joan Bennett after her turn as a good, stoic, dedicated hostess to Leviathan functions. It would have been easy to turn her into Mrs. Johnny Iselin and fork her daughter over to the cult, but you don't come back from that choice. The characters might get their memories erased, but the audience doesn't. Wise to have her go along with Barnabas's plan to take her to an island — any island. There are a lot of audiences for Dark Shadows, but they all can agree on basic right and wrong.

This episode was broadcast February 2, 1970.

EPISODE 955

When Angelique's latest husband tries to burn her alive, can she reunite with an old flame? Angelique Rumson: Lara Parker. (Repeat; 30 min.)

After Sky tries to kill Angelique, she flees to the Old House, where Quentin takes her in. Sky's attempts at reconciliation are rebuffed. Meanwhile, Barnabas pursues Maggie and even gives her the fabled engagement ring, but Quentin stops him short of biting her. Angelique, seeing Maggie as her rival, has her fall in love with Quentin just as she once had Josette fall in love with Jeremiah.

Sometimes, which is most of the time, I just want to talk about why I love an episode. Dan Curtis had a famous dream about a girl on a train. I had a dream about an Angelique TV sitcom pilot. They both came true. I may like the Angelique pilot more.

With a series as sprawling as Dark Shadows, there are almost countless reasons for tuning in. If yours is Lara Parker, you've made an excellent choice. Beyond her obvious beauty, she fascinates due to her incredibly bright, sharp, poised presence. Her background, one part academia and one part fine, southern society, is one of our closest analogues to the world in which Angelique found her American footing. As with Jonathan Frid, wicked wit, an advanced education, and a respectable social background give her a sense of anachronistic exoticism and authority. Unlike him, however, her roots trade his wry, detached, Canadian sense of irony for the underlying, fiery passion so often associated with the American South. Put all of that together, and you have Angelique. Moreover, you have an intensely watchable performance of a frequently reprehensible character. Even when we don't like what she does to people, we like watching her do it. And few others could pull off such intermittent evil and have us rooting for her, anyway. When she's bad, it's for understandable reasons. When she's good, she's usually being evil anyway, and that's towards someone even worse. Again, for understandable reasons.

For many, Dark Shadows is a TV series about Angelique.

If we ever wanted to make it official, 955 is the pilot, lacking only an animated opening credits sequence in which she kisses Barnabas, whips off his tie with saucy panache, and uses it to strangle a toy soldier while winking a huge, celluloid eye at the audience. This is pretty close. Beginning an episode with Felix being thrown onto the streets of New York by his fed-up wife is amusing. What's better? The Angelique series (meaning 955) begins with Sky Rumson barging into her room with a torch, saying, and I kid you not, "I wanted to work it out."

Well, if you put it like that....

From there, we see one satisfying scene after another, fulfilling the Angelique jones we never really knew we had. Quentin even greets her with a bemused warmth set aside for reuniting celebrity frenemies on the Jerry Lewis telethon. There's a kiss on the cheek, of-course-you-can-stay-at-the-Old- House, and warm sympathy for her husband trying to burn her alive. What's most important is that moment of, "Quentin, I think I really did love the big lug, all along," which is her kinda-but-not coming to the same crucial realization that Barnabas will reach in the future past of 1840. This reduces Quentin to mentally stammering like Hank Kimball on Green Acres because — cue laugh track — he just saw Barnabas macking on Maggie, and successfully, too. With Josette's ring! He's a vampire again, so he might as well drink the best. I mean, Joe Haskell's out of the picture. Victoria's out of the picture. What's touching in this is that Barnabas is pursuing Maggie. Not Josette. But Maggie. And it's high time. Naturally, if only Sky had tried to kill Angelique just a few hours earlier she would have beaten Maggie to the punch, but then we wouldn't have the bittersweet makings of supernatural farce.

At least we get the relief of seeing her tell Sky to get lost. I've had plenty of moments of watching women knuckle under to jerk boyfriends who do one horrible thing after another but always get taken back. It's nice to have one of them try it with Angelique. It's like another part of the pilot, but now the pilot has gone from the world of domestic comedy to the socially conscious era of Mary Tyler Moore. Only one more hurdle... Maggie! Who's dressing like Rhoda more and more, but still stands in the way of Barnabas.

You can hear the gears turn louder than "#1 at the Blue Whale."

You know what? Wouldn't she and Quentin make a nice couple? Fans keep picturing them together; they're the Mary Ann and Professor of Collinsport. Let's give them what they want.

The devil's brand makes its familiar return from 1795, and suddenly Quentin and Maggie are locking lips in a way that seems far more satisfying than the case of Josette and Jeremiah. Barnabas only asked this one on a date. It's not like they're engaged. But if you're Angelique, and if your only tool is a love spell, then every problem looks like Kathryn Leigh Scott. At least she picked a suitor who's bulletproof if it comes to a duel again. All that's left would be Angelique telling Barnabas that Maggie needs to see them kissing so that she'll get jealous and dump Quentin. It's for his own good.

"Angelique, it sounds crazy, but it just might work." You know… it just might.

Louis Edmonds turning into a cat tested well with audiences before.

This episode was broadcast February 20, 1970.

GEOFFREY SCOTT was the picture of stalwart.

Dark Shadows was known for actors with myriad positive qualities. When considering the male leads to appear after Mitch Ryan, 'stalwart' isn't always the first word to shuffle up on the Rolodex. Could David Selby, Roger Davis, and Joel Crothers project the quality if called upon? Of course. Blindfolded, in their sleep, on an iced tightrope, in a hurricane, backward, with a drink in their hand... not spill a drop. They could be 'stalwart' with characteristic ease and truth, but Geoffrey Scott simply was. This was, literally, the Marlboro Man come to Collinsport. This was a man so tough that he went from having both legs crushed in a biking accident to resuming a career as a virile, athletic screen presence.

He topped this by moving to the Rocky Mountain area because he enjoyed the skiing. If I discovered that he was powered by the rays of Earth's yellow sun, far from his native Krypton, I wouldn't be surprised. He held his own against the Hulk and Margaret Hamilton at various points in his career, and that cannot be said for many other actors.

He came to us on Dark Shadows with an unenviable task. Thanks to the 1897 storyline, Angelique credibly transitioned from unforgivable villain to a clever, brilliantly strategic heroine with a wistfully sad Secret. It is probably the most overlooked gem in the crown of that storyline. Soon after, we reunite with her in late 1969 to find her married. Dark Shadows fans are protective of Angelique. What kind of man could possibly satisfy this literal Force of Nature? Casting the part of her husband may have been one of the most difficult tasks for the producers in the course of the show. The answer? Again, the Marlboro Man... Hollywood-born stuntman, model, and actor, Geoffrey Scott.

Not just the Marlboro Man, but as the man who walked to the Taj Mahal for a Camel. Only a guy like Geoffrey Scott could do that with an easy confidence that made him look right at home.

As hunky, magnate publisher Sky Rumson, Scott was as warmly likable as he was blindly ambitious when we discovered his true identity as a Leviathan cultist. After the headaches caused by the intense and introspective Collins men, it's understandable why Angelique finds this rugged, all-American, hardworking businessman an uncomplicated relief. And It's just as easy to feel her betrayal when his occult affiliation surfaces. Lara Parker and Geoffrey Scott had an easy chemistry, and that's understandable. Both appeared with Dan Hedaya in the off-Broadway musical, Lulu, and made a darn good-looking couple.

Scott went on to be in constant demand for commercials, television, and film. A frequent guest star on programs like Matt Houston, Harry-O, and Dynasty, he was no stranger to comedy, also appearing on Married... With Children. He was a lead as well, starring in the innovative NBC program, Cliffhangers, with Jerry Reed in Concrete Cowboys (taking over in a role originated by Tom Selleck), and in one of the first made-for-cable series, 1st & Ten. The latter was a role he won out from competing actor, Chris Pennock. No hard feelings. He was simply made for it.

Like John Beck, Geoffrey Scott was the kind of star who refused to be taken down by the bullet of fashionable irony that pursued the unique, American institution known as the square- jawed leading man. There was, and we hope, always will be a demand for actors of the honest and knowing strength epitomized by Mr. Scott. His career began on Dark Shadows, and as one of its alums, he made the show proud by continuing to evolve as a hardworking and welcomed presence across the spectrum of performance. His final film role was as the president in 2003's Hulk. He had my vote.

EPISODE 960

How is Chris Jennings the key to Bruno's plan for world domination? Ask the talkative zombie! Bruno: Michael Stroka. (Repeat; 30 min.)

Jeb is increasingly smitten with the notion of human life. Bruno takes this as a cue to plan his eventual plan to replace Jeb as the Leviathan leader. All he needs to do is chain up Chris Jennings, trick Jeb into getting locked into a room with him, and then wait for the full moon.

High School Confidential captures two zeitgeists at once, and I'm not sure if they disagree, agree, fuse, or simply enjoy a cool, smooth cigarette and agree never to talk about it. Russ Tamblyn has that effect. He's either hipper than the room, Babylon 5, only thinks he's hipper than the room The Haunting, or doesn't even dig the limiting scene of calling it a room, man, because all that's about walls and not a framework for windows, dig, Twin Peaks?

Did you notice how forced and awkward that was coming from me? I could never get it off the ground. Not one bit. And there's only one thing more painful than a square guy in a world o' cool, and that's a square guy in a world o' cool who thinks he's passing. It's one of the reasons why Spiderman 3 is so painful. Peter is projecting an image of cool that doesn't work because he has no idea what he's doing.

Welcome to the Spiderman 3 of Dark Shadows — Leviathan Prime. Aka, the Russ Tamblyn of the series. To me, being the Russ Tamblyn of anything would beat a GBE after my name, every time.

I hate to say that I love this uncomfortable foray into "modern" culture by Dark Shadows, but it's marvelously illustrative of how impossible it became for establishment media to keep up with any kind of youth-oriented culture or fashion. One of the fascinating elements of the series is its display of that cultural numbness. When it began, just thirty- one months earlier, youth culture was driven by adult culture. JFK might have been six feet under, but Camelot still drove fashion. Sinatra was turning fifty, but he was still in the prime of his comeback. James Bond was a colossus, and the man kept snappy and wore a suit.

Thirty-one months earlier, Burke and Joe defined angry (kinda) "youth" on the show. Of course, the arrival of middle-aged Barnabas skewed the show's chronological compass even further away from youth culture, kicking those long-hair, rockabilly, yeah-yeah types to the back seat and letting the Canadian drive.

Quentin's arrival shakes it up a bit, but you're only going to get so much hipness from a West Virginia boy with a Ph.D. Don't get me wrong; David Selby goes far beyond human conceptions of cool, but that's the point. I'm not sure that mattered as much as it did even a year before. Maybe it didn't matter at all for youth appeal. But someone thought it did because we get Jeb and Bruno, and what results is a show by middle-aged writers in youth drag. Now, we don't get Charles Napier cracking his knuckles and jumping for joy because he has a new lease on life for William Malloy, but we get Jeb, Bruno, hair higher than Joan Bennett's, and a lot of people calling each other "man," man. Meanwhile, the now-zombified Sheriff Davenport staggers away with the episode, far more interesting and talkative as a zombie than he was before, proving that nothing's cooler than being room temperature in Collinsport.

That's my takeaway from this episode, a platonic orgy of male unbonding. With no Barnabas and no Quentin, there's not a lot for Jeb to push against except for Bruno. Bruno shows a plucky knack for class mobility when he proposes to himself that he, Bruno, a human, would nevertheless be the ideal next leader for a race of timeless immortals so vast and ancient they have flecks of gold on their dental floss. We can't deny that Jeb wants to be boss as much as have the freedom of one, but with Bruno on one side and Barnabas on the other, he's learning that management means having all of the responsibility and none of the power. All he can do is threaten the frustrated management figure opposing him, one Roger Collins.

Now that Roger is back from Louis Edmonds' vacation, Edmonds represents the silent generation with a ferocity they rarely allow him. It's foreshadowing the establishment backlash to come, and given what a bullying lout Jeb can be, the establishment is sorely needed. And that's another dimension of showing hipsters by way of the unhip.

Cool was redefining itself so quickly that even Roger Corman's youth epics expired seconds after the projectionist cracked open the cans. The angry establishment doesn't need to worry about any of that because it defines itself by its defiance of cool.

The timing is predictably atrocious. Just when DS tries to find a sexy antihero in the guise of a shaggy haired cult leader, Charles Manson became a walking wake-up call that the sixties were over before they were over.

The message? Wear a tie. Trim your mutton chops. And call Russ Tamblyn in situations like this.

This episode hit the airwaves February 27, 1970.

EPISODE 965

When zombies seal Quentin in a coffin, Barnabas knows that love must be in the air. It's a Very Valentine's Dark Shadows, but will a wedding spoil the fun? With Barnabas and Jeb, this much fun just can't be legal! Nicholas Blair: Humbert Allen Astredo. (Repeat; 30 minutes.)

Jeb goes from burying Quentin alive to kidnapping Julia. He wants to be human. Although, at the same time, Nicolas Blair prepares a wedding ceremony that will end with Carolyn being turned into a Leviathan. However, the satanic secret agent is double-crossed when Jeb recruits Barnabas to usher Carolyn away from the Leviathan altar as he destroys the Naga box.

For a lot of us, Dark Shadows is the only soap opera we will ever watch. Given that, I am still amazed at my capacity to see the storytelling as a stunt. Because it's not storytelling. It's anti-storytelling. Storytelling is all about getting to a catharsis. You know, these people learn in their lesson, a few of them die, and the rest of us go home to watch Benny Hill. That's how this is supposed to go. But a soap opera can't end. It's like Data playing Stratagem. The point isn't to win. The point is to just keep playing. It's a narrative shepherd tone, continually descending as it slips in new beginnings destined to also descend. So that's great. Let's take a moment to appreciate that before admitting that it can also drive you a little crazy after a while.

And then there's an episode like this. Boom. Over. Done. Nothing left but a wedding, the death of Sky Rumson, and that embarrassing shadow curse that we really don't talk about with strangers.

You can just feel the massive satisfaction that rolls off of it for everyone involved. Mark your calendar with that red pen that the show only needs about two or three times a year. Something actually happens. Today, wonder team action force goes to work, and they end the Leviathan storyline with a beautifully baffling abruptness that perfectly matches its beginning. It's like a Battle of the Network Stars where every contestant is Robert Conrad. There's an honestly giddy disregard for consequences to be appreciated. Both by the characters and by the producers of the show. The heroes recklessly attack an ancient relic that sizzles with powers none of them understand. The only person who has an inkling of what it means is Nicholas Blair, and when they break the box, he runs like hell. The rest of them just shrug and book a wedding.

The zany ending is a relief for the writers, also. Because they're just having too much fun. Laura's death wasn't this much fun now, was it? See? The very fact that the story can end so extraplusdoublequick, with Jeb doing a 180 without even changing lanes, says it all. Best to just get it over with and pretend it didn't happen. And they keep the good part. In the divorce with the Leviathans, they make sure they get custody of Christopher Pennock because none of this is about him.

When you look at this in the overall life of the show, they are busy elevating Barnabas to the big screen, which is a clear statement of what they know Dark Shadows is — and what ultimately makes it work. Leviathan, schlmiathan, baby, we're going to Hollywood. So, with that prospect in mind, we get a brief and daffy Viking funeral for everything else. The ball drops as Quentin is buried alive, which starts to happen so frequently that he might as well get his suits made by Liberace at Whispering Glades. (After all, the foot curls when rigmo sets in.) And he's buried alive by zombies, who are probably glad to have the company. But it's only two zombies today. He was kidnapped by about four zombies in the prior episode. What happened to the other two zombies? Were they only temps? Was there a budget cut? Did they not test well with other zombies? Were they booked on Password? We will never know.

Meanwhile, Jeb, who really hasn't had time to figure out who he is at all, decides he's going to be a human and kidnaps Julia to do the biomedical honors. I can only imagine this is the most extreme Bris ever conceived. They did not cover this in medical school, but somehow, he wants her to change him completely into another... creature? One that's not a God. I mean, I'm not even sure Julia is qualified to perform a nose job. This is all very specialized stuff. But this was in the days of the HMO, and I guess anything was possible.

Why is he doing it? Why does any villain ever do an about-face on Dark Shadows? Because they're in love of course. That quintessential motif should be obvious to viewers by now, but they make the point again with absolute clarity just to make sure that no one is confused. It's like a teacher doing a review straight out of the test the day before. We are as grateful now as we were back in Enochian school.

And it's a proper Leviathan wedding. You've been to a million of them. Traditional, February, outdoor, Maine ceremony.

And overseen of course by Humbert Allen Astredo in a tasteful but quietly lively sequined gown. The bride, as is the way, is hypnotized by Humbert with his magical cigarette case. Out of sight of the groom, of course. As the vows are exchanged, the groom grabs the celebrant's horned devil stick and beats the sacred relic into nonexistence as Barnabas ushers the bride away to help him finish 30 pounds of deviled eggs that the two missing zombies were supposed to make and have plated as the reception began. But they are nowhere to be seen. Which is why you hire licensed caterers for these things and not the first zombies you see hanging around in the parking lot of Home Depot at 6 AM.

Then, as Humbert flees the exploding altar, the groom clutches his abdomen with the realization that there was no prenup. The episode ends.

Oh, but before that, those love tattoos show back up from 1795 — one of them, still on Kathryn Leigh Scott and the other one on David Selby. So, they declare love for each other for the sole reason that it's a very special episode.

The whole thing is a hoot from start to finish. And I think it was supposed to be. The only thing missing? Collinwood's favorite zombie, the reliably and suspiciously plump Chuck Morgan, who appeared yesterday and will appear again to tear apart Collinwood a few months down the road. I suspect his fellow actors on the show signed a petition to get him temporarily banned because they knew he would have emerged as the real star. And to me, he is.

Chuck makes for a magnificently unlikely zombie. So much that I actually researched him as the episode was going on. I had heard that he was a wrestler, and by God he was, sometimes going by the name of Big Ben Morgan. Texan by birth, Morgan had Show Business in his unitard, also appearing on Broadway in Teahouse of the August Moon. And in this case, I'm not pulling your leg. Look it up. He's buried with his wife vera in a cemetery in Chattanooga, and I think a road trip is in my future. Care to tag along? I think there are some good stories to be discovered about this robust wrestler.

So, all of this and a Texas wrestler, too. Maybe this is the high point of the series. In the words of my academy professor, the guy who made you think or sink, "the more complex the mind, the greater the need for the simplicity of play."

After following up the 1897 Collinsport Exhibition of the Future by making Barnabas a failed villain managing a rather waterlogged Armageddon, everyone deserves a last hurrah like this. Two grim movies, a nihilistic trip to parallel dimensions, a harrowing 1995, the destruction of Collinwood, and a Pyrrhic victory over ultimate evil are all waiting in line.

This episode hit the airwaves on March 6, 1970.

PART THREE

RETURN

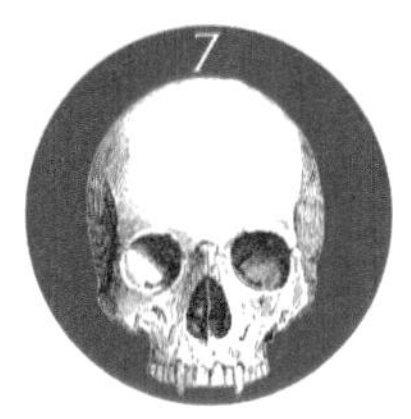

1970
Parallel Time
THE MAGIC FLIGHT

"Night has fallen over the Great House of Collinwood..."

While House of Dark Shadows was being filmed, the show went on. Why not in a parallel dimension, accessed by an unused room in a sealed-off wing? Why not, indeed? Let's wrap up the Leviathans, first.

EPISODE 980

Be careful what you wish for, Barnabas Collins. You just might get it when the Parallel Time room takes you on a one-way trip into another dimension. Sky Rumson: Geoffrey Scott. (Repeat; 30 min.)

A desperate Sky Rumson's gambit fails. In the effort, Jeb plunges off Widow's Hill, Carolyn plunges into depression, and Barnabas forces Sky to shoot himself. With the danger passed, Barnabas is no longer distracted from the desperate pangs of bloodlust. In a last-ditch hope that the rules will be different for him in Parallel Time, Barnabas explores the mysterious portal once more and finds himself trapped there.

Have you ever had the experience of watching a scene on the show, finding it well-acted and dramatically compelling, about matters that are crucial to the characters, but when it was all over, you'll be damned if you can remember what happened? It seemed like something was happening. Everyone was behaving as if something were happening. And yet, turn the corner, and you're still at Worthington Hall. Masters of that particular medium are forced to do what I can only call a form of Zen anti-writing. Everything has to matter. Everything has to have dramatic dynamism. But it must be limited to as little real growth as possible.

And it has to happen in a medium designed to be both constantly compelling and yet accessible by audiences who can't afford to be excessively distracted. They've got ham salad to grind out by 5:30 and still have to give the kids a shot or two of Benadryl before you-know-who gets home. Okay, you can't say that nothing happens. But what was it, exactly? This strange chemistry is the reason that we can't stop watching a soap opera once it begins resonating with us. Why is it so familiar? That unlikely fusion of constant tension wrapped up in the frustrating amber of inertia resembles daily life closer than any form of art that comes to mind. Even Dark Shadows. Maybe, especially Dark Shadows. We spend weeks and months waiting for some sort of inevitable change. When it happens, as it does in "reality," it transpires with a blink-punishing swiftness. It's always satisfying, and yet, it never quite lives up to our expectations. Sometimes, it's better. In fact, it often shames the impulse of having expectations by exceeding them while falling just short enough to keep us watching.

Characters on soap operas see The Resolution as the end of their problems. We know that they serve to usher in new ones. To writers and producers, they represent opportunities. And for the writers and producers of Dark Shadows, they represent the possibility to electrify the culture itself. The saturation of Barnabas and Quentin into the zeitgeist proves my point. Creating them created inadvertent cultural power for the producers. And with that came the pressure to sustain it. To top it. To remain on the cultural vanguard. And, through the injection of novelty, often through novel actors, shield themselves from the power of performers to see themselves as indispensable. Everything after Barnabas, it's safe to say, was an attempt to re-create that success. It's easy to evaluate that success or failure based on how storylines resolve themselves, if they ever even do. I think it's more interesting to look at beginnings and wonder about the aspirations within.

Few transitions are as dramatic as this one. Ultimately, few will be as strangely permanent. Sky Rumson is gone. Barnabas doesn't even bother to bite him. Even if he enslaved Rumson as his blood-bound servant, he wouldn't exactly be a familiar worth bragging about. Sky would probably knock on Barnabas's coffin multiple times a day. Asking for a glass of water or warning him that they sent a new milkman.

Letting go of Sky Rumson's small potatoes; we must concede that Jeb is gone as well. It's not like the show didn't give the character a fair shake. His storyline kept going even after the primary threat presented by it was over for weeks. As much as they tried, Jeb never took off like Quentin or Barnabas. I sincerely wonder what Dark Shadows would have looked like if Jeb had been as popular as the Collins cousins. Would they have needed Parallel Time to cover shooting the movie? Could they have afforded to go at all?

From a certain perspective, Parallel Time is the boldest and most awkwardly optimistic piece of storytelling on the show, designed to please fans while taking away all of the characters with enough saturation to carry an unprecedented feature film. But what if it were potentially more?

I have every confidence that the production team looked at Jeb with hope. After two years of dizzying success, was anything outside the realm of possibility? And if not Jeb, then Parallel Time. Yes, they had every reason to believe that Parallel Time could be a success, also. Why not? They had already done it once. In so many ways, 1897 is a Parallel Time story. It reflects a number of the earlier, more successful plot elements of the classic period but with the confidence and swagger of a show that knows what it's doing. Dark Shadows could have easily continued in 1897, and although everyone would be curious about the events taking place in the present, they were hardly bereft of pure DS entertainment. Among other things, it's Dark Shadows the way it could have been, had Dan Curtis known what he could get away with. After the mixed reception of the Leviathan arc, perhaps the team wondered if they should have stayed with the better mousetrap of 1897. Perhaps this upcoming storyline is a way to correct the mistake, if only metaphorically.

It feels as if the writers are yet again playing their own Monday morning quarterbacks by recreating the show based on even more of what has defined success. This means leaving something behind. The prospect of a successful introduction to Parallel Time explains a number of the more controversial choices of the movie. What kind of film kills off most of its major characters? Maybe one that is preparing audiences for the idea that Dark Shadows can continue without those characters. Obviously, the film universe and the television universe are two separate things, so we are speaking symbolically, not literally. Imagine that Parallel Time had been a roaring success. By the film's release, the franchise would stand redefined. Could Parallel Time have become the series' new home? In a post-Vicki universe, anything is possible.

The potential success of Parallel Time was not in its novel concept. No one speaks of it in the same breath as "Mirror, Mirror." Its strength simply lies in its freedom to rewrite the rules. But with tried-and-true elements that they had discovered, rather than as points of pre-production speculation.

David Selby is a success, so why not make him the head of the household? I would certainly tune in. Kathryn Leigh Scott can clearly do more than just pour coffee, so what if she becomes the Mistress of Collinwood… who is also a stranger? One who can view the mansion's antics with the objectivity of an outsider. In other words, Victoria Winters on spiritual steroids. While Grayson Hall plays a tremendous best friend, she's too good as a villain to waste. So, let her do what she does best. At least, what she does best when not in Gypsy drag. And look at how much more capable and intelligent they allowed Willie Loomis to become. Well, Parallel Time allows for that, also.

Rounding out the ensemble, you have an Angelique who is deservedly a point of attention for everyone, rather than The Other Woman. After all, they had seen exactly what Lara Parker could do, so why not make the spotlight even brighter? It may have been intended as more than a placeholder in the Dark Shadows saga. It feels like a further refinement of marvelous elements they discovered while getting there. And, conveniently, you have your most popular character just waiting to be released.

Why consider this? None of this happened, of course. Parallel Time was not a Barnabas nor Quentin-level success. Neither were the Leviathans. But look at these storylines based on their potential as well as their delivery. Because at this point, it was all about potential. If you've never seen the show, this might be objectively evaluated as the start of the next big thing. When it's not that, it gives the rest of us a greater reason to sit back and reflect on what really made Dark Shadows, at its best, work.

This episode hit the airwaves March 27, 1970.

This next one is notably light. It was one of the first written as the reality of the quarantine was really settling in. I tried to keep it buoyant because God only knew where things were going. Wallace and I attempted to keep a watch-through of the series going on in those early days, but like everything else in the dystopian novel called Reality, it fell apart. Clearly, Dameon's Bea Arthurian pantsuit was made of stronger stuff.

EPISODE 994

When Quentin encounters the specter of Dameon Edwards, do Angelique's former lovers stand a ghost of a chance at keeping it together? Trask: Jerry Lacy. (Repeat; 30 min.)

Quentin is shocked when the ghost of Angelique's former friend, Dameon Edwards, begins dripping blood around Collinwood. Trask, the butler, and Bruno barely maintain their composure when informed of the manifestation.

Four years ago, this was day two of the Daybook, and it was a significantly different animal. It was a good call on Wallace's part, several months later, to limit me to just one episode a day. Over the years, I went from little to say about an episode to sometimes an embarrassing abundance. I often wondered if I would run out of things to talk about regarding the show, and the notion is absurd.

The real star of this one is Dameon Edward's suit. That may actually be true.

The remarkable thing about that is the fact that this tight, haunted episode does not need a fantastic costume or two to eclipse it. With the exception of Amy's appearance at the end, it's a masculine episode… as much as one can be when the costume department raids Bea Arthur's closet. Which, come to think of it, is pretty butch. And my point is proved. All seriousness aside, it is about men dealing with the ghost of a man, all in the shadow of a woman who drove everyone to the brink of distraction or worse. After all, when you see a frosted glass on Dark Shadows, you know it's getting broken. And when you see someone named Trask break it, you know that the worst is in the offing. It's a tight mystery, with David Selby showing what must have been refreshing nuance for his bellicose character in Parallel Time. Especially with Michael Stroka's Bruno, who likewise puts in one of his subtler, most believable turns in the role, Selby plays his notes subtly and close to the vest… but not so close that we, as invisible confidants, don't have an idea of what's in his hand. He's playing the most cuckolded character this side of a Moliere play, and now that Angelique's dead and Maggie is in a fit elsewhere, he has the pleasure of slow roasting his rivals. Even the horror of a bleeding ghost is obscured by a delight at what that means for seventy or eighty other lovers. It's about time they shared in the paranoia. Come on in, fifth battalion, the water's awful.

I always enjoyed Jerry Lacy's too-brief turn as Trask, the butler, showing a kind of nervous and tight professionalism that introduces a new type of domestic at Collinwood, and one we never realized was sorely missing. Of course, he has confidence; he's got the only dignified costume in the installment. The rest are sporting either Collinwood's most quietly outlandish or, in the case of Quentin's brown-shirted nightmare, ugliest ensembles on the show. I can only assume that Mostoller lost a bet with Denise Nickerson, and she got to pick out the duds with all of the restraint someone her age would show at catering. Is it as glorious as a craft services table equipped by Farrell's? Dare I say, even more so.

First, it's clear that Michael Stroka, hair so high I imagine him inflating it by blowing into his thumb like a cartoon character, appears like he's wearing one of Maggie's vest and turtleneck numbers she sports as the governess in primary time. Which may be why he never stands in the episode. I'm sure he has winning gams, but he's no Kathryn Leigh Scott. (Apologies for objectifying both, but when the latest from Junior Sophisticates fits, wear it.)

Dameon Edwards' outfit is truly the astounding star, here though. A futuristic jacket, belted with two buttons on a sash, sans lapel, makes him look like Alan Sues auditioning to play a Bond villain. This is over a shirt with a collar wider than most major home appliances of the age, accessorized by a scarf that would be the envy of even the great, late Deforest Kelly. It's an outfit that could only have come about by Roddy McDowell costuming John Saxon in a failed Gene Roddenberry pilot, and that's where I want to live.

Only a bachelor ghost could have the silent swagger commensurate to carrying off such a suit, and it's an amazing snapshot of fashions they were sure would take off and carry us into a glorious future. It's impossible to watch the episode and not be carried there, also, and Dark Shadows' penchant for showing us a past that never quite was is finally matched by the suggestion of a present that should have been.

This episode hit the airwaves on April 16, 1970.

EPISODE 1049

When a drunken Carolyn announces that she knows the deadliest secret at Collinwood, will she live to tell it? Carolyn Loomis: Nancy Barrett. (Repeat; 30 min.)

Carolyn, thinking she knows the secret of Angelique and Alexis, gleefully taunts everyone at Collinwood. Unfortunately, the killer lures her away and stabs her in retribution.

As a showrunner, Dan Curtis was too far ahead of his time. The Parallel Time sequence of the show is an experiment in and testament to that, as is the project he had running, yes, parallel, the film House of Dark Shadows. An episode like this allows him to test waters and flex muscles that we can see later in his career as a bloodthirsty and unsentimental filmmaker. He sets up the cliches of the soap opera and then shows his frustration by smashing them with an unceremonious sense of ritual. And if he didn't, the writers, reading the room, did it for him.

Even though I've summarized the episode twice, let me take my own go at it, neither doing a TV Guide nor a vaguely quantitative recap. Carolyn, in a miasma of booze, bitchiness, and low self-esteem, plays informational keep-away without realizing the actual consequences that follow. As a result, she gets stabbed to death by the one character bitchier and lower-self-esteemier than she: Roger. Dark Shadows has had enough of that nonsense and starts playing for keeps, a practice that it will follow throughout the final sequence of the series. If you screw up (or even if you keep company with screw-ups), you'll die. In today's world of ruthless "real" television series, killing off central characters is an event that's no longer shocking. Dan Curtis inarguably invented it, so all you other guys, get back in line.

Across town, Curtis is preparing. Although we rarely acknowledge it as such, it's the second Parallel Time storyline that he would present, each one getting uglier and more nihilistic. Each one, more relentlessly transparent in the logic of what it plays out. In 1970 Parallel Time, we see a Carolyn who is also widowed, paranoid, and unstable. Just like in "real life." In her dialogue with a heartbroken Liz, it's not so much a glimpse into a parallel universe as it is into a future that Dark Shadows never quite reached. She's both explosively abusive toward those with failed love and implosive as a reaction to the one she's lost completely. Unlike the world of standard TV (of the era), there's only so long that can go, and the show finally exploits that ugly truth.

Similarly, on the big screen, Curtis will take it a step further. I'm no expert on things that don't exist, which is why

I'm not a theologian, but I can guess that an emotionally shattered hemopathic man who profited from the dehumanizing slave trade and starved for two centuries, will probably dine without sentiment or remorse when released on an unsuspecting world by an incompetent redneck. And someone will eventually take him out once he plays all of his cards by becoming the most prodigious and swiftest serial killer in the history of Maine. Because that's Barnabas 2.0.

This reflects Dan Curtis, himself. Uncle Barnabas the hero is a concession to TV. Barnabas the killer is probably more like the truth. When writers asked Dan where the TV version was, and he responded that he wasn't doing it that way again, we get the most revealing statement about the creator possible. This is the producer who would send writers running from meetings throwing up. And Parallel Time — this kind of blunt, pained, short-timer, unsentimental Parallel Time as we have in this episode — is not necessarily so parallel. It's unfortunately true. The secret to Dark Shadows is not that we've gone to Parallel Time, but that we've finally emerged from it.

This episode hit the airwaves July 2, 1970.

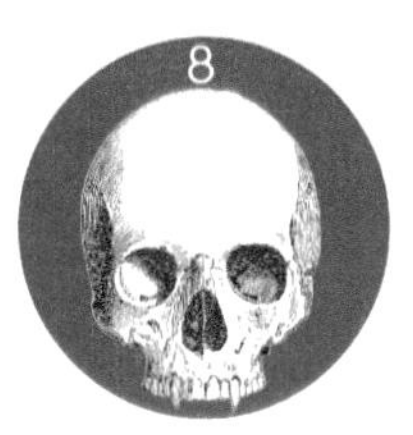

1970
RAGNARÖK

This is probably my favorite storyline in the series, although it's also the least fun. Having gone to 1995 in a sideways attempt to escape parallel time, Barnabas finds Collinwood in ruins and stumbles across a list of events that will precede its doom. He returns to the present, whatever that means at this point, and despite his valiant hand ringing, Collinwood is destroyed.

Well, we can all stop bitching and moaning about the show being about a pen. It's proof that Dan Curtis was capable of epic storytelling without ever leaving his minute studio.
No, it's not about a pen. It's not even about Dark Shadows.

It's about America.

It's about a man from the era of America's highest aspirations thrust into chaos and devastation. Is it the result of his absence or the logical consequences of his actions? That's a sphinx without a riddle. But this is not the program that began in 1966, when we could and would climb out of Camelot's crater, carried on the shoulders of a mighty Texan in Washington, and in his care, soar ever upward to the moon and beyond. Or so we thought. The mud of Woodstock mired us in the belief that this was the best it could get. We buried another Kennedy. And a King. And an X. Charlie had done the devil's work, indeed, and his legacy is written in the soul's blood of pure, erotic ebullience, Sharon Tate. Need security? Call the Hell's Angels. We see how Altamont worked out. I'm sure Cronkite talked about it after disclosing the Vietnam death toll for the day.

So, Barnabas goes twenty-five years beyond all of that and finds Collinwood in ruins. I am not surprised. The town of Colinsport is terrified to even speak the name, "Collins." Perhaps because they destroyed them. Perhaps because they did not save them.

Barnabas returns with a list of events that will signal the Fall. He thinks that he can avert them, but our poor, poor Pulcinello is reliably mistaken. The list is inevitable. He is not a savior. He's the Herald of Galactus. It is a list designed to mock his aspirations, and expecting him to change the events enumerated on it is like asking Patrick Henry to come to our time and prevent the domestic terrorism of January 6. And after the events of that day in 2021, the darkest day in American history, we should not watch this storyline the same way, ever.

Art challenges the status quo by asking us to see the familiar through new eyes. This show will do that before becoming affirmation once again. It is a painful prophecy that unfolds with the helpless desolation of oncology results. It's made more watchable when you realize that it will resolve itself happily. Barnabas will go to 1840. And by trusting the most important woman in his life, he will be there when she rescues the future. How is that affirmational? By example. We are in "the 1840" of some future generation's potential dystopia. Change is up to us.

But before the dawn, we need a little more darkness.

EPISODE 1083

Sebastian Shaw disturbs Hallie with news from the beyond, but will he open his third eye in time to see that Collinsport's most venerable hunk is coming his way? Professor Stokes: Thayer David. (Repeat; 30 min.)

David and Hallie find a dollhouse of Rose Cottage in the playroom and are disturbed by the presence of dolls that resemble themselves. Driven by Hallie's evasions, Professor Stokes visits Sebastian. Although he implies that Sebastian is a fraud, Sebastian demonstrates his powers through a heartfelt vision that ends in the sight of the children sleeping. After Stokes leaves, Sebastian confides in Roxanne that the children were actually dead. At Collinwood, David and Hallie try to break Gerard's spell by burning the dolls. When they return to the playroom, the dolls have reappeared, unharmed.

The irony of Dark Shadows' broadcast history is that, by the time they were making the episodes that would have really given kids nightmares, the kids for whom the show was vaguely aimed were too old to be scared. Or given nightmares by soap operas. Or maybe still watching. But 1083 is a fine candidate for nightmare inducement and a perfectly good reason to walk a little slower on the way home from school. Lately, Jonathan Frid and Grayson Hall are not reliably waiting to greet them.

It's a cursed storyline. Cursed by the fact that we already know they're doomed. Yes, the whole point is averting it, but at no point do our heroes catch a glimmer of hope. In this episode, we have only the third-stringers to rely upon. And I hate to call Professor Stokes this, but the role of skeptic is a strange one for him, and it's a little odd to try and get behind him not believing in something. Especially because he gets it wrong. And that's what they do in the Ragnarök sequence. They get it wrong at every crucial point when getting it right would thwart Gerard. He is a villain whose plan only works because of entropy. An all-star can only get it right so many times. Stokes not only has trouble detecting that Sebastain Shaw is the real deal, but he even fails to detect the only lie told by him: that the children were in no real danger. In fact, he saw them dead. This isn't a testament to Stokes' waning powers; it's a tribute to the insurmountable odds he faces in near ignorance.

Killing kids is one of horror's few taboos, reserved only when the medium has no interest in charming the audience. (And to witness what happens when you effectively break that taboo, revisit Pet Sematary.) Sure, kids have died/almost died before on the show, but never just… because. Heroes constantly outmatched? One of the only things that makes much horror watchable is the knowledge that the forces of good may somehow escape. Or, as with the 1982 The Thing, at least take "it" with them on the way down.

The last victory Gerard wants is a moral one, and it's clear that none will happen on his watch.

1083 typifies the storyline in that David and Hallie are on the front lines of both the attack and the defense. Fewer things are more unsettling than trying to solve a problem you may be unwittingly creating, and episodes like these are strange precursors to the feeling that Candyman gave audiences. There, too, the heroine is a lightning rod for manipulation by the villain. Dollhouses, as I've noted before, are testaments to our desire to control. As David and Hallie try to sidestep its rules by burning the dolls, Gerard must again deliver a memo in inevitability by making them reappear.

Why a dollhouse? Coming up on a future episode, David and Hallie will see themselves replacing the figurines within. It's what I consider to be the single most disturbing image on the show. Gerard's message is a clear one; David and Hallie are already dolls in a dollhouse, themselves: Collinwood, Gerard is its clear master, and maybe he has been for a very, very long time.

This episode hit the airwaves August 19, 1970.

EPISODE 1092

Julia's plan to put Maggie into intentional danger results in Maggie being put into intentional danger. Maggie: Kathryn Leigh Scott. (Repeat; 30 min.)

Julia uses Maggie as bait to find her attacker, but the plan fails. As she and Barnabas continue to decode prophecy and study Rose Cottage, the children are drawn to the playroom by Carrie's taunting voice. There, they see themselves as dolls in the dollhouse.

1970 is Collinwood but not Collinwood when Barnabas and Julia return from Parallel Time and 1995. Roger and Liz are gone, as are any outsiders who are not menacing weirdos like Roxanne and Sebastian. I didn't know how much I would miss Sam and Burke and the Blue Whale, which is the Drawing Room for the Common Man, quite so much. The stories have been so exotic that we really haven't had time to mourn them. But the bread and butter of so much of the show was playing off rich from not rich, isolated from urban, sherry from Stroh's, etc. This perhaps became irrelevant with the introduction of Quentin, a man of pretty common sensibilities with an aristocratic last name. Losing that chemistry is a shame because it grounded the show and the family. Take that away, and disorientation sets in. Never before has the Collins family felt more isolated and helpless. Are these things even going on? Don't bother to look, the mirror was blinded a year ago. The Collinses always saw themselves as the saviors of the commoners, but it's the other way around. The last of the townsfolk, Maggie, is finally being sacrificed. It's the price she pays for climbing Mt. Olympus. She was right to warn Vicki and a chump for ignoring her own advice.

1092 begins with Maggie being allowed to wander the Collins estate so that Julia can track down her assailant. When that fails, she and Barnabas refuse to alert the authorities, which might have been a lifesaving move. It's as if they and the series want her to die. Maggie has been astonishingly indestructible, and it takes a team effort of malice, hunger, and negligent friends to finally pour her into Sebastian's car. But with sensible average folk around, there is no way that the Collinses would have stayed in that house. I mean, it's Quentin, the kids, Barnabas, and Julia. Carolyn, too. That's only a double room at the Collinsport Inn and a couple of sleeping bags. It might be close quarters, but Gerard can have the house. Doesn't happen. In a vacuum of pragmatism, this is what we're left with, and it's intentional. Horror may be the ultimate expression of art because both are about stripping down the essentials until the only remaining choice exists by default.

The children fight inevitability and are victimized by it all at the same time that they symbolically enact it. (Kathy Cody's best acting on the show is her eerie voice work as the gloating voice of Carrie.) Another element that makes this Collinwood-not-Collinwood begins with David Henesy's narration. He's not supposed to be doing this, and his voice is not supposed to be that deep. He and Hallie even argue over whether or not she's a guest, and David gives her the bad news that she's become a lifer. So… is she the next Vicki or Carolyn? Yes, no, too young. All answers apply, ultimately making her another element that doesn't quite fit, and doesn't quite fit… on purpose. It keeps Collinwood alien to us. Because this upcoming trip is not about saving David or Collinwood. Whether he knows it or not, this trip will ultimately be about Barnabas saving himself.

Barnabas continues to wander through a liminal forest, and in the words of Michael Corleone, every time he thinks he's out, they pull him back in. 1897 seemed to be the forest, and 1970, home. It was a specific place to which he could return after Parallel Time, but nothing's the same when he does. The household is different. Even Julia's hair is different. The forest has followed him into a present that may be more unfamiliar than Parallel Time. By the time he returns home to 1971, Collinwood is finally the familiar same, but he is not. That's the irony, and it's not a nice one.

Is he being manipulated? We all are. Viewers and our sympathies. Heroes and their supposed true loves. 1092 is talking about this in loud silences and a final image both chilling and satirical when we realize we are in the dollhouse with them.

This episode hit the airwaves September 1, 1970.

EPISODE 1105

When Barnabas realizes that Maggie is bonded to another vampire, it's time for Willie to raise the stakes before she's gone for good. Willie: John Karlen. (Repeat; 30 min.)

Julia and Barnabas are again unable to protect Maggie from the other vampire, and thanks to Carolyn's mocking help, Willie finally finds her in the mausoleum, attacked again. They later track down the vampire's daytime resting place, and he and Julia are shocked at what they find.

Unthinkable and existential crimes and affronts to Collinwood!

If it existed. But does it? A Collinwood without Louis Edmonds or Joan Bennett is not exactly Collinwood, but has anyone noticed? It just kind of happens. The series lulls us into a presumptuous nonchalance, and when we finally call roll, it's far too late.

1105 brings us into the last five episodes of the prime and contemporary universe in which the series began. It was and is "home," and excluding a brief glimpse in 1198, this represents the beginning of our last and most apocalyptic visit. There is no sweet to the bitter, and if you're looking for sentiment or nostalgia look elsewhere. It's not a home, it's a house. Roger and Liz are gone, and we are a far cry from Roger's declaration to an earlier ghost that, "We'll be back!" Quentin comes and goes, primarily to betray everyone for a fellow, former phantom-out-of-time. Barnabas is compromised to strictly nocturnal operations. All three "residents" — Carolyn, David, and Hallie — are on the road to demonic corruption, with David and Hallie missing. What does that leave? Maggie? At last, even she lacks the wherewithal to defy the vampire's summons, if death doesn't claim her before undeath can. A surrogate guardian for the home, she's unable to guard even herself. I haven't seen Mrs. Johnson conscious lately. Willie, of course, is Willie. Stokes is busy fulfilling a prophecy that said he'd be nowhere near the joint when the chips were due. That leaves Julia as the last and only guardian of the house and what remains of the family. How did she get this assignment? And why should she be stuck with KP when there is not a single, sane, uncorrupted person in the house? When she escapes to 1840, it's not just to save her own life. It's an escape to life. Any life.

It's such a strange and terminal predicament for the ensemble of both actors and characters that makes Gerard's curse feel real. He's been destroying the house for months. It's only now, stepping back, that we actually notice how successful he's been. His work is done. The zombies are merely a flourish.

This is a tough, sad, obstinate storyline, and it defies efforts to love it. Gothic literature knits a strange glamor into its sense of decay, but the Ragnarök sequence doesn't. It's a very real death, and it doesn't even feel reversible with the mechanics the show has established. It's just quietly malignant, and it mirthlessly mocks our heroes. Barnabas loses Maggie to vampirism, which is bad enough, but it's not even HIS vampirism. He can't find or summon the other vampire or even guess its gender. Willie is equally incapable of protecting Maggie, finding her near where he initially found Barnabas, years before. Quentin? Seduced by one ghost and about to be assassinated by another, taunted as a villain he never was from a timeline he never knew. But we did. As Willie is charged with killing the vampire at the end, we realize how unlikely this is… and that it's just a salve. Like Iraq after 9/11, it's not even the primary problem. When the vampire slowly murdering Maggie

Evans is a mere distraction from the real crisis facing Collinwood, you are dealing with a helluva crisis. But what's the real crisis? Because Gerard is the easiest answer, and that elusiveness is both the sequence's strength and vulnerability.

This episode hit the airwaves September 18, 1970.

EPISODE 1106

When Julia and Willie open what might be the box for Barnabas' RealDoll, they discover the RealTruth, which may be a RealPain in the neck! Roxanne: Donna Wandrey. (Repeat; 30 min.)

Julia and Willie discover Roxanne's coffin. Barnabas' love for her prevents them from killing her. Barnabas traps her in the Old House, pursued by Sebastian, who later opens her coffin and aims a gun inside.

The show has seven months left.

A wildly successful storyline in 1897 was followed up by three storylines that command unfavorable comparison. A movie has been released, depicting most of these characters getting killed. They are no longer "just" cultural giants with symbolic weight. They are simply characters. Not icons. No matter how much the public adores them, they are just storytelling pawns for the producers. The show is still successful. It could be argued, though, that it has released just enough grasp on its identity that we can suddenly contemplate the world without it.

It's too late in the series for this, and because of that, it's all the more welcome. Here we are, in the midst of all of this Dark Shadow when... what should break out? Dark Shadows. It was a year ago that the show outgrew its habitat. Like almost any living thing, it had to. After incremental evolutions and explorations, the show found its apotheosis in 1897. And after exploring the wildest potentials of Cold War Gothic storytelling for four years and three different eras, few possibilities seemed left in the genre.

Besides, they had become their own genre. After four years and a very successful summer of learning to break the rules, they were now in a position to make the rules. So, why not cure Barnabas? Is there anything really left? And if you're going to cure Barnabas, you might as well give Quentin a happy ending also. Even though he's only been around for a bit, it seems like he's earned it. Besides, have we really had a leading man who wasn't also trying to kill Roger? Or kidnap Maggie? Or constantly avoid Willie's inquiries about why he has yet to make employee of the month when he is, in fact, the only employee?

So, for the prior year (more or less) the show has been basking in its own glow. Yes, let's have some Paul Stoddard. Heck, we can bring Paul Stoddard in and then turn around and kill him. Why not have a snake cult? It gives things a touch of super-spy panache. Heck, let's make a movie and send the rest of the cast into a parallel dimension. Let Thayer have that pencil-thin mustache he's always pining for.

And it was confident. And it was ambitious. And just very vaguely on the launching pad of desperate. And it is now so confident and ambitious that we career towards the apocalypse by default. Because what's left, really? If the show were a growing person, it has reached the dark and mordant introspection of early middle age. Gerard sits in the center of a postmodern, existential labyrinth, mocking the enlightenment and industrial revolution heroes with rumors of inevitable doom. It refuses to disclose its weapons, much less its terms of surrender. Why should it? It needs no weapons. There are no terms of surrender because there will be no surrender. Only complete annihilation.

Gloomy stuff. Compelling, but gloomy. Profound thinking usually goes there with enough self-actualization. After all, death and cancellation come for us all, even the undead. The show was drawn from some of the finest works of literature. If literature eventually follows the bleak-but- contemporary highway of modernism, so must Dark Shadows. And we've been trained to accept it over the past year and define Dark Shadows by this woeful Weltanschauung. So there he is. Sulking around Rose Cottage with its Weltanschauung hanging out. And then along comes an all-star tribute to Dark Shadows by Dark Shadows. Almost as if the writers were nostalgic for their salad days, when the biggest concerns revolved around life's simple pleasures, like a chained coffin containing one of your loved ones. You know, that special someone who may be up for a stake through the heart, or a lifetime of starving imprisonment with the symbol of a dispassionate God burning a hole through their chest, or maybe just a big, warm hug. It's that kind of episode. Beginning in a crypt with stake-wielding vampire hunters, it remains faithful to the only sets that may matter — the Old House Drawing Room with Capn' Matthew Morgan's Rubbermaid Big Max Love Dungeon behind the bookcase, and another suitably gothic setting where Roxanne's coffin has been waiting for this moment.

And of course, being Dark Shadows, that moment ends up being intentionally unintentionally riotous. Roxanne has been a vampire since 1840. So, for 130 years? Which is far longer than Barnabas has been a vampire. Taking into account elapsed time and all, Barnabas has only been a vampire for two or three years. You would think that she would've figured out someplace more secure to sleep it off. Julia and Willie might know one end of a stake from another, but they are not exactly the team that you call in to test an impenetrable security system. I doubt they could cut line at the Stake 'n' Ale salad bar.

It's hard to tell how many times Roxanne almost dies in this episode. Her coffin is opened constantly. And when it's not opened, there's somebody going in just to stand by it and think about opening it. But the same thing happened to Barnabas when Petofi had him as a prisoner. Captors were constantly opening it up, taking the cross off, letting them stretch, putting the cross back on, closing the lid, and then repeating the process all over again. No wonder Barnabas had to sleep in a coffin. He was exhausted. That wasn't dictated by the rules of the supernatural. It was a political statement to his captors.

If this is full of impossibly active characters who never quite appear. We've already talked about how exhausted Roxanne must be. But the really exhausted and insulted character Has to be Quentin. When Julia comes up with her big scheme to calm Barnabas by confronting him with absolute emotional chaos, she realizes that Willie Loomis isn't up for the job of catering and décor. So, completely off-stage, she sends for Quentin to help move the coffin. I'm sure he's thrilled. At this point, Quentin has so little to do that he's reduced to schlepping wildly heavy crates offstage. We assume it's by hand because I don't think Quentin is the station wagon type in that moment.

It's a teachable moment; check with Julia before giving Liz the keys to the forklift for some big date.

But amidst all of the nostalgia and silliness and morbid merriment, the old-school nature of the episode also serves an important purpose for the plot to come. Even though this is a new world of gods and monsters, so unlike the one just a year prior, it is still inhabited by the heroes who were shaped by that earlier age. And where does it all eventually go? Barnabas loses Angelique after discovering the unalloyed nature of his love. So, everything from there-back to here is a setup for that moment. In a startling fit of maturity, Barnabas muses that he truly is beyond Josette.

Why? Josette was just the most proximate cure to the underlying problem: loneliness. If the show is "about" Barnabas, which, let's not kid ourselves, it is, then his primary concern is the primary concern of the show. It's the most inconvenient of primary concerns. It's one that no one wants to hear about. Again, loneliness. I think this is what drives Barnabas. It rests balefully under the veneer of the pursuit of Josette. And its tendrils stretch across the storylines. The show begins with Elizabeth, whose loneliness is self-imposed, sending for an orphan to tutor a motherless child who, for all we know, has been making his own braunschweiger sandwiches for breakfast since he was four. The entire program deals with the lonely hangover of the fellowship party that ended a decade or two before the show even began.

Stake or seduce, Barnabas? The indecision he faces is emblematic of the entire program. Is Roxanne the ultimate companion, or is she the opportunity for ultimate redemption? Is she the only one who can truly understand the pain of his existence, is she just close enough to seem familiar, or does her ruthlessness demand elimination? Barnabas is paralyzed by these considerations. And it's an important opportunity to just pause for a moment.

It's only the smallest grand decision of his life.

This episode was broadcast Sept. 21, 1970.

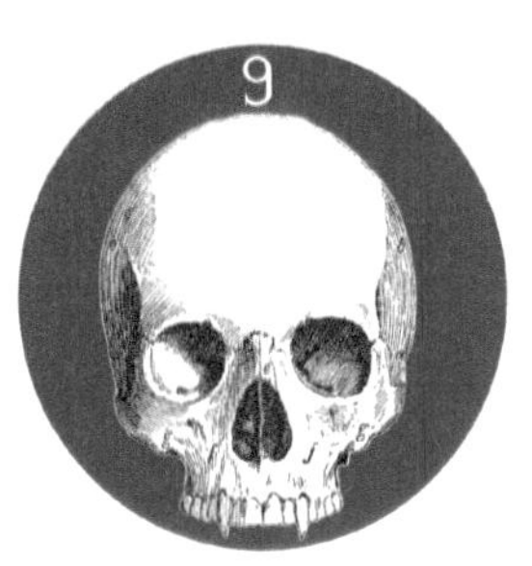

1840
Masters of Both
Worlds

"Night has fallen over the Great House of Collinwood..."

1840 is one of the most obscure storylines of *Dark Shadows* because it was kind of/sort of the end of the series as we know it for the main characters. For several years in the 1980s, I worked for a PBS affiliate that was showing *Dark Shadows*, and the rumor mill around the station stated that the show became increasingly expensive to broadcast via syndication as it went on. I guess the thinking was that viewers would get hooked and then they would have no choice but to pay a King Johnny ransom to satisfy them. Well, as far as we knew, no one was satisfied. I did not see these episodes until the mid-1990s on VHS. It is a strange and rambunctious and sometimes plodding storyline, And I think one of the things that distances it to this day is that none of its repercussions can be enjoyed in the future episodes. everything else gets its chance to influence later events. But not this. It also upsets the expected romantic fate of Barnabas by having him reveal that he's in love with Angelique. OK, OK I understand why some of you see this as a non sequitur.

Yes, the writers were making this up as they went along. However, once a text is finished, you have to look at it as one complete story. At that point, the methods of its construction are trivial. It could very well be that Shakespeare wrote Hamlet while standing on his head. Who cares? If you go back and watch the series with the secret of Barnabas's love in mind, that knowledge and your imagination will have you finding clues and evidence constantly. It becomes a more challenging story. It becomes a far more interesting story. And it becomes a story that doesn't just stop. It has a legitimate and beautifully painful ending.

EPISODE 1111

Julia responds to the need to pass for normal in 1840 by unleashing a blood-crazed monster she claims is her brother. Daniel: Louis Edmonds. (Repeat; 30 min.)

In 1840, Julia hatches a plan with Ben to pass as a Collins. She meets Daniel, the insane patriarch, and Gabriel, his disabled son. Gabriel may have evidence to her real identity via a stolen earring or he may choose to wear it to compliment his girlish bouffant. Julia goes to the mausoleum to unleash Barnabas, displaying the sound, evidence-based thinking that preceded her in the field of medicine.

1111 is a breathlessly dense episode, introducing (or reintroducing) audiences to scads of characters. Welcome to 1840 proper. It's a Dickensian time, and the coincidence of so many important characters being in a single Dark Shadows episode at once is, well, one worthy of Dickens. The writers have gotten almost too good at this by now. 1795 and 1897 felt as if they rationally meted out new casts of characters very few at a time. In this case, we meet or hear of nine or ten. It's almost dizzying. But above all else, it's brave. This is not an incipient universe, but one fully formed. They drop us off in the middle of it, send us a care package, and wish us the best.

It's easy to admire the guts behind this. What's not as easy is caring as much as we should. When you meet the characters just a few at a time, you have the luxury of building sympathies with each before the next round comes in. Well, by the time Flora and Gerard enter, I'm exhausted. On the surface, it's easy to conclude that the cast so far isn't particularly likable. Ben looks more grotesquely malignant than aged. It would be easy to appreciate Daniel more if he didn't introduce himself by confessing that he murdered his wife. The character of Gabriel is designed to be one of the villains of the series, and Christopher Pennock has yet to be given the opportunity to enhance him into a delightful one. Not only is Flora a gullible dingbat, she is executed with a voice that really drives the point home. (Note, Joan Bennett does a hell of a Tiny Tim impression.) We meet Gerard and hear him speak for the first time, but we already know where his character will wind up, so confirmation bias goes crazy as we look for him to slip up.

There's an interesting storytelling lesson here. When Barnabas goes back to deal with Quentin, we already know that the solution to the problem resides in solving the mystery of who Quentin was and how/why he died. While Gerard certainly is responsible for what happened in 1970, he still feels somewhat secondary to all of this.

Of course, the sympathetic character in the midst of this is Julia. She hasn't always been the easiest character to like, and her pluckiness here and strange optimism about releasing Barnabas lift her standing even more than seeing her battle zombies. Her first act in the episode is getting into a rumble with a walking, talking story theme. The aged and mentally bereft patriarch, Daniel, introduces himself by mistaking her for the wife he murdered, and tries to murder her all over again. As he does so, he begs to know how many times he will be confronted by this.

What a reflective statement by the franchise. Everything here has to do with sins of the past. Everything here deals with people sacrificed for reasons pertaining to love and the convenience of love. How many times does the show take us back, with the optimism that, if we can just go back far enough, to the right enough place, we can prevent even the need to make amends? In his madness, there is wisdom, and it could very well be that Daniel, the show's once and future child and patriarch is the ideal character to represent all of it. Played by both David Henesy and Louis Edmonds, Daniel is, at times, innocence, corruption, father, and son. He is both ends of the spectrum that we know too well, and he unites generations of both actors and characters under similar and disparate roofs.

Of course, we will learn that Gabriel is desperate for his approval. Even to the point of faking his own disability. And even to the point of murdering him to succeed him. Daniel is the ultimate Collins. In the fusion of generations and actors, he has no female equivalent. In a show with such a female heavy audience and female heavy ensemble, which begins with a female protagonist, the fact that the ultimate Collins is male is another quiet way that the show spreads focus and opportunities between the genders.

It is appropriate that Julia, vaguely androgynous herself, is our surrogate here. It's high time that Barnabas, her other half, who also has a blend of the complementary gender in his persona, arrives. They have a storyline to save.

This episode hit the airwaves September 28, 1970.

EPISODE 1113

Barnabas Collins decides that the only man who can help him avert the apocalypse is the last man he can trust: himself. Barnabas: Jonathan Frid. (Repeat; 30 min.)

Gerard thinks he has Julia by the short hairs when he dangles a newfangled earring in front of her as evidence that she comes from another time. Her explanation is credible enough to send Gerard away, leaving her time to conspire with Ben Stokes about recruiting Barnabas for the campaign. Ben finds Barnabas in the Old House, saying goodbye to Josette's portrait... and dominance over his future. As he reasons with the Vampire, the present day version of Barnabas consults with Ben's descendant. Surrounded by an insane Carolyn and a suicidal Quentin, Barnabas is compelled to use the I Ching wands to take the battle to 1840. He immediately encounters the vision of Julia's grave.

Dark Shadows is turning to its most forbidden topic: endings. The job of a soap is to perpetuate misery. It resolves one source only after it slides in another. But this phase of the show is replete with endings, conclusions and assorted apotheoses. We've seen Collinwood destroyed, and that's how the ending begins! How do you top that? That kind of question surges within 1113 with urgent power. It begins with fatalism and then asks, "Is that all you got?" This is the perverse optimism that you find only at funerals. Because when the universe falls apart, the only certainty is change.

With Barnabas, we even see double! The show continues its audacious presentation of parallel storylines — two different centuries with overlapping casts and one character appearing in both. The most unique acting challenge for Jonathan Frid is playing two different versions of Barnabas, both of whom have their counterparts in the relative future. And Dark Shadows is the only show where the future is 130 years in both directions. This storyline has a bad rap for being confusing. I suppose if you struggle to do things like drop pennies and straighten unknotted rope, you'll find this baffling. But if you can manage those arduous tasks, 1840 is a pleasure.

Barnabas Collins may be the long suffering and occasionally non-beating heart of Dark Shadows, but Julia

Hoffman is its soul. (Drop me a line if you can really explain the difference. But it sounds good.) Following her into 1840, it's clear how far she has come. She began as a conniving, intellectually ruthless, arrogant invader. If Collinwood tortures its beloved sons and daughters, you can imagine when an outsider puts it in a bad mood. Julia pays her dues. Now, she is on the other end of that process.

Her scene at the beginning of the episode is a well-earned tribute to smugness. She deflects Gerard's smarmy interrogation with a cool efficiency that borders on decadent relish. Julia knows that she could die at any point. She knows that she is far over her abundantly-coiffed head. Not only is she fearless, but she has learned to take pleasure in hoisting her enemies with extra petard. Supernatural bullies specialize in lording forbidden knowledge over the rest of us. As Julia frustrates their efforts, her sense of "take that" is not only admirable, it's infectious. Had Victoria Winters remained on the show, this is the main character we might have gotten. Although I doubt it. Julia's age, gumption, and guile are impossible to imagine with anyone else. We are seeing Dan Curtis's dream, after all. Just by way of the real world.

Meanwhile, Barnabas finally takes down the painting of Josette. After all, she let go of him. And she has given him the permission to move on. That's on her end; this is a matter of his own choice. It involves the sort of courage that people can only show when they are too close a tragedy. There is a grace period in the time immediately following a tragedy before its burdens become a part of us. Oddly, decommissioning Josette is a job that could only be accomplished by the 1840 version of Barnabas… and the 1970 version of Barnabas. Anything in between had had just enough time to become obsessed with his loss, but not enough experience to contemplate life without it.

Barnabas is speaking for himself and the writers when he boasts, "the word safe has no meaning for me."

It's an extraordinary point of freedom... everything is possible because nothing is possible. It's the same kind of desperate bravery shown by the producers as they introduce a backward echo of Pansy Faye, with the nobler ancestor, Leticia Faye. It's a character whose existence has no practical sense but has such a poetic ring of truth that pedantic cavils are undone before they can be spoken. Leticia is there because it's the most interesting continuing character that Nancy Barrett crafted, and because Nancy Barrett intrinsically belongs at Collinwood as its neurotic and self-punishing ray of light. And who has the time to wallow in trivia when they have a 50-year-old soap opera to write about? One of the story's primary themes is the decay of our aspirations over time. The introduction of Leticia manages to accomplish this... backward. Somehow, Leticia is an ancestor of Pansy. And somehow, and it may just be the semiotic impact of a more natural hair color, Leticia feels a little more humane and relatable.

And she's not the only double in the episode. Leticia is confident in her use of the supernatural. But Nancy Barrett also plays the vaguely psychic Carolyn in 1113. Her encounter with the paranormal has driven her quite mad, pitting the two characters against each other. Similarly, we have a scene in 1840 where Ben Stokes reasons with his former master to show courage and trust. This transitions to a scene over a century later, in the same house, where Elliot Stokes shows a newly dawning sense of hesitation and Barnabas must rally him into action.

Moments before, the 1970 Barnabas is introduced under a looming portrait of himself from haughtier and happier days. He is attached to his chair, Hamleting himself to the point that a skull may appear in his palm at any moment.

Barnabas is either on the verge of implosion or explosion. He seethes with Stokes' report on the funerals for Carrie, Daphne, Elizabeth, and the assassinated future of the Collins family, David. These are unthinkably bold and permanent strokes of storytelling, and they engage Barnabas as they engage us. He has spent his second and third lives doubting his place in the future, and it has suddenly passed him by.

It is in this moment that Barnabas truly appreciates the ability that makes him unique. He alone can use the curse of immortality to travel within his own lifespan in either direction.

For the trip to 1897, this discovery was an accident. Now, its invocation is a mandate.

Barnabas rallies to a rare moment of decisive and ferocious action at the thought. He can only be haunted by the past for so long. Within the space of just a few lines, this gentleman of the past again becomes the last best hope for the future. A year ago, this might have been executed with a sense of insouciant elan worthy of Alexander Dumas. Frid avoids letting any twinkle spark his eye. Too many people have died. Too many regrets filled the ledger. Yes, he is answering the call to adventure, but it is with gravitas and respect. And yet again, the series reinvents itself.

Too often, he is written off as a villain literally defanged after his first few months. I will admit, he spends a frustrating amount of time doubting his next move. But even when Barnabas is at his most mournfully indecisive, he is, to me, the Great Man. It's in scenes like these, today, that we see why. In fact, those other moments of ethical denial and over-intellectualized paralysis are what make episodes like 1113 such a joy.

And the universe surrounding him seems to be in agreement. Even Elliot argues with him about the risks of such a journey, Carolyn glides downstairs for a late afternoon cocktail and yet another nervous breakdown as Quentin tries to hang himself upstairs. As if to prove Barnabas' point. Once Barnabas tries a tentative trance, the first thing he sees is Julia Hoffman's tombstone from 1840. A call to adventure, indeed.

And you wanted to talk about risk, Professor Stokes? Let's talk about risk. Risk may be James T. Kirk's business. But for Barnabas Collins, it is his very life.

And I can say the same for Dan Curtis.

This episode was broadcast September 30, 1970.

EPISODE 1118

Will Gerard's plans for dominion over Collinwood change when he meets its long-sleeping guardian? Barnabas: Jonathan Frid. (Repeat; 30 min.)

Barnabas establishes a relationship with Daniel as he challenges the story of Quentin's drowning. Meanwhile, Judah Zachery attacks Ben Stokes.

It's like the past two years or so never happened, and that's a surprisingly good thing. It's good because, for all of the expanded mythos and wonder brought by Nicholas, Quentin, and Count Petofi, we've spent the past couple of years expanding the mythos without always connecting it. It's tough to realize until you see Daniel Collins and Ben Stokes ruminating about the doomed nature of the family as a primal force of nature, Mr. Beale. Even though Daniel is a different actor (and he really isn't, in a cosmic sense) and Ben's face is an unrecognizable topography of the malignant, we know we're home. Beyond Liz and Roger seething over brandy and Things Unsaid, this is home. And when we hear them — these heralds and descendants of Elder Gods like Joshua and Naomi — speak of the Bedford Murders, we take it seriously. It's akin to hearing parents talk about some heretofore-unmentioned childhood disease that almost got us before we could understand what it meant to be sick.

1840 is just close enough to home, and by that, I think we all know I mean 1795, that its tarnish hurts more than the strangeness of 1897. When Louis Edmonds' Daniel shows lucidity, our hearts soar as profoundly as they crash when he descends into babble. In this episode, his embrace of Barnabas and his insistence that he take the Old House, both save time and ring with a rightness that makes him one with the viewers. It's about effin' time, and it's what we would do, too. After all, who is Daniel but the first of the first generation of kids to grow up watching Dark Shadows? That strange energy resonates through the character and right at the viewers. At last, Barnabas is not a stranger. Is Daniel crazed enough to see him as safe or sane enough not to listen to his inner child whispering murmurs of danger? Who cares? Barnabas is back in business with considerably less situational guano to wade through.

Early in the episode, Ben correctly notes that Barnabas isn't the same man that he was just scant moments before. The transformation from beleaguered baddie to decisive hero is a tribute, naturally, to Jonathan Frid and the writers. But it's also a reason to reflect on the uniqueness and relative longevity of the show. These are vastly different characters and completely, understandably the same man. (Just like Daniel.)

Barnabas has ascended twice, now. If his seizure of the heroic mantle didn't grab us the first time, in the choices he makes regarding Eric Lang and Nicholas Blair, then we cannot help but cheer him on now as he fully rebounds from his fall with the Leviathans and failures in Ragnarök. 1897 was a not a fluke, nor was it fantasy roleplay. You can bet your Lindens that it was Barnabas's training ground, and it was proof to him that just as no time is truly his, all times are truly his, as well. His comfort with command and decisive problem- solving speaks to the best that he will be — all of who he was in 1897 with the mellowed knowledge of how rare and precious that status is.

Like Freder in Metropolis, Barnabas is a protagonist somewhere between the hands and the mind. Whenever either is the solution, he and we are quietly pleased, because we didn't know he had it in him. He's smart, but he's no Nicholas Blair. And he's strong, but few (save fireplace poker-bending Eliot Stokes) are stronger than Adam. It's fitting that the Last Son of Collinwood appears in the same episode with his match, Judah Zachery, a being of — literally — pure mind. It's a tribute to the alien intensity of actor Michael McGuire that Zachery is a character of such credible opposites. There's blazing-eyed malevolence mixed with a strange, fearful sense of being lost that I would imagine accompanies being a nearly omnipotent, disembodied head in a glass box.

All kidding aside, after the foes Barnabas has bested, it's appropriate that he stare down, not just one from the past, but of all pasts. His nemesis is the embodiment of the abstract. Defeating him will require not just Barnabas's wit and physical prowess, but the exploration of the inhuman heart. He cannot solve Judah Zachery while being the kind of binary thinker that created Judah Zachery. Barnabas has reformed morally.

1840 will require him to go further. The first order of business is to force him to do so without Ben Stokes.

You can't go home again. Home always changes. Yet it might be a place that forces you to change with it.

This episode was broadcast October 7, 1970.

EPISODE 1124

Can Barnabas evade the son of the man he murdered before Judah Zachery claims another life? Lamar Trask: Jerry Lacy. (Repeat; 30 min.)

Armed with a letter disclosing the potential true identity of Barnabas Collins, Lamar visits Collinwood to force the brash Englishman's hand. Meanwhile, at Rose Cottage, a man once possessed by the head of Judah Zachery confronts a haunted Desmond, dying in the process.

Maybe today this isn't the Dark Shadows Daybook. It might be the Trask House Daybook. Because I think we've stumbled into another series. What a marvelous episode that charges out of the gate, giving us, just in the opening narration, an absolute banquet of intrigue, occult weirdness, and reasons to keep watching. The episode absolutely delivers, with actors like John Karlen and Nancy Barrett still finding new colors in their performances and a script that has genuine intrigue and dread. If you've seen the rest of the series, parts of it may feel familiar. And? Bolero quickly familiarizes us with itself, and that's the point. It's a burgeoning experience that intentionally maintains a simplicity that reveals a mounting complexity and grandeur, each go-round surprising us with what it contained all along. Yes, Bolero. But with Donna Wandrey instead of Bo Derek, and that's a pretty good trade. After all, Donna Wandrey never said, "They're washing me like a horse," while expecting to be taken seriously in subsequent features. Only Thayer David could pull that off.

Even though it's at the start of the much-maligned 1840 storyline, this is a solidly rambunctious way to introduce someone to the series. When it begins, Desmond is possessed by a haunted head, Quentin has drawn the Death card in a tarot deck, we find out that Kate Jackson is there to murder Quentin, and Barnabas is doing everything he can to win the current woman of his dreams away from, well, himself. He's always had to live down his nocturnal activities, but this is the most extreme case yet, as he tries to make up for the cad, he was just a few days and yet hundreds of years ago. Kind of. Compounded. That's really before any dialogue starts. What a welcome to Collinwood! Considering what people have to wade through in the first episodes of the show just to get to the whole vampire part, this is like pressing the accelerator on a McLaren. And then you kill off Abe Vigoda. Nothing against Abe, but if it worked for Coppola, it could work for Curtis. Abe, it's just business.

However, wedged in between that terrific opening and a climax where supernatural forces victimize Vigoda (and feel free to go back and read that phrase as many times as you want), we are actually stepping into a parallel universe. Well, kind of, and more interestingly than we ever did with parallel time. Because for just a moment, we step into the sister series of Dark Shadows.

It's the series that never got made, but the series that makes all the sense in the world. Its star? Jerry Lacy.

Is he the villain? Yeah, if you're a Collins. But that's a particularly pretzeled moral bar. Take a step back. Get an objective view of the ethical landscape that mercifully vanishes at Widow's Hill. We take a degree of heroism for granted on the show because vampires are cool, and we like Jonathan Frid. It's easy to forget that these are pretty reprehensible people. Is there an alternative? Maybe for a blip in 1840: The House of Trask. For a period, they are the other white meat of prominent Collinsport families. Yes, they are working class, and, yes, they haven't been there as long, and no, they don't stay as long, but they nevertheless have a place. And you could very easily make a multi-generational supernatural TV series just based on that dynasty.

One of the things that brings this into focus is the stunning performance of Jerry Lacy, an actor so good that we take him for granted. It can be a curse of good actors because they make it look so effortless. In 1124, Lacy could easily win a bet on who the dashing and dark romantic lead really is. He is just as intense, unpredictable, and determined as any vampire. And perhaps as commandingly seductive. When he is alone with the women in the episode, he summons up a surprisingly deep well of passionate intensity. Yes, judgmental, but not without a powerful sense of desire.

As he draws Leticia Faye into using her psychic abilities for his own ends, he shows a new and powerful side to the Trask archetype. For once, nothing is forbidden to him by the cloth. Poor Barnabas only comes back into the drawing room to save his own keister, seconds from being outed. With Lacy in brief control of the drama, Jonathan Frid plays the weasel pedal to an extent that even outshines the best of John Karlen. As hard as he possibly can. It's a delight, and he continues when he gets back home. Like a cartoon character, Trask has let himself in there, also, and is so calm and collected, I am surprised he's not smoking Barnabas's pipe and correcting his crossword puzzle.

Briefly, Trask the hero of a different show has somehow wandered into a program where the victors of history have written him and his family as the bad guys. His father was a badass witch hunter, reportedly tortured and starved to death when he dared to pursue the servants, lovers, and associates of a vengeful and aristocratic vampire. He never knew the old man, but he certainly knows of his legend and suffered his absence. Fascinated with the strange dance of life and death, unable to afford medical school, Lamar Trask has clearly studied voraciously. He's well-versed in the law, of course. A historic trial cost his father his future. Even in 1840, the only way to learn about bodies and anatomy, short of becoming a music hall entertainer, was to become a mortician.

Makes you think. Maybe he didn't get into that line because he's creepy. He might have followed that pursuit for entirely logical reasons. The Collins family is a menace! Look at the Collinses that he has to deal with. There's Gabriel, who is not exactly the life of the party. Then you have Quentin and Desmond, who have the incredibly poor judgment to do things like build unguarded, unstable time portals, become best friends with Gerard Stiles, and consider the severed head of a nefarious occultist to be a great gift for his brother.

The whole town loses either way there. If you think it's the perfect gift, you're a danger to the entire town. If Flora is so nutty that it IS the perfect gift, you're a danger to the entire Western Hemisphere. As a warmup. Yeah, these are the normative characters. These are the people we are supposed to trust. Topping it, Trask has a letter from his father absolutely outing what went on shortly before his mysterious death, doing so with eerie specificity. And who shows up? The "identical son" of his father's killer, wielding ungodly social power and wealth. A man who potentially. has the powers of hell at his fingertips. And he's suddenly on a first-name basis with your former Lois Lane.

Bolero again. But not just ascending. By this point, it's inverting and twisting like a trapeze artist determined to see how far their bravery and recklessness can take their art. In 1840, the show is still in midair, and maybe that's where it remained. Of course, the eventual fact that Lamar is a ruthless and unethical bigot has to crash the party, taking Dark Shadows back to reality, which is not only where it belongs, but what it defines.

This episode was broadcast October 15, 1970.

EPISODE 1149

Barnabas is none too pleased when he discovers that Roxanne has put Trask under her vampiric spell, but will she get the point before daybreak? Randall Drew: Gene Lindsey. (Repeat; 30 min.)

Roxanne attacks Lamar Trask, putting him in her thrall, but Barnabas and Randall rescue him before contemplating Roxanne's destruction.

As Tom Jennings learned, there's nothing like being a vampire who is hunted by another vampire to really ruin your day, even if your day is at night. That Barnabas is on the hunt to undo Roxanne is both therapeutic and painful, like a holodeck psychodrama. Symbiotically so. Roxanne is the result of his actions of the past and the present. The act of discovering and hunting her is an exorcism as much as anything. She actually is the Josette who rose as a vampire and is yet another failed love interest, doomed more by bad luck and being in the wrong place at the wrong time than by conscious action. Of course, the fact that she gets to give Trask a little taste of life on the other side of the cemetery wall is a bonus that saves Barnabas the trouble of doing so himself. And of course, the situation is made further therapeutic by the fact that he simply gets to set up her death and leave it to Randall, so his hands stay relatively clean. She stands as a sad reminder of his toxicity more than as a foe, tying the inexplicable loss of Parallel Time's happiness to the mess in which he's again found himself. Still, as Barnabas engineers her death, we know that 1840 is headed into its final act.

Of course, it's easy to speculate that, had Roxanne remained necrotically alive and victimizing Trask, she might have taken the eventual blame for all of the bizarre activity at Collinwood, thus saving everyone the trouble of the trial and perhaps even preventing Trask from assassinating Angelique. But no. She may be therapeutic, but she's no Dr. Sidney Freedman, just a bitter reminder both of what Barnabas is trying to escape and what he'll never have. We once again learn the lesson Dark Shadows frequently extols, namely that taking responsibility for your actions is a good idea only in the abstract. Sometimes, it magnifies the consequences even as it vaguely delays them. In the sixties, life was easy; when in doubt, blame Willie Loomis. To revert to the class structure so dear to the Weltanschauung of Barnabas? That is Willie's proper role in life and the proud station into which he was born. But it's 1840. In his absence, I guess he could blame Laszlo, but that fez brands him as even more ineffectual than Aristide.

Gene Lindsay is headed towards his final performance, and his appearance as Randall Drew is one of the show's most curious anomalies on a strange checklist. An important character with vital ties to other characters, leading man appeal, and the stalwart, Dan Curtis look. Giving him copious screen time and opportunities to take story-changing action only to dump him after five episodes? Rather than seem like a waste, this seems almost like a luxurious creative indulgence. The show is so awash in ideas that they can afford to use an actor and pivotal character like that in even a small part. He feels like someone destined for bigger things, and his quick departure is a marvelous portent of how lethal this storyline can get.

1840 returns several times to Dark Shadows' most familiar theme — "Strangers at Collinwood" — but unlike other storylines, I think the strangers outnumber the residents. They all create a sense that Collinwood exists in a context of a larger world, and the benevolent, bland Randall Drew is the storyline's best attempt to suggest that not every visitor to Collinwood is a vampire, alluring witch, or severed head in a box. There are normal people out there, too, and they serve as a pleasant reminder of the peaceful life for which our characters strive. It may be boring, but as fans of Star Trek: The Motion Picture will tell you, sometimes boring can be nice.

This episode was broadcast November 20, 1970.

EPISODE 1165

Tad finds out that justice can be a mother when Samantha performs her wifely duty of trying to get her husband beheaded. Tad: David Henesy. (Repeat; 30 min.)

Even though the county prosecutor quits his job over the inanity of Quentin's trial, the figures of Official Justice insist it goes forward anyway. When he's replaced by someone played by Humbert Allen Astredo, Quentin knows it will not go well. Meanwhile, although Tad begs his mother to testify on Quentin's behalf, she instead takes the stand against him. Quentin responds by sitting around and pretending not to notice how handsome everyone thinks he is.

It's David Henesy's last day on the program. It's a sad graduation. It's a quiet graduation. It's the kind of graduation that means a lot more to the adults than to the people actually going through it. Like all graduations, I guess. It's hard to tell whether or not they intended this to be his last appearance. He was at an awkward age for the program. You couldn't get away with any of the juvenile plots of him doing something out of naïveté. Yes, he could be turned into a delinquent, but that's a move the show might not be ready for. Even in the world of David Cassidy and

Bobby Sherman, he's not quite old enough to be an official teen idol without it feeling just a little bit creepy. All of this... packed into someone of middle teenage vintage who nevertheless has a voice deeper than Brock Peters.

His farewell to the program consists of one scene, and it shows the influence that Tad should have on his world. With his father accused of witchcraft, Ted expects his mother to testify on her husband's behalf. Virginia Vestoff does a wonderful job trying to bend and weave around Tad's expectations, preparing herself to survive whatever kind of confrontation will follow whatever stunt she pulls on the stand.

Although no relationship in life improves after the first date, it is the last conversation that permanently frames us with each other. Given that these characters, via specific actors, turn up over and over and over again in era after era, it's pointless (in some regards) to see them as anything other than one figure with many masks. All of the David Hennessy characters might as well be just one David Hennessy character.

And if we look at it that way, what do we learn from this?

Well, for one thing, this character was much better at talking people into things back when he decided the rules were meant to be broken. Like Britannicus in I Claudius, I feel like he's become obsessed with "putting on his manly gown," maybe because he doesn't wanna wind up mistaken for Laszlo. Either way, he may be becoming all leading man (at least on the chalkboard in his dressing room), but his decision to play it straight comes at the cost not only of his humor but his overall cleverness. As is reflective of youth culture at the time, if he were any more painfully earnest, we would only see him crying an Iron Eyes Codependent mono-tear over the river of deceit and betrayal that runs through Collinwood.

So he's growing up. That's a bookend. He's decided to take life seriously. That's a bookend. And he is desperate to stand up for his father, who is getting railroaded on false charges. It feels like he has earned the right to do this. "He" began as a character all too eager to see his father railroaded over allegations the paternoster projected onto, well, who knows? Maybe his other dad. I think we've all had those thoughts. Whether he's doing it for reasons of malice, reasons of justice, reasons of love, or as a five-dollar menu combo of lovingly malicious justice, the David Henesy character begins and ends as someone trying to align his father's legal standing with reality. And it's refreshingly uncynical that he should go from a boy trying to get a guilty father convicted (or at least in hot water) to a kid trying to get his father out. Of course, the two fathers are vastly different. The primary similarity is that the mothers are either physically or emotionally absent, and neither have his best interest at heart. But he is the only person at Collinwood who has yet to see family as more of a mess than a bastion, and so he sticks by the institution with admirable loyalty.

And Samantha does get up on the stand. Of course, she does the opposite of what Tad wanted her to do. She's ready to betray Quentin with zesty abandon. But The Henesy's not around for that. It's almost as if this last blast of optimism collides head-on with one final betrayal from an untrustworthy mother. And perhaps that's all that the David Henesy figure can take. He disappears after that. The message? Very few parents are what they appear to be. Especially mothers. Eventually, that destroys the child within.

Dark Shadows teaches its lessons in cycles. Moral development in Collinsport is not a straight line. It's a corkscrew, both moving forward while covering the same ground over and over again. The sometimes surrogate mother figures in this character's life have been fire demons, completely absent, suicidal alcoholics, reanimated occultists, and at last, an untrustworthy shrew. As much as the show is meant for women, the female figures that David encounters, no matter the name, have stunningly little to recommend them. Although Victoria is hired to be his companion, she, like all adults, becomes enraptured by events that pre-date David. In that case, for nearly two centuries. Who can compete with that? Carolyn is likewise lost in a hopelessly lost romantic union, which generally makes her lousy conversation. Liz is obsessed with death whenever Joan Bennett wants a vacation. And Maggie is at Windcliff. So much for female nurture in Collinsport.

Fortunately, for someone with a sniveling, cowardly, alcoholic louse of a father (at least for the first year or so), David finds his modeling and nurturing in the men in his life. At various times, Barnabas, Quentin, and Tom Jennings all follow in Burke Devlin's footsteps to provide David with good advice and understanding moral support. At a time when most male relationships on television were based on macho buffoonery, this is revolutionary and refreshing. If you could take anything away from the David Henesy character, it's that three uncles can make a hell of a mother.

This episode was broadcast Dec. 11, 1970.

EPISODE 1169

When Angelique declares her love for Barnabas and lifts his curse, Judah realizes that the former vampire's human side is a dangerous place to be. Judah Zachery: James Storm. (Repeat; 30 min.)

Barnabas interrupts Gerard's daytime quest for his coffin by appearing quite human, having been made so by a contrite Angelique. Meanwhile, as Angelique reveals her history as Miranda Duval, Gabriel is haunted by the ghost of his murdered father and attempts to kill Gerard. Everything has to grow up.

It would have been just as school was letting out for the holidays. Kids were three years older than they were when they spent their first (significant) DS Christmas break in 1795. I know that the show wasn't expressly aimed at them, but, well, it was, anyway. Sam Hall was the father of a twelve-year-old boy, and thus, was not only aware of their evolving sensibilities, but of their schedules, as well. School was letting out. Although kids were home all the time, they also had more things bidding for that time. The show would kick it up accordingly. 1795 existed to show the knotty nature of pursuing passion's industry. It's appropriately two- dimensional for kids first learning about the basics of new love, infidelity, and the occult. Three years later, the lessons of ep. 1169 are far more nuanced, dealing with last loves, true loves, and a love so enduring that it grows past romance and into actual respect, affection, and admiration.

It's my understanding that the ratings were not as problematic at this time as history later implied. Still, Dan was increasingly restless, they had a star who was desperate to play anything other than the show's sensation, and not being a genre writer, Sam Hall himself was growing exhausted and bereft of fresh ideas. It's a natural time to start asking where this is all going. Dark Shadows was not a sustainable organism because of its very strength... the wild ideas that sparked the story and the vast number of episodes they had to enliven. While that may seem kind of sad, it makes it the Roy Batty of daytime TV, finding a life with shape and meaning because of its limited lifespan. Other soaps may have memorable storylines and characters, but are they a memorable story? It's impossible. But as unwieldy as Dark Shadows seems to be, there is a story within it. Like the Garden of Earthly Delights, it may be a massively complicated and surreal mess, but there's a frame, and if we step back far enough, it's all there to be seen at once.

1168 makes us acutely aware of that. As a piece of dramatic structure, it suffers from the endemic curse of its medium: the most vital moments are in the first act. Why? Today's first act is actually the resolution of yesterday's climax. So often with Dark Shadows, the episode begins with yesterday's crescendo, but unlike the countless other entries in the saga, it does more than pad the running time until setting up the next episode's big beginning. Hall is cleaning house, taking chances, unwrapping surprises, and, seemingly, hanging out with dear friends he knows are going away.

So, if they are going away, what can he do for them? How can he thank them? You know, "them" being not only the characters, but the actors who were his inevitable collaborators.

Let's start with James Storm, who has the opportunity to delve ever deeper into the character of Judah Zachery. Zachery, at this point, is so close to victory that he doesn't seem to care. Storm has enjoyed one of the show's rarest delights as he subverts one deceitful character for another entirely different deceitful character, but never really taking the spotlight as he should. He's competing for airtime with the program's most saturated and robustly charismatic male ensembles. Given that, he's practically Elvis, and the field of near-metadrama is his '68 Comeback Special.

How many layers? We have Sam Hall writing for James Storm playing Judah Zachery possessing Ivan Miller pretending to be Gerard Stiles. That's not confusing. It unrolls at a stately pace. Rather, it's generous. Storm is so nimble and meticulous in his performance; you'd think it would turn clockwork. No. His singular magic is to fuse that almost pointillist precision of thought and language with the Halloween-night joy of simply performing. And he's in marvelous company because Christopher Pennock is allowed dazzling range here as a Gabriel pushed to the edge. Planning, calculating, and swearing vengeance, he's a murderer trying to shift the blame onto Gerard. And from a certain point of view, he's correct. But like a twisted riff on Hamlet, he's tortured by the ghost of the father he murdered, and this spectral patriarch may not be omniscient. He's still there to take it out only on Gabriel, and you would think that, in death, he would see the puppet strings of both Gerard and Judah, at the very least spreading the blame. But Daniel seems myopic to this, and the frenzy of ghostly guilt and greed seems to galvanize Gabriel (hang on, let me catch my breath) into taking his first actions to preserve the Collins legacy. In Dark Shadows, you don't even bother to hope that your ancestors will go to a better place. You just double it on the pass line and pray they didn't see what you did.

On the blueprints, the dullest and most thankless part on the show had to go to Grayson Hall, who's not crazy, supernatural, newly human, possessed, nor haunted. Her edge comes from the fact that Sam had to sleep sometime, and if he thought he was going to turn her into a wandering sounding board for exposition, he'd better sleep lightly. Having only guts, common sense, and enough experience to know that Blairs and Petofis come and Blairs and Petofis go, she's one of us looking in. Judah doesn't stand a chance.

In her attempts to reason with Barnabas, we see each appreciating and suffering the lack of what defines the other. Julia is memory. Fact. Common sense. Barnabas is a creature high on the fumes of pure relief and affection. Is it possible that Angelique is staging all of this for a royal screw worthy of Wile E. Coyote? Yeah. But… you know… it's also possible that she's sincere. We have no evidence. So, yeah, she did this out of some newfound goodness in her heart. It's possible. What? Stop lookin' at me like that. It is. And as it turns out, I'm right.

Lara Parker plays the dishwater-dull role of Proving She's Earnest and then Giving History Lessons. That kind of goody-goody nonsense and trip-down-memory-lane-ing is deadly for actors. However, these are also profound turning points for the character. Someone who's lived only lies — down to her very name — or centuries is changing the dance. That's a powerful lesson, and Parker plays it with a fierceness that communicates the absolute necessity of compassion and honesty. She's tried everything else. If 1840 is anything, it's a woman's attempt to protect the man she loves from the machinations of a deranged ex-boyfriend. From the implications she drops about Judah, it's clear he was a love of her past. How different he was from Barnabas, and perhaps that's the point.

And this positions our craggy, hand-wringing hero to have moments in the sun at last… again. We see him through the eyes of Julia and Angelique as everyone tries to reconcile that, yes, we have the capacity for change. Even the worst of us. Jonathan Frid, a man who, three years prior, was damnably uneasy playing youthful innocence, now portrays the same man with ease. It's an innocence that's organic. It comes from knowing how complicated humans will make the world, and what a relief it is when they drop the act. Innocence like Barnabas's doesn't come from a lack of experience. It comes from seeing how little can actually come from it. And relishing pulling the rug from beneath Gerard? As well as showing off his Mrs. Peel? It's been a long time coming.

This is all in 24 minutes, and that just begins the goodbye.

This was broadcast December 17, 1970.

In rereading this, The importance of cycles to DS is the stand- out concept. Yes, OK, the show repeats itself. These were not horror writers and it could be argued that Dark Shadows, while containing elements of horror, was not a horror show. My best friend in the analysis of the show has been the habit to look at an ostensible flaw and ask if it is actually an advantage. Repetition is a good example of that. Is it repetition or is it reiteration? One tool in education is an acronym called ROPES. It stands for "review, overview, present, exercise, and summarize." And how many times does Hamlet doubt himself, fumbling around issues of confidence long after the audience has made up its mind? How many songs and pieces of music revive pieces of melody as they push forward?

In its practice of repeating itself, Dark Shadows clues in on a vital paradigm for looking at life. We tend to look at progress as an arrow, flying ever forward. But what if it is not an arrow? What if it is not a straight line? Yes, it technically is moving forward. Check. But what if it's a corkscrew? I've probably used the analogy before, but as we near the end of the show, it's important to, yes, repeat. Technically progress is linear, but it often has to revisit the same lessons to see how experience changes our approach to it. To look at Dark Shadows and see only the internal similarities is to willfully miss the point. Instead, ask yourself what's different. It's a scary question because it reflects back on us. It challenges us to ask what we have changed. As I get older, it's easier and Easier to Distract myself By complaining about meeting the new boss, same as the old boss. Instead, we should take repetition as a given. The only thing that should not be repeated is how we behave given that vast experience. If you watch Barnabas and Angelique, those changes are the essence of their drama.

EPISODE 1186

Just when you thought it was safe to go back to the east wing, Parallel Time is here to stay. But will Daphne go with it? Morgan Collins: Keith Prentice. (Repeat; 30 min.)

Quentin is sentenced to a beheading and denied an appeal as Barnabas schemes for a new plan of action. Meanwhile, Gabriel overhears Edith and Gerard in the throes of passion and subsequently kills her. Daphne stumbles onto the Parallel Time room where her double confronts a sister, Catherine, who is ambiguous over a marriage proposal from Morgan Collins. She is still in love with a prior flame.

The future coughs significantly in the wings as 1840 begins fumbling for its boarding pass, and the transition is a complex, rich delight. It's easily the most nuanced storyline transition of any on the show. It has become a huge universe, and a "transish" should not be a tidy thing.

1186 is typical of the 1840 storyline. It packs in all of the thematic and ritualistic good stuff we look for in DS and skips the repetitive running-in-place that so often turns off new viewers. I know, because I watched it with someone who had only passing familiarity with the program, and it kept his attention on more than a polite level. In one episode, we have…

- The results of a witch trial, where the real world contends with the supernatural, and vice-versa.
- The remorse from one friend toward a troubled other, defying expectation and ending with threats over the stewardship of Collinwood.
- The revelation of romance within. Quentin's Theme as ghostly bait.
- A seemingly disabled man stands and kills his wife.
- Someone ventures near Parallel Time.

It's an almost dizzyingly dense combination of show elements. Are the writers getting desperate or are they just tired of ploddingly plotting at the strangely arrested pace demanded by the medium? It's cosmically irrelevant. By this point, Dark Shadows has become its own medium and it is finding a tempo commensurate with the intelligence of its audience. Hey, you guys… the ones complaining that we suddenly have to tune in for every episode? Yeah, please go watch General Hospital or something. The rest of us like tuning in for every episode, and now we get even more great stuff per installment.

It's a brisk, witty, suspenseful installment full of satisfying moments and strange wonder. Anything that begins with the threat of a beheading can't be all bad, and the surrounding treatment of government bureaucracy should please anyone in the jaws of a mindless machine. When Barnabas appeals the impending separation of Quentin and Head, he's told that, since there's no precedent for that kind of crime & punishment, there's no precedent for appeal. It's reasoning that's delivered with all of the confidence we expect from a bureaucrat who has no idea what's going on, and who cares even less if you know it. With a week before the inevitability of death and axes, you'd think that Barnabas might want to, you know, send to Boston for a real lawyer, but he's too busy working himself up to more harebrained schemes. What? We'll have to find out.

This is an intensely head-oriented storyline, and as we see Gerard in vague remorse for Quentin, it could be that it's both genuine and strategic. I never really know how much of what we see at this point is Gerard and how much is Judah Zachery, and I like to believe that it's far more of the latter. Meanwhile, Christopher Pennock, perennial hero of the Daybook, knows that Gabriel is going into the windup for his exit and is relishing it. Gabriel may be the most dynamic and unpredictable limited-lifespan character on the show, and after brief, saving salvos of help and wit, he's going for the Gloucester award with gusto. It's a shame to see Terry Crawford go since Edith is the opposite of the simp that was Beth, but what an exit. 1840 admirably mixes the supernatural monsters with the real. The buildup of Gabriel in the wheelchair is suspenseful enough that a double dip of rise-and-kill is completely welcome, and Pennock's towering height adds to the menace.

Speaking of double dips, it's back to Parallel Time. Has Dark Shadows finally admitted that it works best as a period piece? With the exception of about 1710-1760, 1860, and 1920-1940, Dark Shadows has explored its timeline thoroughly, and even the treat of visiting one of those periods would be a challenge given the strictures of the mythos (not that it ever stopped the writers before). At this point, the only way forward is sideways, and the introduction of Morgan Collins and a mysterious "other man" expands the DSU and harkens back to its sudsy origins. Morgan is in the classic mold of the Dan Curtis tall-dark-and-baritone leading man, who sets up a great bait-and-switch when Bramwell enters the picture. I don't begrudge Jonathan Frid wanting the opportunity to play an earthier leading man. Less fun, ultimately, for Lara Parker. She's commented that Angelique was too much of a goody- goody, which is true when the character's not trying to murder children, and if that is the case, Catherine may be the chance to Be Real Pretty, but I'm not sure she's more interesting as a figure of agency.

The underrated 1840 is entering its climax and denouement. Shifting completely to an entirely new storyline, with no substantive crossover, may be the program's biggest gamble. Any ongoing crossover character would have been an ill fit, anyway, and the strangely mature 1841 Parallel Time storyline finishes the show in a manner both familiar and strikingly different. Look beyond the surface, and what seems like "more of the same" is quite the opposite. Dark Shadows is about cycles, and the only thing left after 1841 Parallel Time is Vicki's arrival in 1966 Main Time… followed by the rest of the series, chronologically. The eventual and stable union of Bramwell and Catherine is the opposite of the seething mistrust and betrayals experienced by both Roger and Elizabeth in their Main Time marriages. It shows us the arc — not of "the characters," but of Characters in the story of Dark Shadows. Only at Collinwood is the brightest future in the distant past… and in a parallel universe, at that.

This episode was broadcast January 11, 1971.

EPISODE 1190

When Quentin escapes from jail, will he and Daphne tie the knot before Gabriel ties her down forever? Daphne: Kate Jackson. (Repeat; 30 min.)

Gabriel's attempt to kidnap Daphne is ineffectual, and the lass escapes. Meanwhile, Joanna stumbles upon Gabriel and Melanie in Parallel Time as she searches for Daphne. Nonetheless, Gabriel seizes Daphne from the shadows.

Of course, the 1840 storyline is contrived. Of course. It's not the character study of 1795 or the lusty, sprawling bacchanal of pure imagination of 1897. True to its industrial revolution-era setting, it's a piece of clockwork, cleverly designed to include the apotheosis of Barnabas Collins among dozens of other storylines. The network of interlocking agendas becomes deeply impressive, three steps back, and yet I cannot accuse it of seeming contrived. It simply feels like the owner of the hand of destiny is showing his receipt and telling us all where we can get one. Quentin is out of the way for Trask and Gerard, leading to a witch trial where Barnabas takes up rhetorical arms against a sea of troubles, and by opposing, winds up with Angelique shot.

Which has its own clockwork beauty of dark and ironic inevitability.

Elements of 1190 are so emotionally mature that I wonder if the show is still Dark Shadows. Joanna Mills quickly concludes that Quentin just is not that into her, and she frees him. Good for you. In this case, she defies the jealous lover stereotype, and for all of her blandness, gets the Victoria Winters Award for intrepid house snooping, while Daphne is doing the same thing in hidden corridors that seem designed to store old paintings on the walls. Staying steady among the rampant Dutch angles ("Boff!" "Pow!" "Insinuate!"), Joanna even has a moment to stop by the ultimate secret passage, the Parallel Time room, where Christopher Pennock and Nancy Barrett star in the costume version of The Lost Weekend. The portrait of an alcoholic is convincing, and it will need to be. 1841 Parallel Time is easily understandable as the show's downfall when you consider that it gave them, realistically, nothing connected to the prior four years of world building. Yes, running dry on ideas, we've heard it. Running even drier on Frid-as-Barnabas? Clearly. It's simply a shame that no one thought to extend a tendril of continuity between the universes again. Needn't even be a big gun.

When the Parallel Time cutaway happened today, I found challenge in mustering extreme enthusiasm, even though the final result (1841 Parallel Time) is a gem of a storyline. The highlight of the episode, reliably, is Christopher Pennock, the James Cagney of the DS ensemble. Here, he plays two Gabriels, and neither gent is a prize... but in totally different ways, implosive vs. explosive. The difference is arrestingly subtle, down to movement (no, not the legs) and tempo-rhythm. This is the case where relentless training really pays off.

Meanwhile, away from the wistfully sad portrait of a charming alcoholic's mastery of rationalization, the other Gabriel seems to appear in this episode as sponsored by Ronan Farrow's most paranoid suspicions. Pantingly lustful, even a priapic Rev. Wilbur Glenworthy would try spiking Gabriel's Ovaltine with saltpeter. And yet, there is such a goofy quality to Gabriel's authentic melodrama — straight out of Love Rides the Rails, complete with tied-up damsel — that any sense of transgressive violation just seems like... it ain't gonna happen. He eventually rejects Daphne's come-on in a disappointing burst of common sense. He makes up for it, however, by showing off his counterfeit good-guy badge while commiserating with Joanna. It's an orgy of irrelevance. At this point, they're both short timers for totally different reasons. But so are we all in the world of Dark Shadows. However, the show is a möbius strip, and the twist is coming up — some time after 1841 Parallel Time and before the next episode, #1, in Main Time, so far behind us that it's the next stop on the horizon.

This episode hit the airwaves January 15, 1971.

EPISODE 1192

Samantha learns the terrifying secret of Joanna, but will it be enough to save her from becoming the next ghost of Widow's Hill? Joanna Mills: Lee Beery. (Repeat; 30 min.)

After a startling imprisonment in Parallel Time, Quentin and Daphne escape to encounter Joanna Mills. After Samantha's bullets pass through her, Joanna lures her onto Widow's Hill, where she reveals herself to be a grotesque ghost, bent on revenge.

1840 continues to be the best-kept secret on Dark Shadows. It's largely known for the surprising denouement of the Barnabas/Angelique storyline, and while the other arcs don't have that kind of canonical weight, they can be tight, smart, and intriguing.

Watching the Joanna Mills mystery conclude, we're reminded of that. Like the beginning of the Leviathan story, 1840 seems to present both a main arc and an anthology running concurrently. In 1198, it wraps up a section of that anthology. The segment might be a challenge to get into (because of the ensemble of unfamiliar shor timers) but it pays off when you do. It's one of those brief dimensions of the show like "The Stopping Off Place" story that ran a year before — easily forgotten despite deserving of a mental dog-ear. I'm bending the page corner now.

If the episode has any message, it's "don't tick off a ghost." Up until Joanna Mills, ghosts on the show reveled in their supernatural powers, and while they were incredibly powerful, there's always the sense that they are limited to abilities like telekinesis and mind control. Joanna, though, successfully pulls off a hoax on a level that redefines what a ghost on the program can be. If Josette had possessed these powers, Angelique would have been the next unsuccessful cliff diver on Widow's Hill. She's intensely corporeal, fooling scads of people into believing she's real and saving her big reveal for maximum impact. Actress Lee Beery brings a sense of placid control to the part, making her the perfect foil for the tightly wound, humorless Samantha as delivered by Virginia Vestoff. Her postmortem reveal is genuinely horrifying in a luridly Basil Gogos way, and in my book, that's Louvreable. It's another moment for parents of the age to have every reason to keep kids from watching, and even more reason for kids to go as Jim Phelps as possible to outwit household Standards & Practices. This kind of entertainment merits Ace bandage slings tied to bed frames, probably-lethally suspending kids upside down from the second floor, hovering like Spider-Man outside the family room where the forbidden images would spill forth.

1192 even gives a goose to Parallel Time when Quentin and Daphne are briefly trapped there, sucked back to Main Time only because two Kate Jacksons in one place created a Crisis of Infinite Daphnes. For a moment, the story has intrigue and suspense beyond the typical Parallel Time voyeurism. We even learn who discovered Parallel Time — Ernest Weisman of the University of Vienna. It's a great nugget of trivia from Quentin I, worthy of Eliot Stokes, and it ties the seemingly random events at Collinwood to a larger mythology that longs to be explored by future writers. It pays to keep watching — back to the beginning of the show — after wrapping up the "present" of 1841 Parallel Time. Taking the larger context of the Dark Shadows mythos with us, what we lose in mystery and wonder, we gain in intrigue and detail.

As an aside, Joanna Mills was, of course, the reason that the song, "Joanna," was written. It's one of the lovelier, if "airport loungey" pieces of music from the show, but because it appears so late in the series and in the less popular of the MGM films, the piece remains obscure. Even more obscure are the lyrics, which I wrote last spring.

JOANNA
MUSIC BY ROBERT COBERT. LYRICS BY PATRICK McCRAY.

I'M WEARING PANTS.
THEY'RE MADE OF LYCRA
AND THEY CLING TO ME IN OH SO MANY WAYS.
THEY'RE JUST PANTS, YOU SEE,
BUT PANTS FOR ME,
TO WEAR FOR ALL MY DAYS.

WHEN I THINK OF ALL THE LEATHER LEDERHOSEN
THAT PEOPLE WEAR IN FAR-OFF GERMANY...
WHEN I THINK OF HOW THEY CHAFE,
I GUESS I AM SUPPOSING,
THEY'RE PROUD WE SEE THAT THEY ARE FIRM OF KNEE.

I'M WEARING PANTS...
THEY'RE MADE OF LYCRA
AND THEY CLING TO ME IN OH SO MANY WAYS.
THEY'RE JUST PANTS, YOU SEE,
BUT PANTS FOR ME,
TO WEAR FOR ALL MY DAYS.

TO WEAR FOR ALL MY DAYS.

This episode was broadcast January 19, 1971.

EPISODE 1196

"Head Alert!" Judah Zachery brings Valentine's Day a month ahead of schedule when he robs Angelique of her powers just moments before Quentin's planned execution. Angelique: Lara Parker. (Repeat; 30 min.)

Angelique's plan to fight fire with voodoo fails when Judah Zachery removes the powers he gave her, 100 years prior.

After persuading Charles Dawson to free her by gently beating him to death with a candlestick, she races to the site where Quentin and Desmond are about to go head-to-head in a laundry basket that will probably never be used as such again. Today, I may be on Judah Zachery's side. And I didn't realize that until I sat down to write this. I will have to go back and look at what he did that was so terrible, but the 20th and 21st Centuries have made up their minds on the witchcraft issue. Those who don't believe in it aren't exactly going to be holding trials. Those who do believe are more than likely participating in it.

Structurally, this episode falls in an awkward place. The most exciting part of this sequence of action was yesterday when Barnabas explained to Angelique that she's just not a member of Club Corporeal, and so they can never really have a substantial love life. As many times as I have watched that moment in 1195 where Barnabas denies her desires because of her occult nature, I have had a hard time understanding it. I have always operated under the assumption that the endowment of her powers has, by its very nature, robbed her of something crucial. I think it's something that Barnabas senses more than he can fully intellectualize; his objection is not so much about her being "a witch," with the moral baggage that comes with it. Instead, it is about the detachment that comes with that much power.

A relationship is an endeavor primarily driven by emotion. Emotion isn't always pretty. The more power someone has to act on them, the more damage they can do. Angelique swings back-and-forth between benevolence and rampant awfulosity. The latter nogoodnikism that trails around her in the DS "timeline" is a bloody testament to my point. It's all good and well to breathe and count to 10, but what does it mean for someone who can reverse time?

Barnabas reacts from the mindset of an abuse survivor, and as sad as that is, it's about time he moved proactively on that. Because he does measure his response to her love by her capacity to do damage. And, okay. I fess up. (pause) Yes, it's very convenient for this universe to then remove her powers shortly after this conversation with Barnabas. But let's look the army medic in the eye; writing fiction means dusting for the fingerprints of coincidence. Dark Shadows simply doesn't have the time left to disguise that obvious fact with a finesse we've all outgrown.

Writers of fiction are very quick to have characters reject godhood. A little conveniently so. Frankly, I find the person who rejects power without at least browsing the catalog to be a little suspect. Yes, Uncle Stan told us that, "with great power comes great responsibility," and far be it for me to question him. But at the same time, there are a lot of corollaries.

For one thing, maybe it's not as much responsibility as it seems. Or maybe the exercise of that responsibility isn't really that difficult. Ultimately, I think most writers are taking the lazy, easy way out when they have characters make these antitheistic pronouncements. This is pertinent to Angelique because she doesn't voluntarily give up her powers. Judah Zachery giveth. Judah Zachery taketh away.

And Angelique is no idiot. She's going to hold onto these abilities because, as a mortal from the 1690s, she knows exactly how miserable life can be. So, where does that leave Barnabas?

By curing him of his vampirism, she has made a more profound sacrifice than we might initially think. Okay, Barnabas might believe it's a stretch for a mortal to love a witch, but it's an even greater leap to expect any immortal, nearly-omnipotent being to love a creature who is going to age and wither astonishingly quickly, all things considered. Although the vampire's curse was meant as a punishment, perhaps subconsciously, she also realized that it was the only way they could be together. How else was he supposed to accompany her through time, given that the power to make or break a witch seems to be unique to Magus Zachery? By the 1790s, she has been like this for 100 years. And even in that time, who knows how often she has ping-ponged throughout the centuries? For her to stifle her abilities and risk everything to travel to the American wilderness for this man is perhaps more admirable than anything done by her rival. Josette agrees to an arranged marriage to a guy she loves, picks up a free mansion in Maine, and calls it a day. That's about as brave as picking out a value meal at Subway.

Judah Zachery is doing her a favor. Think of the size of Angelique's sacrifice when she turns Barnabas back into a human. She is condemning him to die the death of an ordinary man, and she is serving herself the punishment of having to watch it, anticipating nothing but a nearly-eternal life without him once he passes away.

It's a perspective that changes things just a tad. And before you stop me from crying too athletically into my Gibson, that degree of love could explain the degree of wrath that she's shown so many times. One hundred years of immortality might be enough to detach anyone from the experience of being human, and perhaps that's why Barabas rejects her. Judah Zachery is not exactly Santa Claus, but by turning her back into a mortal, he has (even if accidentally) given Angelique the gift of human relatability. The gift of her powers helped her find Barnabas. Rescinding them is the one thing that could help her keep him.

This episode was broadcast Jan. 25, 1971.

EPISODE 1197

As the executioner readies his ax, Angelique, Barnabas, Quentin, and Desmond unite to destroy the ultimate Curse of Collinwood. Barnabas: Jonathan Frid. (Repeat; 30 min.)

Angelique arrives at Quentin's execution with the head of Judah Zachery, identifying it as the prperty of... (checks label)...

one Charles Dawson. Desmond uses the distraction to shoot Gerard, finally releasing him from Judah's hold. When the head of the warlock dissolves into a skull, Angelique's story has new resonance. She is held for questioning and Barnabas sees his own son, Bramwell, attempt to win Catherine back in the Parallel Time room. Barnabas determines to express his own feelings to Angelique. When he approaches her to do so, Trask bursts in and fires a pistol at her.

1197 is rife with some of the most profound moments in the series… some that are really there… some that play out in my mind's eye based on implications and wishes. In classic, Dark Shadows tradition, it's also bang-up entertainment. And it's the start of goodbye.

I can't ignore that when I watch it. The idea makes my chest tighten, and the execution has a strange, terminal excitement that exists in no other installment. It's a resolution without a price — until the very, very final seconds. Before that? It begins with a sequence so satisfying that I want to take up smoking just so I can have a cigarette afterwards. Appropriate salute for a show of the era.

It's still hard to imagine that this is the penultimate installment in the whole thing. But it is. Keep that in mind. 1841 Parallel Time is underrated, and it's also an epilogue, existing outside the continuity we care about. Most viewers will be lost without thinking abstractly… or approaching it first, as the only Dark Shadows they know. But this… episode 1197? This is the real beginning of the end. It's the series saying goodbye. It's how nearly 1225 episodes of continuity depart without knowing it. And what was it like for viewers at the time? For the more aware, every day was alpha and omega. With no seasons and no full bundles dropping on Netflix at once, each episode was the next, and the last, and a cliffhanger for more, and the final chance any of this might ever, ever, in any form, be seen.

Dark Shadows is a ruthless-yet-delicate show. For one with such a male-heavy cast, it is often effete. But not here. Not now. There are too many feelings at stake for the show to be obsessed with preserving them under glass. It may be a saga that begins with Louis Edmonds passive-aggressively sneering at Joan Bennett, but it ends with David Selby swaggering off the blindfold on an execution block. He's got a backbone like the Rock of Gibraltar, and as a Victorian scientist to the end, it's never at the expense of his precision and dignity. Ending the show on a flashback gives us a sense of progress and a point of departure against which we can measure the very first episode. On no other show can we reflect on how far we've come and how far we've strayed, all at once.

The bravado of Desmond and Quentin — and even poor, sad Gerard — make wonderful counterpoints for Barnabas. Especially true as the great man commits to the most dangerous truth and choice of his life: true love. The pivot for him is the Parallel Time sequence. At this point, the Parallel Time sequences have become the Dark Shadows equivalents of lame musical guests on SNL — time to hit the head, check text messages, and light some hookah coals. But in 1197, the interlude is a beautiful metaphor, screened for Barnabas by a godlike Dan Curtis to spur him to take the chance he must. Seeing your own son and twin from the present and future at once is an Escheresque mirror without equal. Then to watch him struggle to overcome the loss of the duplicate of the love you've denied yourself because, for one reason, she's not adequately respectable? A woman denying you for someone even more respectable than yourself?

That'll get to a guy. For Barnabas, it's a Marley's Ghost moment. He's completely transformed for the first of several times in just a few minutes. My favorite moment of potential energy is just after he's seen off his shadow brother — Quentin — into his new and free future. Alone in the foyer, having seen someone leave him and Collinwood smiling for once, Barnabas turns toward the drawing room, where he knows Angelique awaits him.

And for just a fraction of a second, you know he catches a glimpse of his portrait. Is he imagining his first moments in the Collinwood of 1967? How can it not? The entire journey allusively flashes by in an instant. It's a moment of everything, abridged. Like the end of Cyrano, it has a genuinely terrible ending, and I mean that in the best way. Lara Parker gives a bit of a melodramatic twist to her depiction of having been shot. Anything realistic would have been too much to watch. We need the cushion of art in a moment so incredibly cruel. In episode 411, Barnabas discovers the nature of Angelique's curse. He responds by executing her, and if that chain of moments forms the nadir of their relationship, 1197 is the summit. If we look at the 1795 flashback as the start of his story, then 411 and 1197 bookend his journey. In both episodes, only Barnabas survives.

Is it a ritual? To what end? Why does death await Angelique at either end of this spectrum? Miserable survival for Barnabas. Of what possible benefit is this? Especially twice. None. Because he's not supposed to benefit. We are. The audience. We benefit by watching where his choices lead him. In both instances, Barnabas's central sin is dishonesty with himself. It's easy to understand why he's initially blind to his love in the year 1840; he's seen Angelique torment the inhabitants of three separate centuries. It's harder in 1795 because his denial is more complicated. Maybe it's a matter of social class and family pressure. Maybe it's timing. He certainly loves Josette, and she provides none of the challenges posed by Angelique.

Love, especially in fiction, and even more especially in pop fiction, is so tempting to quantify. A bit like a character stat in a video game — an achievement you unlock by revealing Judah. It's far more complicated, and its unclarity leads to the inevitable fan cry of the true believer, "How could he love Angelique more than Josette... especially after all that she did?!"

I don't think it's an issue of more nor less. For one thing, Josette isn't here. Hasn't been, by Barnabas's internal clock, for about 175 years or so. I mean, not really. Her ghost has given him the permission to move on. And it's clear that Roxanne seemed like a good idea at the time, but, you know, um, yeah.

Swipe left. That leaves Angelique by default, but how can he look past her misdeeds?

The only salient fact is that he does. Yes, it's uncomfortable. Baffling. Yet, it's strangely, horribly, wonderfully, inexplicably, infuriatingly, and unfairly right.

That's what makes it love.

This episode was broadcast January 26, 1971.

EPISODE 1197 (A Second Look)

Guess what happens when the characters do all of the right things and suddenly have the prospect of happiness welcoming them with open arms? Miranda Duval: Lara Parker. (Repeat; Our Entire Lives)

Angelique interrupts the execution of Quentin and Desmond with the severed head of Judah Zachery. When its flesh dissolves with the death of Ivan Miller, even jaywalking tickets are forgiven by the judge. Unable to live with this outbreak of rampant justice and happiness, Lamar Trask shoots Angelique just before she can hear that Barnabas loves her. The End.

"Attention must be paid."

So said the Widow Loman at the grave for someone prized only for his insignificance.

I have come back to these episodes more times than any other. This year, it feels irresponsible to devote more words to them. And yet, it feels irresponsible not to. A show the size of Dark Shadows is more than a television program; it is a companion. If you spent three hours on a hobby with a friend, twice a month, for six years, you'd develop an understandable bond. That stretch of time is how long it would take you to watch this story. It's a feast of a tale. Many times, in ways good and bad, it feels endless. The story accrues around the edges, in no more rush than the real lives it punctuates. 1967 is always fresh. 1968 is always a rich and intriguing core sample. 1969 is always better than we deserve. 1970 always pales by comparison, trawling for us to apologize for it. 1971 is always too short... a reminder of what it's like to still love something when everyone else stops.

I remain unshaken in my assertion that Dark Shadows is the most realistic show on TV. It just kind of putters around, threatening to do something significant and then just kind of... usually not. Most of the news is bad. We get used to it.

And then someone is shot and killed.

I'm not being glib when I say that. No, not every tragedy is a sudden and fatal gunshot wound. But I guarantee you that there is someone out there reading this who has lost someone precious, precisely that way. And that's how this episode ends. The most famous quote about television is that "the medium is the message." In other words, the means by which we consume art is as significant a statement as the art being exhibited. Dark Shadows is many things that it had no intention of being. (Newsflash: this goes for all art.)

Like all art, however, it is a teacher above all else. Primarily, it teaches us to look at ourselves from a completely different point of view. But if you watch the entire show, the very storytelling, itself, is the most significant message. Maybe more than one.

The most immediate one is, in the words of Folcroft Sanitarium director, Dr. Harold W. Smith, "Thou shall not get away with it."

The assassination of Angelique is a convenience. The actors want to move to a fresh storyline. The writers are probably hoping that new characters will give them new ideas. And the ritual of storytelling inevitably veers toward drab moralizing. In this modern world dominated by an antediluvian ethos, we certainly hear a lot about forgiveness. And at the same time, we also live in a culture that absolutely revels in just desserts.

We love forgiveness because it makes Oprah happy. It's what we are supposed to do because somehow it will liberate us. It will certainly liberate the people in our lives who are sick of hearing us complain about something. It's vaguely godlike, so I guess it's got that going for it.

But is it just me, or does a lot of the forgiveness we hear about seem to have its fingers crossed behind its back?

Why? We just can't stand the idea of someone getting away with it. Any of it. And because we can't make up our minds which of these things — beatific forgiveness or righteous punishment — we will fetishize more, we look to fiction to give us both at the same time. And who has to pay the tab?

Angelique.

So, of course, Trask has to plug her. The fatheaded, arbitrary rules of the ritual that is fiction decree it to be so. There are plenty of Dark Shadows fans who love to sweep in at this point with a list of all of the horrible things Angelique has done, and I guess this… helps? But I hope you have a list of all of the rotten things Barnabas has done because he's just as deserving of the naughty step. And he pays, also. He pays an ongoing price too terrible for the show to make us watch.

And culture smiles on us for having it both ways. We applaud their 11th-hour moral reversals safe in the "irony" that they are being punished anyway.

Extra! Extra! Read all about it. The one thing these characters learn is that the past belongs in the past. All we have is the present. All we have are the decisions we are making right now. I spend 90% of my day apologizing for what I say the other 10%, and when someone is really going to town on me, I gently remind them that it won't build a time staircase to allow me to make different decisions in the past.

The saddest part about episode 1197 is that the present is the one thing these characters are denied. That's nothing to feel good about. That's nothing to applaud. And perhaps, it's nothing to applaud in our art. Perhaps that's the message we should actually be taking away.

When significance erupts in the mundanity of our everyday lives, it is shockingly sudden. There's no taking it back. And then, the show ends. There's no montage. There's not even a funeral at which Barnabas can insist that attention must be paid.

If you're going to forgive, mean it. Move on. Do it in the name of the future that Angelique and Barnabas never got.

This episode was broadcast January 26, 1971.

It became a ritual to write about this final episode of Dark Shadows, and by that, I mean the Dark Shadows of the main storyline, not 1841 Parallel Time. A soap opera is one, huge, sustained cliffhanger. And if you spend 450 hours hanging off of a cliff, it's important to study what happens when you finally go over. As I compare this version with other essays I've written about the end of the series, I'm struck by the fact that it's less sentimental than my earlier takes, rather than more.

EPISODE 1198

As Barnabas embarks on a determined mission of cross- dimensional bloodlust, is he the victim of a larger trap? Barnabas Collins: Jonathan Frid. (Repeat; 30 min.)

Shot by Lamar Trask, Angelique dies in the arms of Barnabas, not hearing him proclaim his love. Savage in his response, Barnabas chases and stabs Trask, who finds himself trapped and dying in parallel time. Emotionally decimated, Barnabas returns to the present with Julia and Stokes to find that they have successfully altered the timeline for the better. Meanwhile, Leticia Faye and Desmond catch a brief glimpse of parallel time where Julia Collins discovers Trask's body.

1198 is a dangerous episode. As the resolution of the primary series, it trolls fans as much as it fulfills their desires. There is no 11th-hour return of Kathryn Leigh Scott. There is no tearful reunion with Josette. Instead, Barnabas discovers happiness in the arms of a one-time enemy. As the program does what it can with what it has, it shocks more than satisfies. Seen now, it also divides viewers like few other decisions made over its run.

Do we see Barnabas discovering his authentic love for Angelique or merely convincing himself that the only game in town is what he always wanted? Is the series putting viewers in the same position? Are fans of the Barnabas/Angelique romance responding to something illuminating in the text or are they just making the best with what they have, convincing themselves it's what they wanted all along? Are you on Team Angelique or Team Josette? It might depend on when you saw it.

For millions of viewers over several decades, the climactic twist of Barnabas's true, romantic direction is something they saw only once... or never saw at all. Without VHS, DVD or frequently cycled reruns, his "real" love is more of a rumor or fever dream than a fondly remembered highlight of the series. Until the mid-00s, there was no way to review the moment, nor scour any of the series for clues. Good thing, because there were no clues. The writers were making it up as they went along, and if they had known that Barnabas's true love was Angelique, they would have telegraphed it years before. Of course, the show might have benefited from this. But the fact that they can't even hint at his unrealized love makes it more of a surprise. And it makes the whole argument irrelevant. In 2021, Dark Shadows exists as a complete entity. The details of its authorship are just those: details. This is the reality of Barnabas Collins because it's now part of a finished work.

The answer to the Josette vs Angelique question may not be so clear-cut as just choosing one over the other. I used to think of Angelique as the hero because of her last minute transformation and the tremendous sacrifices she makes along the way. But upon this viewing, I was struck by a possibility I had never considered before. As a director, something I always tell actors is that any character, at any point, may not be telling the truth. Even if the author makes it appear as if they are, they might not be. So, in terms of her grand transformation, what if Angelique is making it all up? Or some of it up. After all, she has always been perfectly happy to use her powers to influence Barnabas's decisions. How he came about loving her was always less relevant than the fact that he simply did. No love spells (on him). She simply mastered the fine art of influence. First off… threats to family. That's in 1795. Then, threats to him. That's in 1968. In 1897, maybe jealousy over Quentin?

But in the end, none of those things worked, did they?

Not like making yourself the hero against your past villainy, wiping out a larger threat, and then creating loyalty by curing your own curse. Has Barnabas been manipulated by a vast disinformation campaign? I say this because his decision is ultimately swayed by, yes, the involvement of witchcraft, years after her initial efforts. If it's ineffective to use your occult powers, simply impress everyone by removing them. One way or the other, you're still exploiting the occult. One way or the other, you would never be in the position you are if it were not for witchcraft. Clever. And strangely Zen.

Take the implications to episodes that never happened. We have no evidence that she's really given up her powers. It's not like there's a Butterball popup timer we can check. If she can suddenly cure a near-incurable curse, she can make her abilities appear and vanish at will. Faking her own death is the longest-but-strongest game possible. Had the 1971 Primary Time storyline happened, it might very well have seen Barnabas exploring the timeline in pursuit of Angelique.

At last, she would be desired and sought on a level to rival Josette.

At last, he would have her right where she wants him. It's just an interpretation. Just a what-if, True Believers.

Yes, a bleakly cynical one of multilevel manipulation, but you have met Angelique, right?

Or maybe it's just preferable to the idea that she's gone.

This episode was broadcast January 27, 1971.

1841 Parallel Time
Callback to Adventure

"Dawn breaks over the Great House of Collinwood..."

It's a show about loneliness in many ways. Ironic, because it can be a lonely proposition to watch it. After it alienates friends and lovers who prefer more traditional narratives, the show is often the only company left.

That puts misunderstood "monsters" on both sides of the screen. On the show, most of them simply want to be like "everyone else," whatever that means. Of course, *we* know that they are special and wonderful, and that they would stop being special and wonderful if they assimilated. But it's easy for us to say. We're not the ones who have to live like that. Especially with what Philip Todd charges for rent.

Did the Dark Shadows writers know that they were writing a story about loneliness and alienation when they sat down at the clavichord? I think so. And maybe all soap operas deal with this to certain extents. They tell stories fueled by secrets and secret desires. Dark Shadows does this and more. Because it populates its tales with time travelers of questionable mortality, the program's reflections on hidden truths take on existential weight. Especially when it ponders the murky nature of good and evil with a skeptical eye toward solitude abusers.

After all, if Sarah instructs Barnabas to literally "be" good, that goodness can only be measured by how it changes the lives of other people. Challenging, because if there's one thing Collinwood stands for, it's isolation. The town from the state. The house from the town. The mansion's wings from its center. Even some of the rooms prefer hiding themselves in other dimensions.

When I first looked at the relationship between Episode One and Episode Last, I saw Collinwood as a fortress that excuses itself with "because tradition."

I have little use for tradition. I've always seen it as a convenient and cowardly exploitation of sentiment to sabotage innovation. For Clan Collins, it's cherished as the longest and most arduous path to a slow and certain demise. Unless they fight it. Starting with Vicki Winters and ending with Bramwell, we see that Collinwood can only survive by blending tradition with novelty — welcoming the divergent rather than ignoring them.

Look at 1841 parallel time. Easy to ignore. Seemingly unrelated to the show… except for proving its point.

The whole business with the lottery and the haunted room can feel rrelevant. In fact, my own prejudice in that regard can be seen in the fact that this volume contains no Daybook entries for 1841 PT at all. Apologies for that. It was only after the Daybook Unbound found its way into Kindles that the final storyline suddenly came into focus. The Inner Lebowski awakened as new perspectives made this storyline the micturated-upon rug that genuinely tied to the haunted room together with the rest of the house.

Short form: in the final episode, both Bramwell and Catherine enter the haunted room, while Brutus does his best to drive them into murderous madness. He fails. And by failing, Brutus releases the family from his curse.

He is an honorable man after all.

So, perhaps, the final and first curse of the multidimensional Collins family was not so hard to break. So, how did they do it? Quite simply, they changed the dance. And they changed the dance by going into it together rather than alone. It's just that simple. Their ancestors were so afraid of questioning tradition that they doomed themselves, generation after generation, to suffer from it. They were victims of this false dichotomy — "either we send some poor sap in there alone or the entire clan is kaput."

But as St. Anton of LaVey teaches, enlightenment rests in challenging old orthodoxies and finding third alternatives. Even if it's kind of accidental.

So, what is so special about going in with an ally? Without one, a haunting is controlled only by the source of fear and the person who dreads it. That third voice is reality. It's validation when we need it and a force of doubt when can no longer survive without it.

The series begins with it. Liz changes everything when she brings in Victoria. The house in 1966 primary time might as well be one massive, multi chambered "haunted room" for Elizabeth Collins Stoddard. And for the sake of argument, let's acknowledge that the voices of Roger, David, and Carolyn are too close to really count. Liz needs the example, counsel, and companionship of someone truly from the outside. Well, it doesn't get much more "outside" than an orphan from New York City.

Like a bubbly bodhisattva, Victoria is a walking koan who teaches through questions more than answers. But Victoria is a self perpetuating cliché summed up in "I just don't understand."

This is judged too hastily. *We* only understand things that she doesn't because we are watching Dark Shadows at 4:30, and she's too busy doing her job to waste a half hour in front of the tube when David has an Esperanto test to pass. So, we hear the private conversations that she never does. Maybe she doesn't understand things because they are genuinely incomprehensible to her. They are just as incomprehensible to her as they would be to us.

It's only by Vicki insistently asking her signature question that Liz is forced to confront the secrets, lies, and absurdities that she has taken for granted. The companion is a reality check. The companion is a voice of the living present who can finally be heard over the echoes of the past. Vicki may end up trapped there as a result, but Liz and the audience move on.

The same goes for Bramwell and Catherine.

And maybe us, too.

EPILOGUES

A LAST SUNSET: BEN CROSS

Ben Cross was the last of his kind, truly. A regal actor for fantasy roles that required a star to speak clearly, command the room, and, you know, shave and bathe. They were parts that called for a man of both truth and imagination. A master of theatrical size and total sincerity. He was Captain Nemo. He was Ambassador Sarek. He was Barnabas Collins.

While he was never the first to essay those roles, he had the insightful integrity of a man who made each totally original.

For some, he was their Captain Nemo and their Ambassador Sarek. And although the productions in which he essayed the roles are not definitive versions, Ben Cross delivered formances that were as indelible as those who originated the parts.

For many of us, he was our Barnabas Collins. Not that we weren't deeply familiar with Jonathan Frid, but the 1991 series spared no expense to give us all of the corners cut in the 1960s. It was a reward for loyalty.

Although it was not the original, it was the creator of the show standing atop the towering successes of the Wouk miniseries, determined to make every element the finest he could. Star Trek returned with Patrick Stewart as the lead. Well, Dan Curtis saw Gene Roddenberry's Patrick Stewart and raised him a Ben Cross, matured beyond Chariots of Fire. Capable of bringing equal classical artistry to television fantasy's other great saga.

And he was every bit Stewart's equal. He was ours because, for many of us, Dark Shadows left the air before we were born. But, as with Next Generation, we had the excitement of following the production through its initial announcement to the first photo of the next Barnabas Collins.

Cross's performance matched that first, soulful photo. Intelligent and ferocious, he lacked Jonathan Frid's endearing neurosis, but that allowed him the chance to explore the role of Barnabas Collins with his own judgment. Both men are martyrs to loss and betrayal, but while Frid was determined to rebuild, Cross was bent on revenge. It's a less subtle performance in that sense, but wholly appropriate for the beginning of an arc that would only last for a tad over three months. His game was all too brief. His performance matched it, burning hot and fast. But it was never without delightful humor and humanity.

This is what he brought to Dark Shadows. His Barnabas had a texture, energy, and life all its own, and as such was Richard Burton to Frid's Laurence Olivier. They gave two vastly different interpretations of the great man, and thus, neither encroached on the other. Instead, they are colleagues, and they both gave us the finest performances in the role that we could want.

The same for his Nemo. The same for his Sarek.

At 72, the loss was stunningly premature. It was exceeded only by our fortune that, if batons were to be passed, his was the hand to grasp them.

DARK SHADOWS
The 1991 Primetime Series

EPISODE 1

When a boozing handyman decodes the secret location of a wealthy family's long-lost treasures, he uncovers the deadliest legacy of all. Can the new tutor for the family's troubled heir unravel the mystery before becoming a bride of the living dead? Loomis: Jim Fyfe. (Repeat; 1 hr.)

All-around scamp Willie Loomis unleashes Barnabas Collins, a vampire trapped in his own coffin for two centuries. Masquerading as his own descendant, Collins reclaims his dilapidated ancestral home and is compelled to woo his family's newest employee, a soulful governess who resembles the bride he lost centuries before.

When Ben Cross died, I remember writing that the 1991 Dark Shadows "revival" was the first expression of the franchise that felt like mine. It was the first Dark Shadows production of any kind to roll out in my lifetime. More or less. I was born just a few days after the program went off the air, and let's put the cards on the table, I'm not really sure Night of Dark Shadows counts except as a metaphor for the Fine Art of Settling for What We Got that was the albatross of being a fan back then. Few gigantic pop culture phenomena required as much of its fans as Dark Shadows at that time. This was a program you were lucky to even catch on TV. In 1990, many of the fans had never seen the entire series and had no real hope of doing so. I worked for public television at the time, and the rumor around the station was that Worldvision was asking so much for the final package that absolutely no station would carry it. True? False? I don't know. But I don't see Gerard Stiles around here, do you?

Following the success of Star Trek: The Next Generation, the idea of a prime time, big-budget, hour-long television series on the most powerful network on television was like a reward for loyalty. And it immediately created a strange sense of conflict with the original series. To this day, I feel inexplicably disloyal saying nice things about a TV series that could have hired almost all of the original stars, the oldest of which, among a certain age bracket, wasn't even 50.

Still, putting that aside, this was an incredible proof- of-concept. This was an affirmation that Dark Shadows was not just a TV series. A recognition like this is like finding yourself on the pop culture equivalent of the periodic table. Attention was at last being paid. And honestly? The fact that the original actors were not featured was, strangely, a compliment to them. It was an acknowledgement that they created something so indelible that it became larger than their individual personalities. If anything, it was a tribute to their immortality... just a few inconvenient decades early.

In my lifetime, there was no better time to be a Dark Shadows fan. Twin Peaks had cleared a path for a nighttime supernatural mystery soap opera. Anne Rice was going great guns and had yet to go through that weird, post-9/11 Jesus phase. The Lost Boys wasn't that long ago, and if the Bernard Hughes character isn't the prototype for what they did with Dave Woodard, then... well... I don't need to bother coming up with something to finish the sentence. He clearly was the model.

And you've got to love that. However, therein lies the ultimate reason for the show's failure. Bernard Hughes. Mastermind of Iraq's invasion of Kuwait? You tell me. The future staff of Dark Shadows goes to see The Lost Boys and the hot property they come back with is a character kind of like

Bernard Hughes. Yeah, that's the takeaway, apparently. Keep in mind, I exist in a world where Bernard Hughes defines male sex appeal. But there are times when I wonder if I am actually the entertainment industry's key demographic.

Not that 1991 Dark Shadows has to be the Lost Boys, but it was state-of-the-art. And the 1991 Dark Shadows was not.

I don't lay the failure of the show on the Gulf War. I had a reason to watch the show because I was a Dark Shadows fan. So, I did what a person did at the time; I read the newspaper and I read TV Guide and I followed the show around like Waldo wherever it might pop up on the schedule in between Iraq's regularly scheduled missile attacks on Israel. I never missed an episode.

So, if motivated, it was scientifically possible for a viewer to keep up with the crazy schedule of the show. But the rest of the nation was not properly motivated. Logic dictates that the program, despite its quality, did not significantly motivate viewers en masse. And that's what happened.

Dan Curtis was 39 when the original Dark Shadows went on the air. To put this into perspective, not only was he a relatively young man, but his greatest inspiration, Tod Browning's Dracula, was only 35 years old when the original TV show premiered. Yeah, it was only five years older than the Dark Shadows remake is now. It was all pretty fresh, cosmically speaking. In fact, the original novel was less than 70 years old at that point. But by 1990, Dan Curtis was 63. Horror had reinvented itself at least twice since he was a prime mover in the field. And while no one would call him tired, he produced a Dark Shadows remake that had the kind of dated swagger that comes from someone who helped invent a genre. Because of that, maybe he doesn't see a lot of need to check in with what has become of that before jumping in again. I kind of get the feeling that everyone around the office considered Dark Shadows 1991 relevant because Dan Curtis said it was relevant. Unfortunately, the Zeitgeist didn't get the memo.

In the long run, I think this serves the 1991 Dark Shadows series better now than it did at the time. It has a stately confidence that grows as the series moves on. But I don't know many people who hang out at the water cooler gushing about how excited they are to see more stately confidence that night on TV. Perhaps, in 1990, God help me, it needed a blond Barnabas with spiky hair and a leather jacket. That was the fashion back then, and at least it would be a tribute to paying attention. And that's great. They didn't do that. After all, conservative clothes never go out of style. It has an admirable stodginess that a 63 "year" old guy who had just spent a decade waging World War II would look at and say, "Yeah, that's about right."

Yes, let's admit it, we answered the question, "What if somebody gave a Dark Shadows and nobody came?" Because it was not Twin Peaks. It was a response to the zeitgeist of 1967 that got made 23 years too late. Me? My idea of a great band back then was and still is the Ink Spots. So, I like the fact that the show is not some winkingly postmodern flavor of the month, diagnosing the audience's sperm motility the old- fashioned way with a high style that can't make up its mind if it's parody or sincere. Like Twin Peaks. Instead, that show just bullies you by condescendingly Lynchsplaining that whatever tonal interpretation you have of it is wrong. But my real beef with that show is that it was successful and reportedly good, and a lot of people liked it and instead of priming the audience for Dark Shadows, it created a situation where Dark Shadows was criticized by many for not being it.

And because the man works his ass off to run this particular Bartertown, I have to acknowledge the head of the Historical Society here. It would be ooky not to. You get the Daybook, I believe, because Wallace McBride has big executive stuff to do. The guy is a fantastic writer. Go back and read Monster Serial if you want proof. Look at the first line of his Alien review. It is rhetorically sublime. The man knows what he's talking about. One day, if I'm lucky, I will be able to hook a reader with a simple first sentence like the one he uses there.

Wallace loves Twin Peaks, and he's smarter than I am to an extent that makes me a gym coach who's gotten stuck trying to muddle through an organic chemistry textbook because the actual teacher has jury duty. He loves Twin Peaks, so go watch it.

I'm just cranky because what kind of a world is it where a guy dressed up like Barnabas Collins (Dale Cooper in his natty black suits) gets all of the cultural cachet while the new Barnabas Collins struts around in vaguely dated turtlenecks that make him look like Ron Burgundy's mortician? Barnabas Collins was not a man with much need for business casual circa 1979. I swear to God, I think Willie just raided Roger's latest donation to AMVETS and convinced Barnabas that it would impress Victoria. I'm sure he talked Barnabas into slathering himself with Paco Rabanne, wearing a gold chain under the offensive turtleneck, and probably Sansabelt slacks just to complete the ensemble.

Ben Cross brings a uniquely regal sensibility to Barnabas, and it works best in the context of the 1791 flashback. That's really where the character comes into his own, and since everyone knows what the mystery of Barnabas Collins actually is, I wish they had simply started the series there. It would have given a fresh sense of sympathy and relevance to his quest for Josette, allowing them to enter the modern era with Barnabas as an understandably reluctant vampire. That was a magical choice that the original series had to discover through trial and error.

There's no need to repeat the learning process. Let the story itself do the heavy lifting. Unfortunately, Cross is forced to play an almost cartoonishly suave and confident vampire who is largely interesting because he's named Barnabas Collins. I wish they had allowed him to explore the nervous, fearful, and paranoid, dethroned aristocrat that I always think of when considering the essence of Barnabas Collins in those early episodes. Cross was reportedly a man with a tremendous and ebullient sense of mischief, and I think he would have risen to that challenge with a lot of gratitude.

Having had fun at the expense of a show I actually like, let me list what really works in this pilot. The cast is incredibly strong. Joanna Going is positively luminous as Victoria Winters. Alexandra Moltke strikes me as playing a loving caregiver for a disturbed boy who also does what she can as an educator. Joanna Going gets to play a highly credible educator who also happens to have a skill at reaching this disturbed young man. It's an important distinction, and it makes it easy to root for her as a character capable of solving Collinwood's mysteries rather than someone I'm just kind of concerned about.

The rest of the performers spend most of their time doing what casts do in a pilot; they recite exposition. But they execute it with a sense of investment and stakes. Roy Thinnes's natural presence and dark integrity help to create a different type of Roger Collins, but one I am just as interested in seeing revealed. This is a man who has been married to a fire demon and has lived to tell the tale. And it's wonderful to see Jean Simmons out of makeup, despite having rock and rolled all day and partied every night.

In a cast of standout performances, there are several unexpected ones that work exceptionally well and are worthy of special praise. Dan Curtis and the team make lightning strike twice with the casting of Joseph Gordon-Levitt as David Collins. Like David Henesy before him, he has a blend of maturity, menace, confidence, and vulnerability that does the impossible by making a child character just as interesting and unpredictable as any of the adults. Equally terrific is Barbara Blackburn. She combines Caroline's necessary youth with a mature intelligence, sense of wit, and honest, smokey-voiced eroticism grounded more in those inner qualities than simply relying on her bone deep physical beauty. As with the women of the original Dark Shadows cast, Hollywood really missed the boat by not casting her in everything possible for the next 30 years.

My favorite of all of them is Saint Jim Fyfe. His audition was reportedly an explosive exercise in risk-taking that commanded his casting... despite being nothing like John

Karlen. Because the character is so distinctive, he gets to have far more fun than anyone else in the cast. Fyfe and the writers know that this character is destined to be a sympathetic everyman, loyal to Barnabas more and more out of an instinctive sense of his master's nascent humanity than fear. It's only now that I can see a series where Willie is the audience surrogate more than Victoria. Making Willie the troubled inheritor of the Ben (Stokes) Loomis mantle grounds his sense of loyalty in something larger than himself, and it is the thread that so beautifully ties together the two eras occupied by the show.

No, he's not John Karlen. But he does what I think Karlen would champion; he makes the character his own rather than an imitation. It's a trait shared by his castmates, but he gets to explore the furthest dimensions of it. There are few episodes of the series where he doesn't make me laugh and tear up just a tad. Fyfe embodies the single most important adage in selecting performers: choose the most interesting actor, not just the most naturalistic.

If Dark Shadows 1991 failed to be a show with numbers demanding a second season, and if it falls short of being the late-eighties music video nightmare that might have gotten all the gang talking at the sock hop, it doesn't matter. It sustains its half-season with a unique, compelling, and headstrong voice that doesn't need to ask for anyone's approval. Dan Curtis' braggadocio may have created a strangely anachronistic show, but given the nature of its lead character, that may have been the most loyal choice possible.

EPISODE 7

Victoria's done with seances after a doozy from Maggie lands her in 1791 and seeing double! Josette Dupres: Joanna Going. (Repeat; 1 hr.)

Victoria awakens outside the Collins manor house (later to be known as the Old House) in the year 1790. She calls Barnabas by name and passes herself off as the new tutor for young Daniel and Amy until she can find a way back to the present. Unfortunately, her strange clothing and mysterious origin draw suspicions from Barnabas's Aunt Abigail, who, convinced that she is a witch, summons a maniacal clergyman, Reverend Trask. Meanwhile, the actual witch, Angelique, roams free and tries to reignite her affair with Barnabas from years past. She is unsuccessful, and vows to take control of the situation. The first to fall under her control is Ben Loomis, Barnabas's faithful manservant.

This episode may be my favorite of the 1991 series. It has a sense of rambunctious enthusiasm and confidence that dominates the screen. When the daytime version goes into its first flashback, you can feel the sense of risk and danger behind what they were pulling off. The revival's flashback lacks that sense of risk, trading it for a giddy confidence.

Dark Shadows – both the broad strokes and details – had proved itself a lasting success. In the approach to the 1991 series, you can feel that. It has a strange swagger, and the 1791 flashback is Exhibit A. Knowing that Elizabeth would be Naomi, etc., etc., affected the casting with a foresight the daytime series never enjoyed. The double casting of the 1795 sequence feels like a stunt. The 1791 sequence in the nighttime show is clearly a choice. It's where Dan Curtis reveals, if anything, the real program. Really, for such a young series (or young incarnation of a series), everything works. Making Barnabas, Peter, and Jeremiah a triumvirate of dear friends was a warm touch that humanizes the sequence immediately. The characters are well-drawn, anyway, and they serve as revealing foils for Barnabas.

Barbara Blackburn and the writers find an entirely new way to make Millicent a nightmare. Stefan Gierasch's Joshua is a stingy prig trying desperately to forget that he has a decent, loving heart. Lysette Anthony does all she can with Angelique, but this is the one misfire of the sequence. For all of the evil of Lara Parker's Angelique, I believed that the love was genuine, and I saw traces of kindness whenever her mask would slip. Anthony goes a far more one-dimensional route, and the results are not the success they should be. Oddly enough, I love the snarling, long-haired zealot Trask played by Roy Thinnes. Both Jerry Lacy and Thinnes are forces with which to be reckoned, but in Thinnes's case, I fear he might bite my fingers off while sending Vicki to the gallows.

At this time, the Gulf War had done its damage to the ratings by incessant preemptions, the Soviet Union was falling from within, and Silence of the Lambs was a box office champion.

This episode hit the airwaves on February 8, 1991.

EPISODE 8

If bad-boy Barnabas is the one hopping beds with fiancees and chambermaids, why is he hearing demands for satisfaction... from his brother? Jeremiah: Adrian Paul. (Repeat; 1 hr.)

Barnabas and Josette enjoy a lusty reunion while Angelique casts a spell to unite the prospective bride with Barnabas's brother, Jeremiah. Her plan is so successful that the two escape to Boston and elope, but Barnabas pursues them. After the two men are reduced to physical combat, Jeremiah reveals that he and Josette have married. Having been bested in battle by Barnabas, Jeremiah demands the satisfaction of a duel.

Victoria's family history tells her that this is how Jeremiah died, and tries to thwart the duel alongside Sarah, but to no avail. Barnabas vows that no harm will come to his brother, and when it comes time to load the pistol, he pockets the ball. However, Angelique casts a passionate spell that fires a separate blast, killing Jeremiah when Barnabas pulls the trigger. The family is shattered, and Abigail blames Victoria for the sorcery behind Jeremiah's death. Meanwhile, in the present, a confused Phyllis Wick arrives from 1790 in Vicki's place, dying of diphtheria. Modern Barnabas is terrified; he recalls her dying from it. Could the same fate befall Victoria? And if Mistress Wick dies, will that strand Vicki in the past?

Like the episode before it, episode 8 betrays a series running at full steam, seasons ahead of most successful shows. The 1790 flashback is an underrated triumph for Dark Shadows, economizing in many ways, luxuriating in others, and taking (some of) the best of that storyline and distilling its essence from a marvelous wine into a powerful grappa. As with an HBO series season, the promise of seven episodes begins to pay off around the eighth. The cast is now more than confident; they are enthusiastic. Ben Cross may seem a bit lost as the Barnabas of 1991, but the Barnabas of 1790?

Completely in his element.

The casting of Adrian Paul is spot-on, as well. He has a minuscule portion of two episodes to make an impression as a vital catalyst for Barnabas, and the man succeeds. (I've heard a rumor that he was to play Quentin had the show continued. But I've also heard that Dan Curtis offered the part once more to David Selby.) Soap operas are often about the repression of emotion. You know, quiet desperation and all that. In this, emotion — Hollywood-sized — takes the top bill. Sentiment is somehow more heartening. The anger is justifiably explosive. Regret is at operatic levels, hold-the-soap-thank-you.

And the passion? It feels ahead of its time for 1991. The love scenes between Barnabas and Josette have honest, raw, lusty abandon. And the magic forged by Angelique? Is it just me, or does it look like the unseen Magic Wand she uses while casting her spells was made by Hitachi? Lysette Anthony is shameless in the best way, behaving for all the world as if she'd wandered off the set of a Ken Russell movie and couldn't tell the difference. That doesn't interfere with the pathos of the story. If anything, it puts it into a context that makes this version of Angelique all the more perversely hateful. She revels in the pain of others not only because the result brings her pleasure, but it also seems that the process itself does, as well. Intense, romantic, and ripe with supernatural intrigue, this episode reminds me just how much I enjoyed the 1991 show as it evolved.

This episode burst from the chests of television screens on February 15, 1991.

EPISODE 10

Barnabas is determined to attend the grand opening of Collinwood even if he has to rise from the grave to do it! Millicent: Barbara Blackburn. (Repeat; 1 hr.)

The family buries Barnabas as Josette prepares to leave for Boston, pleased that the book from the future was seemingly inaccurate about her date and mode of death. Joshua moves everyone into Collinwood, and when Barnabas rises, the new vampire finds considerable privacy in the Old House. He feeds off of Millicent and a local prostitute while gaining the curiosity of Trask, who sees him as a demon. Shortly before she is to depart, Josette goes to the Old House, where she sees Barnabas as a vampire and embraces him, nonetheless.

With the rising of Barnabas, the core of Dark Shadows finally solidifies. As with all of the 1790 half of the 1991 series, this is a beautiful, polished, classy, and passionate retelling. The writing has energy, economy, and poetry. Overall, the most outstanding dimension of the remake is in the cast. Dan Curtis has a remarkably keen eye for crafting an ensemble, and each performance feels more winning than the last. As I noted before, they really solidify in the 1790 sequence, and their confidence with the characters and each other is evident in the sincerity of the drama and the wit (in this one, it's largely thanks to Jim Fyfe, whose Ben Loomis is the straight-shooting, enthusiastic, ironic best friend every hero needs).

If there is any element in the episode where the storytelling loses its footing, it's in the interpretation of the vampire. It's a shameful, music video depiction, leaving Ben Cross looking like a hybrid of Billy Idol, Jeff Spicoli, and Craig Wasson at the end of Body Double. He hisses and snarls and just... no. What's more poignant about all of this is that Cross makes great choices under this drag. He plays the soft pedal with clarity and humanity as he alternately represses, reveals, and even revels in his new condition. It's the makeup and mugging that detracts from it all.

Favorite and most subtle moment? After his first night, Barnabas awakens in a cellar. The first thing he does is run his fingers under his teeth, checking for fangs. His reaction, a very slight flicker of relief that never settles. Perfect. Just perfect. The rest of the cast bucks up just as admirably, and it feels as close to Masterpiece Theatre as Dark Shadows got. Take a decent actor, put them in contemporary clothes, and you see a, well, decent actor. What is it about aristocratic, historic garb that makes him look like a genius? This is really clear when we flash-forward to 1991 and the whole thing just feels leaden. 1791. A grand story for a grand cast.

As a (then) Californian when the revival first aired, I can attest that the Gulf War made watching the show a nightmare due to constant interruptions and reschedulings. And trying to get a friend to watch? They were even more hopelessly lost. Dark Shadows.

Sometimes you seem cursed. By this point, the war was over, but the damage was done. Look at how the dates line up. The show premiered on January 13 and 14, with the first three episodes. Highly rated. So far, so good. Three days later, on January 17, military operations began. The next day, January 18, episode four aired. On the east coast. On the west coast? Just before it begins, Iraq launches SCUD missiles at Israel. So, yeah, no show that night for us. At least, on time. This was a really crucial episode because it would have been the first in the regular time slot, training the public about where the show was. Episode five, on January 25, aired on the day when Iraqi troops spilled millions of gallons of crude oil into the Gulf. Something of a news item. There were three unpredictable episodes in February, and by the time the show wrapped up with its last four episodes, the war was over. But the damage was done.

Other trivia. This episode was directed by Rob Bowman, who abandoned the WB Dark Shadows pilot many years later to direct Elektra, which was its own reward. Unfortunately, the new director, P.J. Hogan, largely crashed the WB pilot with nutty stylization.

On this day in 1991, US troops arrive home from the war and Iraq releases a number of journalists and two captured American soldiers.

The day came when I had to write an epilogue for DS91. With the death of Dan Curtis, episode 12 of the 1991 Dark Shadows became the last real exploration of his original vision. The entire series is a troubling subject for me because it was a v very public failure. And if a full blown, lavish, big budget, beautifully acted, prestigious "Criterion Edition" of Dark Shadows failed, the sinister implication was that the Dark Shadows concept itself was fundamentally broken. I don't know if that's true. I certainly don't want to think that that's true. Perhaps the thud heard in 1991 only meant that there was still something missing in the execution. Perhaps it meant that Dark Shadows was as a creature in a very specific period of time.

None of these arguments grab me. Ultimately, I believe that the show was too reverent.

Dark Shadows 1966 was a response to its time. Dark Shadows 1991 was not. Instead, it was a very pretty rendition of that response, 25 years too late, thinking that it was the last word in cool simply for giving it a go. It reminds me of Star Trek: The Motion Picture — a very attractive movie, paralyzed by its desire to legitimize itself. But that's not what the original Star Trek was doing. As I've said before, I think Star Trek II: The Wrath of Khan is one of the Rosetta Stones worth our study. Perhaps it was not a response to the 1980s, but it was a response to Star Trek, itself. To the sense of family that the audience found within the corridors of the Enterprise.

That's why the best moments of DS91 are between Willie and Barnabas. Those are moments where, even if that series is not about 1991, they are most certainly about Dark Shadows. Which is the reason we are there, too.

EPISODE 12

Highly-paid executives at a top television network claim poor viewership to cancel a show they first made impossible to watch. Head of the Network: Brandon Tartikoff. (Repeat; all too often in Hollywood)

In 1791, Vicki awaits execution while Barnabas accidentally drives his mother into near-catatonic, delusional madness. A snooping Abigail meets her end at Barnabas's hands, and Joshua, discovering this, arranges for Trask to visit via Ben Loomis. Barnabas and Ben extract an admission of Vicki's innocence from Trask, before walling him up for the public good. Peter Bradford takes the document with him to a magistrate, but Angelique's powers cause it to be forgotten.

Meanwhile, Sarah dies, having hidden from Barnabas on a cold Maine night. Daniel barely lives, thanks to Vicki's knowledge of treating fevers. Barnabas begs his father to kill him, but he cannot. Instead, he assigns Ben to chain his son forever in the mausoleum. In the present, Maggie breaks Julia's strange possession, only to become possessed by Angelique, herself.

At a certain point, it almost resembles the end of The Wild Bunch. Cold, nihilistic, with a slash-and-burn viciousness regarding its own body count, the episode feels as if they know it's a swan song after the royal rogering of the Gulf War and NBC's lackadaisical management. Not the case, however. This was filmed in November of 1990, months before they would go to air. Still, it exists in the context of "The Best of Both Worlds" and even if they weren't Trekkers, the creative team now lived in a world where genre television went there.

Again, there's almost nothing unsatisfying about these 1790 episodes of the 1991 series. Grand and sumptuous in every regard, they use handsome appointments to highlight what's already the star: the writing. These are dense episodes, full of action and plot-plot-plot after the occasionally pokey first six installments. I don't know how they play for those unfamiliar with the show but – excluding the missing Nathan Forbes — this really demonstrates how arguably labored and plot-piebald the 1795 sequence in the original series could get. Especially in episode 12, we get a constant barrage of heartbreaks and triumphs, including wacky exorcisms and the end of Abigail, Sarah, and a drunken Trask.

The performances are as fine as the best in genre television, with special kudos going to... well, the entire cast. Stefan Gierasch and Jean Simmons handle Naomi's descent into madness with tenderness and dignity, and Gierasch's stony heart continues to crumble as he becomes perhaps the saddest collateral damage of all of this: the one cursed to survive. Along with him is Jim Fyfe, playing a deeply sentimental man with a subtlety that adds a resonant counterpoint to the broad approach he explored as Willie.

I remember communicating over Prodigy with young Joey Gordon Levitt, who implored fellow Prodigians to hector NBC, which I did. I knew it was hopeless, but it was something.

I would have been far more perturbed about the cancellation, but... the show ended on a satisfyingly high note and never got a chance to get bad. The Gulf War can always be blamed for its ratings failure, and I rarely show it to people who don't deeply enjoy it. The show is a great ambassador for the franchise, and I hope it will continue to be honored as such.

On this day in 1991, NBC made a big, dumb mistake.

MITCH RYAN REMEMBERED, TWICE

Mitch Ryan died.

Normally we use euphemisms for these sorts of things. "We lost so and so." Or, "such and such went too soon," as if there is some more appropriate time. But of all of the Dark Shadows cast members, none projected honest and uncompromising integrity like Mitch Ryan. It feels fundamentally disrespectful to dress it up with something other than a plain and honest fact when referring to his death. The word is as straightforward as the character he played. And as pained.

Burke Devlin was the show's first "troubled hero." We absolutely wanted to get behind him, but his extremity held us back. And besides, we're sort of trying to root for the Collins family. But there he is. Episode after episode. He's there for Vicki. He's there for David. He's there for us. He was a menace. He was a friend. And in every phase, he was believable.

I can think of few other actors who could project that kind of tortured ambiguity. It was a human mystery, and it compelled Victoria's imagination as much as any ghost or phantom parent. He welcomed us to Collinsport in every sense, and alongside the writers, Mitch Ryan set the Escherseque moral landscape that defined the series and drove it forward.

Mitch Ryan and Jonathan Frid shared the same, most important quality. In their performances, they were able to embody two diametrically opposed states of mind without creating a contradiction. The fascination generated by that strange and unique ability compelled viewers to keep watching, unable to guess where those men might ultimately go.

Ryan was no stranger to conflict. His exit from the show was driven by a poignant battle with alcoholism, and the evidence becomes increasingly obvious as his time on the series goes on. The struggle led to a break from acting. For most, that break would be a permanent one. It is to Ryan's credit that he took the recovery process seriously and rebuilt his career within a few years. Soon, he was co-starring in the Dirty Harry sequel, Magnum Force, almost nabbed the role of Picard, essayed the villain in Lethal Weapon, took a memorable and recurring role on the hit series, Dharma and Greg, and played a pivotal part in the Halloween franchise.

Easing into retirement, Ryan found continued opportunities to explore art in painting and writing, publishing his autobiography quite recently. He revived the Burke Devlin character for Big Finish Audio and framed the recent Dark Shadows rep production of A Christmas Carol with a fine narration of alternating warmth and gravitas.

I interviewed him on Christmas day seven years ago and found him to be exactly as warm and accessible as you would imagine. He was a fellow Louisville native, having grown up just a few blocks from where I grew up, myself. We are a strange and unique breed, in the company of Tod Browning, Muhammad Ali, and Hunter S. Thompson. Mitch Ryan was a fine addition to the list.

A Korean war veteran, he began his career on the stage at the Barter Theater and remained loyal to live performance, even appearing in A Long Day's Journey into Night at the Pasadena Playhouse in 1993 with fellow Dark Shadows alum, Alan Feinstein. He was a lifetime member of the Actors Studio, appearing in Wait Until Dark and The Price on Broadway. Smoothly transitioning to film, his judgment and leadership won him the presidency of the Screen Actors Guild Foundation.

Few performers have rebuilt their careers with such dignity and range. It would be a cliché to point out that his self-generated revival made him somewhat of a phoenix, but considering that he battled a Phoenix on the program, we'd be remiss not to make a note of it. He built the very definition of a worthy life, and that's exactly the kind of personal character necessary to give Collinwood its true foundation. He welcomed Vicki and the viewers to the beginning and the end of the world. Thanks to his work, though, that salutation may always be in the wrong order.

When I wrote the obituary for Mitch Ryan, I also had a show opening that night. In a letter to a friend, I went a tad deeper....

The piece was a bear because he was a virile guy, and although he slipped into old age with exactly the kind of crusty dignity that you would imagine, it was one of those things where it was not unexpected. Kind of like Jonathan Frid. When someone went too soon, like Chris Pennock, or they roiled away in a miasma of personal conflict, like John Karlen, the words come really easily. Mitch Ryan was different.

I have a lot of regrets about not meeting him. We got along extremely well when we chatted. Kathryn Leigh Scott was really happy with the interview I did. Every word I wrote about his warmth and enthusiasm was genuine. The fact that we could reminisce about Louisville was a huge bonus. I grew up in the very last years where vast swaths of Louisville institutions somehow had carried on from his childhood. I don't know exactly where his house was down to the mailbox, but I could take you within a few blocks. And it was pretty much a house like mine. He went to the same high school as my mom, and I had to dance delicately around the fact that it was about a decade after he graduated. (He was eight years older than she was.)

I mean he was just a sweetheart. I was going to bring a book on his neighborhood (and my neighborhood) to the Dark Shadows convention in 2016. When he couldn't make it, I vowed that I would send it to him. I never got around to it. I'm sure he forgot about the whole thing seconds after I made the offer, but it's one of those weird human moments that just kind of hangs on my conscience.

Now, now that the play is over, I actually have the time to sort of sit back and properly mourn. I honestly think he is what made the show what it was at its very core. I think he provided the essential first mystery and sense of masculine ambiguity that propelled the series. It was the baton that Frid picked up.

And it's a marvelously happy life. It's a life where he took the kind of problem that normally dashes people forever and he simply overcame it. Well, I'm sure there was nothing simple about it. But he overcame it. I regret that he didn't get the role of Captain Picard. By the time Patrick Stewart took the part, he had already had a wealth of brilliant opportunities to explore acting. And although Ryan did some great stage work, it was maybe not the same as working year in and year out with John Barton at the RSC. That show would have been a jaw- dropping vehicle for him to show and discover what he was put on this earth to do.

But despite that, he was just the very best kind of credit to his profession, to the show, and to what we all can be.

A CHRISTMAS CAROL (2021)
with the Dark Shadows Ensemble

There are times when an idea moves beyond the intention and becomes an unexpected wonder. Dark Shadows fans enjoyed just that in Richard Halpern and Ansel Faraj's recent Zoom production of A Christmas Carol, which 'aired' on December 19. Not only did the producers bring us an adaptation of Orson Welles' radio play, but David Henesy and Alexandra Moltke Isles returned to join the ensemble. You probably know that. You probably also know that their return should have been the story. If it had been limited to that, it would have been a successful moment in history, but a failure as a drama. And there is not one unsuccessful second in this production.

At its very marrow, this production of A Christmas Carol is the most artistically successful follow-up to Dark Shadows since the show went off the air. The budget was not vast. But that doesn't matter. Did it ever?

Because fans of the show don't necessarily want more Dark Shadows from our Dark Shadows. We want more of the ensemble. And we want to see them given the chance to show us and the world why we love them.

This was that opportunity. The script is a strong and economical distillation of the story, supporting the actors yet staying out of their way. I can't necessarily say that for other Dark Shadows productions. And while it's not a Dark Shadows production, it is, resoundingly.

As wacky and perfunctory as the project could have been, it manages, above all else, to be tasteful in its risks, with everyone participating. It's improvised and compromised around the edges, and that lets us see what the actors bring to the execution via quirky and personal contributions. From wonky top hats, cozy scarves, and appropriately fire-engine-red reading glasses to David Selby's tieless tuxedo, the visual world of this show intersects immediacy and literacy, and, most prized of all, fun.

I mean, there is an inherent ridiculousness to any production via Zoom. It's hard to bring James Tyrone to life if it looks like Peter Brady is about to appear in the square next door to announce that his voice has changed. But that kind of visual language is used with discretion and strategy by Ansel Faraj. He trades out widescreen oomph for spectacle that works on a more resonant and emotional level. That becomes clear when Mitch Ryan delivers the touching and spare epilogue. His adoring cast members look on with professional satisfaction and affectionate gratitude for the chance to hear him have the final word. And it's just as moving for us.

Of course, the impossible luck of seeing this ensemble assembled is going to put any audience of fans in the right mood. Yes. That's especially true in a year where, I believe, we have lost more cast members than I'm comfortable counting. Everyone is both having fun and bringing their A-Game, with about as much prep time as we are used to seeing them have on the original show.

This was not an easy presentation to pull together with little notice. But its success is a minor miracle. It's what happens when determined professionals get to do what they do best. The result is a production that, although brief, connects us with the emotional realities of the actual text, serving up sobering truths about aging, regret, and envy with equal measures of believably-earned hope.

And there is esprit de corps and an intense sense of teamwork. But at a certain point, someone has to be Scrooge and stand out even further.

So, David Selby.

In a performance that should define the most extraordinary horizons of what quarantine theater can be, Selby is somehow able to capture true theatrical size with the cerebral nuances afforded by the intimacy of the webcam. In the midst of nothing but technology, David Selby delivers nothing but humanity. I kept waiting for his "bah humbug," and other trademark phrases, eager to hear his unique spin on them. Well, there was no spin. I was seeing Ebenezer Scrooge making a point to other characters rather than a self-conscious actor trying to top earlier Ebenezers. David Selby is a fine writer who represents the author, not himself. I suspect that we are seeing the performance he would want from actors in one of his own productions.

As the production unfolds, we see a character desperate to hide the pain he associates with lost loves and friendships. This is ostensibly a play about the unfair privilege of class differences. Here, I sense a parallel story: the unfair privilege of relationship differences. Scrooge, having earned it, wears his alienation with the pride of a man sure of nothing else. Selby's Scrooge feels wisely reverse-engineered from the middle of the play outward in either direction. The relatable sadness of his miscalculations and deviations from the Fezziwig standard chain him as much as the weights encumbering Jacob Marley. As a character haunted by Marley's Christmastime passing long before any literal ghosts appear, Selby takes great care to believably connect with the details of Ebenezer's past. With nothing but his face and voice, he brings us the depth of Dickens with a rare purity as Scrooge is reintroduced to everything he's lost.

When Scrooge finally exults in perhaps the most heartfelt "Merry Christmas" I may have ever heard, I felt like I was seeing a man finally given permission to forgive himself. Scrooge connects with a world ever ready to offer second chances, and if anything makes this a "Dark Shadows" production, it's that. Again and again, that's the message of the show, and that's the message that we see here.

Partly because of our connection with the work of these actors over decades, the show was emotionally exhausting, yet was never overwrought. Honesty may not always be pretty, but if it is explored with range and sympathy, it is inevitably the most satisfying part of a ritual like this.

Back to context. Rarely, if ever, does a franchise give its loyal audience a gift of this much heart and finesse. I don't know if we will see the ensemble assembled like this once more. I think everyone is aware of that danger. Like the story itself, this was an opportunity to express a simple truth — moments to express respect, admiration, and love may never come again. Don't be stingy with them.

James Storm is once again the reliable chameleon, embodying principled strength with compassionate eloquence. Jerry Lacy conjures up a Marley with precisely the grim relish to catalyze the journey. David Henesy has lost none of his ability to nail every single line with impudent sincerity. Nancy Barrett completely erased any sadness I might have at her absence from the screen by reassuring me that her spark and wit are still screen ready for the producer smart enough to cast her. Marie Wallace brought her native warmth and sense of life with every bit of the immediacy we enjoyed in 1968 and 1969.

Yes, the story is a bit of a boy's club. Nonetheless, Lara Parker elicits the nimble delicacy of the language with naturally cerebral verve. Kathryn Leigh Scott mixes a sense of ethical sincerity with the hint of sardonic mischief that is her laudable trademark. Leave it to accomplished authors to know exactly how to handle language of mirth and strength.

Alexandra Moltke Isles could have coasted on novelty, but she doesn't. There is a dark and intense forthrightness to her presence, and I am too busy watching her character to be distracted by the rare and long-awaited return of their actor. It took a long time for us to see more of the range she wanted to explore on the program. It was worth it.

Finally, Mitch Ryan inaugurates and resolves the story with an easy, reserved gravitas of reassuring authority. It takes the brightest of actors to observe the action with an improbably passionate neutrality. Mitch Ryan was and is that bright actor.

When the Dark Shadows Universe (a thing extending far beyond the actual production of the show) said goodbye to Ryan, Moltke Isles, and Henesy, a critical balance was lost. Thanks to this production, this can now be seen as only momentary. Dark Shadows is about home, often for those without one. Watching this made me feel as if the doors to Collinwood were open again. 2020 and 2021 took more from us than we deserved. This gesture, at this time, is an essential reminder of what we still have.

Too often, the love of a franchise reveals itself in the desperate acquisition of props and autographs and photos and handshakes, all of which are noble, but all of which distract us from the real reasons why we love the people who brought it to life. Richard Halpern and Ansel Faraj take full advantage of this rare opportunity to see them doing what we love most: acting. They have not only given this ensemble yet another great story to tell together, but they have given us the opportunity and intimacy to share it.

AFTERWORD

As a writer, I lost my knack for fiction far back in 1992 with the death of my mentor and publisher, the great Todd Loren. That is not meant to be maudlin; it's just that the truth sometimes is. I thank Dark Shadows yet again. It elicited a tad of show-don't-tell from the depths of that sadness.

A few days prior to Christmas, I found myself in a conversation about The Offer, a TV show depicting the making of The Godfather. My friend and I pondered what a making-of series about Dark Shadows would look like. I'd often wondered about that. It's a story more dramatic than the show, itself. I wasn't sure how it would begin, but I instantly knew how it should end. In a flash, a Paul Thomas Anderson-style montage unfolded. It's written informally, even for me, but this is how it came out.

NB -- James Aubrey is the MGM executive who ordered the savage cuts from Night of Dark Shadows.

```
FADE IN:
EXT. MONTAGE
We hear the Gayane Ballet Suite No. 3: IV by
Aram Khatchaturian, last heard as Dr. Frank
Poole jogged endlessly through the Discovery in
2001: A Space Odyssey. Sad, slow, sweet,
thoughtful.

INT. JAMES AUBREY'S OFFICE
```

James Aubrey orders Dan Curtis to cut 45 minutes or so of Night of Dark Shadows. ANY 45 minutes. But NOW. Curtis sees that he is now exactly the opposite of what he once was... an artist at odds with a suit.

INT. TEST SCREENING - NIGHT
The audience is filling out cards, circling numbers to state how much they dislike the movie, not understanding what they are watching. Curtis sits there, powerless. The camera pans over to James Aubrey, doing a crossword puzzle during the big climax.

INT. LOBBY BATHROOM - NIGHT
Curtis throws up in the test screening's bathroom. He comes out to see Sam and Gordon staring at him in the lobby. He turns away from the writers and passes James Aubrey, who casually shrugs.

CLOSE UP of Curtis' face, tightening up into a rage and then yelling, "Fire!"

EXT. BATTLEFIELD - DAY
Close-up of guns, blasting away. Then tanks, and we pull out to find Dan Curtis, many years later, commanding Winds of War.

INT. AWARD CEREMONY - NIGHT
Curtis, getting his Emmy. Smiling that enormous smile once again. Aubrey golf claps. Dan Curtis, with all of his 397 teeth, grins straight at him and casually shrugs.

INT. POKER GAME - NIGHT
The Emmy is now in the hands of a pudgy, mustachioed John Karlen, putting it on the table. Everyone shakes their head "no," and the guy next to him takes off his own watch and puts it down as the wager for Karlen.

The camera CLOSES IN on a solitary poker chip in Karlen's hand. It fades to an AA chip in Mitch

Ryan's hand, which he flips between his thumb and forefinger.

INT. MITCH RYAN'S OFFICE - DAY
We see Mitch nodding sympathetically as he speaks to someone on the phone. An assistant brings Mitch a script to look at, but he waves them away, instead giving his focus to his phone conversation, the camera tilting back to the chip.

EXT. RODEO RING - DAY
Bulls charging at the camera! James Storm's eyes are huge. He grabs for something. A red cape? No, a camera! He's in a rodeo ring, snapping photos, never happier. CLOSE IN on his lens.

EXT. SET OF THE GREAT GATSBY - DAY
Pull out on another lens. A handsome man in a safari jacket, Ben Martin, snaps a photo of Kathryn Leigh Scott, being made up in beautiful 1920s clothing before she elegantly glides onto the set of The Great Gatsby. Life is good.

INT. LARA PARKER'S BATHROOM - DAY
Lara Parker, in the arms of some man who tells her something that she doesn't like to hear. She strides confidently into a bathroom where she reaches into a drawer and pulls out… a murder weapon? No. It's a bottle of Head and Shoulders.

INT. SHOWER - DAY
Lara is now in the shower lathering up her hair. We pull back and realize she's just filming a commercial. Cut to: her serving dog food in another commercial. Then her in yet another commercial. Someone yells cut, and she looks incredulously at the script. No, no, no. She crosses out dialogue and begins writing her own, if only for her own sake. That's better.

INT. BOOKSTORE - NIGHT
Lara signs autographs at a release party for
her novel, ANGELIQUE'S DESCENT. She's in her
element.

INT. THEATER WINGS - DAY
Chris Pennock is writing a comic book about his
time on the show. He laughs at his drawings.
PULL BACK to reveal he is in doublet and hose.
A floor crew member hustles him away from his
drawing nook in the theater wings and onto a
stage.

EXT. RURAL GAS STATION - DAY
A car pulls up, full of fans. One has a VHS
tape with Don Briscoe's image. They look at the
overweight attendant whose badge reads, CECIL.
The fans study him, compare his image to the
guy on the box, and nod to each other. They
wave the box at him. Even though gas is still
pumping, Cecil backs away, shaking his head
"no." He locks the office door. The fans bang
on it, relentless in their quest for the almighty
autograph. He curls up in a ball and rocks back
and forth. He looks up at the bare, hanging
lightbulb. It gets ever brighter until it
explodes into...

EXT. MANHATTAN HIGH RISE - DAY
Flashbulbs! ALEXANDRA, elegantly dressed,
leaves the building. The awaiting press
explodes into unwanted questions. A nearby New
York Post headline reads, "Dark Shadows
Heroine Testifies in Murder Case."

INT. AUTOGRAPH SHOW - DAY
JOEL CROTHERS, handsome, mustache brimming,
signs headshots. CLOSE-UP of his hand. As the
person takes the autograph away from Joel,
they smile at one another, and the star notices
a small, wine-colored spot on his hand. He
politely gets up and walks away, into the
crowd, numb.

INT. FALCON CREST SET - DAY
DAVID SELBY, in a black suit, charmingly
menaces a business flunky. That person pulls a
pistol. Selby whirls around to grab the katana
off his wall. There is a crash of a proximate
lamp. Selby is very serious for a moment and
then laughs. He gingerly places the katana on
his desk and backs away, shaking his head with
a grin. The more things change...

INT. SOAP OPERA PRODUCTION OFFICE - DAY
SAM HALL unpacks his typewriter. He wanders to
the set, sees a boring scene of a doctor talking,
imagines the doctor turning into a vampire. Sam
smiles. CUT BACK to the doctor, not a vampire,
but an actor on a soundstage. Sam nods,
realizes this, and walks back to his office,
where he plunks away at the typewriter, bored.
He looks at GORDON RUSSELL'S familiar coffee
cup. Sam just puts pens in it. The office is in
the same configuration as the writers' room on
Dark Shadows, but where Gordon's desk would
have been is now a solitary, vaguely dying
rubber tree plant. CUT TO Sam's bedroom. He's
reading DON QUIXOTE. The font is too small. He
tosses it aside and picks up the remote, looking
at it with contempt. He looks over at a long pile
of junk mail on his bed where Grayson once lay.
The contempt softens.

EXT. FUNERAL - DAY - MONTAGE
Quick montage of funerals in the rain. With
each cut, the crowd gets smaller and smaller.

MINISTER (V.O.)
And we commend Clarice V. Blackburn... (fade
to) David Thayer Hersey... (Fade to) Louis
Stirling Edmonds... (Fade to) Joan Bennett
Wilde to the earth.

INT. DREAM SEQUENCE

FADE TO:
TOTAL BLACKNESS. In relief, slow-motion
skeletons menace a frenzied Jonathan Frid. They
lunge at him, just like the zombies prior to
1840. He can't get away.

PULL BACK to reveal it's a Cinco de Mayo
celebration in Mexico, where we've heard Frid
threaten to retire.

He's dancing. He's happy. A WAITER comes out,
bringing a phone on a long cord.

                    WAITER
              It's from LA.

Frid thinks for just a moment.

He smiles.

He laughs.

He knows that at last, he doesn't have to do
anything he doesn't want to do.

So, he rejoins the Cinco de Mayo celebration and
keeps dancing into the night.

FADE OUT.

                THE END

Welcome to the beginning and the end of
the world.

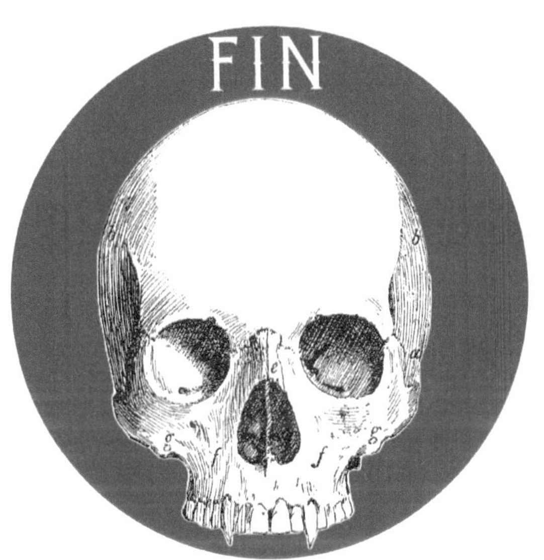

FIN

ACKNOWLEDGEMENTS

Bigger book. More acknowledgments. This book would not have been possible without the notable contributions of Ms. Lara Parker, Mr. James Storm, Mr. David Selby, Mr. Roger Davis, Peter H. Gilmore, Peggy Nadramia, Brother Butch Rosenbalm, Greg Mank, David Raines, Jonathan Alexandratos, Apryl Kelly, Josh Bigwood, Davie Morrill, Jule Saynes, Danielle Gelehrter, Danny Garland, John Wirenius, Gordon Dymowski, Jamie Peck, David Crowder, Dean "Dino" Robertson, David Conover, Christen Pierce, Nancy Kersey, Mark B. Perry, Cara Tillitz, Mark Gilman, Lee Sauer, Riley Watkins, John Hudgens, Tiffany Tallent, Mary D. Johnson, Phil Nobile Jr, Colonel Tom Hotz, Patty Pope, David Hargis, Zack Mitchell, Evelyn Peterson, Anna Grace Gilbert, Jean Helbig, LeAnne Johnson, Brad Cantrell, Joe Letitia, Kendrick Shope, and Ron McCray. To all others who helped, you know who you are. To those, who hindered, you also know who you are, and what you can do.

This book, in the largest sense, would not have been possible without Wallace McBride. The column and its mission were his ideas. His patience is what gave me the time and room to get there.

All gratitude must go to Mr. Lowell Cunningham, who taught me to write all over again. No mission ever had a more stalwart and unerring captain.

Special thanks to the elemental Ms. Kathryn Leigh Scott for everything.

ABOUT THE AUTHOR

Patrick McCray entered the Dark Shadows community in 2012 when he successfully screened all 1225 episodes in only 45 days He joined the Collinsport Historical Society staff the next year. A native of Louisville, Kentucky — he was raised mere blocks away from both the home of Roger Davis and the house where Mitch Ryan grew up.

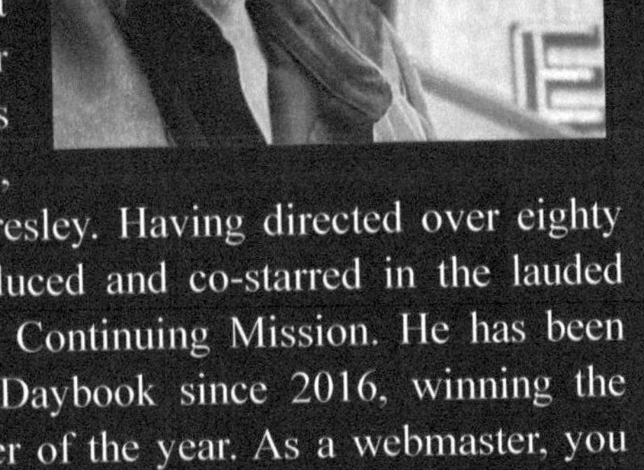

Prior to earning his MFA in stage directing, Patrick helped launch Babylon 5 in the art department and was a comic book author for Revolutionary Comics, creating the underground cult hit, Elvis Shrugged. He later wrote top selling biographies of Betty White, Jack Dorsey, Britney Spears, and Elvis Presley. Having directed over eighty stage plays, he also co-produced and co-starred in the lauded audio series, Star Trek: The Continuing Mission. He has been writing the Dark Shadows Daybook since 2016, winning the 2018 Rondo Award for writer of the year. As a webmaster, you can see his work at kathrynleighscott.com

Barnabas Collins will return.

Yankee Rose!